Misogyny in
Philosophic

Misogyny in the Western Philosophical Tradition

A READER

EDITED BY

BEVERLEY CLACK
Senior Lecturer in Theology and Religious Studies,
Roehampton Institute, London

First published 1999 by
MACMILLAN PRESS LTD
Houndmills, Basingstoke, Hampshire RG21 6XS
and London
Companies and representatives throughout the world

ISBN 0–333–63423–3 hardcover
ISBN 0–333–63424–1 paperback

A catalogue record for this book is available from the British Library.

This book is printed on paper suitable for recycling and made from fully managed and sustained forest sources.

10 9 8 7 6 5 4 3 2 1
08 07 06 05 04 03 02 01 00 99

Printed in Hong Kong

Dedicated to the memory of my grandmother Vi
and my godmother Win

CONTENTS

ACKNOWLEDGEMENTS

Thanks are due to my colleagues in the Department of Theology and Religious Studies at Roehampton Institute, London, who listened to this at various stages in various seminars, and who also read and commented on this work; and also to the Media Services Department at Froebel College, who helped with the presentation of this work.

My thanks also go to Brian Clack for bringing the works of Oswald Spengler and Otto Weininger to my attention. And finally, my thanks are due to Robert Lindsey, not just for his careful and thoughtful editing of the works of Thomas Hobbes, John Locke and David Hume, but for his support and encouragement over the last two years.

The publishers and authors who have allowed work to be reproduced in this collection are acknowledged at the appropriate point in this work.

Every effort has been made to trace all the copyright holders but if any have been inadvertently overlooked, the publishers will be pleased to make the necessary arrangement at the first opportunity.

Introduction: A Fling with the Philosophers

Introduction

When surveying the development of philosophical ideas, it should be noted that a significant part of what passes for the canon of western philosophy goes unnoticed or is consigned to silence. Margaret Whitford writes of the surprise she felt when she realized the extent to which misogyny determines the thoughts of the 'great' philosophers of the western tradition when they turn their attention to the puzzling question of the nature of 'woman'.[1] Who is woman? What does 'she' want? Almost uniformly, such passages offer answers to this 'question' which describe women in deeply unflattering terms. Women are described as 'the devil's gateway' (Tertullian). They are 'big children their whole life long' (Schopenhauer). According to Aristotle and Aquinas, a woman is a 'misbegotten male'. Encountering such passages can be problematic for women who are involved in the attempt to develop a distinctively feminist approach to philosophy. The works of these philosophers form the basis for philosophical debate. What is the feminist philosopher to do with the misogyny contained in these texts?

It is at this point that the question of methodology arises. It would be a gross exaggeration to suggest that all the key texts of western philosophy are misogynistic. Discussion of the nature of woman appears in relatively few philosophical texts. The philosophers' primary aim has been to analyse and explore the 'human' condition – although, of course, what they have to say about women will undoubtedly affect their understanding of humanity! Can the 'wisdom' of the philosophers be separated from the misogyny, or are the two intimately connected? Does a feminist philosophy find its foundations in the western philosophical canon, or should feminists seek an alternative grounding for their ideas?[2]

In her writings, the French philosopher and psychoanalyst Luce Irigaray confronts this central problem of the misogynous element present in the western philosophical tradition. At the same time, she is concerned to address the question of how women might 'learn to speak'; in other words, how women might develop their own distinctive language. This might suggest that Irigaray believes the best way forward is to ignore the philosophical canon with its masculinist ethos. This is not the case. Rather than ignore what she terms the 'phallogocentrism'[3] of the philosophical discipline, she claims that it is vitally important for feminist philosophers to know their enemy, to be intimately equated with 'his' arguments, and through a process of 'mimesis' (or mimicry) to subvert those ideas which dismiss women and their achievements. Once the weakness of these arguments which parody women has been exposed, a radical alternative can be offered. In describing this process of critical engagement with the text, she suggests that we might 'have a fling with the philosophers',[4] a process which will be explored towards the end of this introduction.

Misogyny in the Western Philosophical Tradition

The major figures of the western philosophical tradition have consistently denigrated the importance and status of women. This attitude has been perpetuated in two main ways. In some texts, a blatant misogyny is in evidence. The language used of woman and the concepts derived from her are strictly negative. In others, a different approach is taken. Woman is described in apparently positive terms. Her role in life might be different from that ascribed to man, but it is equally important. Behind this language of 'difference' is an implicit hierarchy of values. Values equated with the 'masculine' (and moreover the male) are of higher status than those equated with the feminine (and consequently with the female). Ostensibly, such texts might seem to offer fundamentally different views on the nature of woman. It may be more appropriate to see such approaches as using different discourses to maintain the inferiority of woman. Both approaches accept a hierarchical understanding of the relationship between man and woman. Man, as the 'norm', defines the human, and woman is defined in relation to man.

Negative Approaches to Woman

In defining woman, some philosophers have formulated their views in purely negative terms. Woman is defined in relation to man and is found wanting. While such accounts are explicitly contemptuous of woman, a uniform account of her nature is absent. Rather, different writers emphasize different aspects of woman's 'nature'.

(a) The Lack of Reason

For philosophers such as Aristotle, reason is the defining mark of the human being. It is this capacity for rational reflection which differentiates humanity from the animals. Or rather, it is this rational capacity which differentiates *man* from the animals. Indeed, Aristotle is at pains to make a distinction between woman's (inferior) capacity for reason and man's (superior) rationality. The difference between male and female lies in the 'fact' that woman does not share the rational capabilities of man.

The claim that she has limited powers of reason has dominated discussions of woman. Schopenhauer, writing a considerable time after Aristotle, continues to claim that woman's inferior powers of reason have an impact upon her ability (or inability) to be moral. In denying that woman has sufficient powers of reason, a second and significant way of defining woman enters the discussion. If man is equatable with reason, woman is equatable with nature.

(b) Woman = Nature

At first glance, it is not immediately clear why an identification with nature should imply a negative account of woman. In the contemporary western world the anthropocentrism which has contributed to the abuse of the natural world is being challenged by environmentalists and others. Considering this context, the identification of woman with nature could be seen as highly complimentary! Indeed, some feminist writers have suggested that the abuse of nature can be paralleled with the abuse of women.[5] If one wishes to adopt this identification in a positive way, one must be aware of the negative connotations which this connection has had historically. Three influences have contributed to this negative rendition.

(i) *The influence of religion* In the writings of Tertullian, woman is identified with the biblical figure of Eve, whose name means literally 'Life'; thus Eve is 'the Mother of All Living'. As the first human mother, Eve can be identified as the matrix of the physical world. Likewise, women have been identified with the process of reproduction, and thus with nature.

A further factor contributes to this identification of woman with Eve. Eve's actions led to the fall of humanity, and responsibility for the heinous state of human existence is transmitted to all women as her 'daughters'. Tertullian, in expressing this idea, connects the Fall with the sensuality of Eve. Woman's concern with sensuality, dress and physical beauty reveals the concerns of unredeemed humanity as opposed to the concerns of those committed to the life of the spirit.

The fifteenth-century Dominican Fathers Kramer and Sprenger, responsible for the *Malleus Maleficarum*, maintain this identification of woman with Eve. Woman is identified with the fecundity of nature. Her fundamental concern is with procreation, and thus she is defined in terms of her sexuality. As a sexual being, she, like Eve, is at the mercy of 'the Lord of this World', Satan. It is interesting to note that while 'anti-religious' philosophers such as Hume may have rejected the mythical framework of Christianity, this notion of the insatiable sensuality of woman is maintained.[6]

(ii) *Reason/Nature* Philosophers in the western tradition have consistently made a distinction between Reason and Nature. While this distinction has been used to shape attitudes towards the natural world, it has also defined the relationship between the sexes. In Aristotle's philosophy, the female is identified with the shapeless matter which needs to be formed by the rational principle embodied by the male. The basis of such ideas in the now discredited and defunct realm of Aristotelian biology may have been questioned; the fundamental division remains. This division forms the basis for Kant's discussion of masculine and feminine, a discussion which in turn informs his account of morality. It finds its fullest expression in the little known work of Otto Weininger. According to Weininger, only man is capable of immortality. His 'reasoning' is simple: the rational man can transcend his environment; woman is too sunk in nature to achieve such transcendence.

(iii) *'Biology is Destiny'* In identifying woman with nature, reproduction comes to determine the 'answer' to the 'question' which is woman. Famously in the writings of Sigmund Freud, one's biological functions determine one's destiny. Similarly in Rousseau's writings, the identification of woman with the role of motherhood determines the form her education should take.

Taken together, these elements contribute to an oppressive interpretation of the apparent 'connection' between woman and nature. Just as the natural world is to be suppressed and overcome by the dictates of reason and order, so woman is to be fashioned, shaped and controlled by man.

Apparently Positive Accounts of Woman

Purely negative approaches to woman may pose less of a problem than some of the more subtle contributions to this debate. Plato's writings are a case in point. In his *Republic*, a highly egalitarian approach to the sexes – or at least to the members of the privileged group in his ideal society – is in evidence. The training and responsibility given to his 'Guardians' is, broadly speaking, similar for men and women. However, a survey of his other works reveals a less positive understanding of woman's role. In the *Symposium*, love of woman is considered subordinate to love of man for man. Indeed, in the *Timaeus* Plato suggests a hierarchy of creation in which women are closer to animals than are men.

The Enlightenment of the eighteenth century heralds a seemingly less aggressive, but ultimately more ambiguous approach to woman on the part of the philosophers. In Kant's writings, for example, an account of male/female relations is offered which stresses the complementarity of the sexes. There is a need for masculine *and* feminine qualities; women should be women and men should be men. But *both* roles are equally important. However, when Kant's views on morality are encountered, the qualities deemed necessary for living the higher moral life of 'duty' are discovered to be those which he identifies with the masculine.

Likewise, Rousseau's account of the education appropriate for women suggests an appreciation and respect for the 'difference' of woman. If Rousseau respects this difference, he expounds an understanding of woman which describes her as the passive helpmate for the active male. Woman *is* important, but only in relation to male desires and needs.

Implicit Misogyny in the Modern Era

With the rise of feminism and increasing pressure for equal rights legislation, the modern era, not surprisingly, sees a sharp decline in material where male philosophers explicitly discuss the nature of woman. Explicitly misogynistic passages seem few and far between in twentieth-century philosophical texts. Indeed, the philosophies of Weininger and Spengler stand out as distinctive for their explicit attacks on women. J. R. Lucas's paper, written in the 1970s, was the last philosophical exposition of the nature of woman that I could find. It is tempting to see the absence of such literature as evidence that modern philosophers have taken account of feminist concerns, and have accepted the need for non-sexist language, presuppositions and assumptions. And yet a close examination of contemporary philosophical debates suggests that the misogyny which shaped earlier philosophies is still present. Indeed, it could be argued that such ideas form the unspoken context for contemporary philosophy. Consideration of the Philosophy of Religion and the work of one of its major practitioners, Richard Swinburne, illustrates this undercurrent.

The language which Swinburne uses to expound his philosophy is distinctively masculine. While aware of debate surrounding the use of inclusive language, especially in relation to God-talk, Swinburne rejects the claim that the male pronoun is gender specific:

> The English language, unfortunately, does not today possess a pronoun suitable for persons without seeming to beg questions about gender. As the pronoun 'he' has been used in the past for reference to a person without seeming to beg questions about their gender, and 'she' has never been used in this way, I shall use the pronoun 'he' to refer to any divine individual, without the implication that the individual is male.[7]

It is hardly surprising, then, that Swinburne has no qualms about using the male generic when writing of humanity as a whole. More telling, however, are the kind of examples Swinburne uses to clarify his work. While Swinburne does not claim that women are incapable of reason or subordinate to men, the examples which illustrate his work strongly suggest this conclusion. So:

> In the actual world, very often a man's withholding benefits from another is correlated with the latter's suffering some passive evil either physical or mental. Thus if I withhold from you certain vitamins, you will suffer disease. Or if I deprive you of *your wife* by persuading her to live with me instead, you will suffer grief at the loss.[8]

The use of such examples suggests that the audience for which Swinburne writes is male; he assumes that his readers are male, having wives, being fathers.[9] As such, Swinburne does not need to state explicitly that women are incapable of reason or subordinate to men; it is enough for him to use examples which suggest that this is the case. The male is the rational subject of his philosophy, the female the passive object, worthy only of inclusion as 'the philosopher's wife'.[10]

Swinburne is not alone in assuming the philosophical community to be composed of males. Alvin Plantinga uses this somewhat titillating example in his discussion of the ontological argument:

> Now if a person can have different properties in different worlds, then he can have different degrees of greatness in different worlds. In the actual world Raquel Welch has impressive assets; but there is a world RW_f in which she is fifty pounds overweight and mousy.[11]

Ms Welch may, according to Plantinga, have more noteworthy features than the typical philosopher's wife, but in using such an example it seems that Plantinga intends her sensuality to be shared and enjoyed by the male philosophers who constitute his audience.

A short survey of trends in modern philosophy suggest, then, that if misogyny is not as explicit as it was in the past, a highly ambiguous understanding of woman remains. Careful analysis and reading of contemporary philosophical texts may suggest that while misogynistic views may not be explicit, an implicit misogyny continues to inform the assumptions of philosophers. This is hardly surprising if one considers the historical development of philosophical methodology. The misogyny which formed the context for the writings of the earliest philosophers is maintained through the transmission and development of the key philosophical ideas of the western tradition.

The Development of Philosophical Method

In developing one's ideas, it is common practice to use the work of previous philosophers to support one's argument. This gives it a sense of grounding, shows knowledge of the history of ideas, and establishes the basis of one's ideas in the development of the tradition. Arguably, this method may perpetuate particular ways of understanding reality which arise from sexist presuppositions supported by key thinkers within the tradition.

The way in which methodology can perpetuate sexist structures of reality can be illustrated if the historical development of dualism is considered. A dualistic understanding of reality can be shown to support philosophical understandings of reason and rationality, which are in turn reliant on particular accounts of male and female roles. The dualism Plato advanced makes a distinction between the shadowy world of impressions and the brilliant reality of the World of Forms or Ideas. Aristotle develops this understanding of reality to include the linked dualisms of spirit/matter, mind/body, reason/nature and ultimately male/female.

The purported connections between man and reason, woman and nature, are made explicit in Augustine's writings. Kim Power in her compelling study of Augustine argues that careful analysis of his work reveals a movement from gender-language concerning the mind to a 'sexualized' understanding of reason versus nature.[12] Power claims that in his discussion of the mind as the locus for the *imago Dei*, Augustine uses gender-language to contrast two features of the mind. Augustine distinguishes between Wisdom (or 'Sapientia'), which, unusually, is defined as masculine, and Knowledge (or 'Scientia'), which is defined as feminine. Both sexes possess both faculties (leading to the conclusion that 'the mind has no sex'), but for Augustine the image of God is located in the faculty of Sapientia. Scientia is a tool to be exercised by Sapientia, but it must be vigorously controlled. This is necessary, because the way in which Scientia accumulates information from the physical world necessitates a close connection with nature and thus with the ways of the flesh. While Augustine is at pains to claim that both men and women share these functions in the mind, the way in which he genders Wisdom/Knowledge feeds into his understanding of male/female roles. Ultimately, the gender language used for the faculties of the mind leads to the sexualizing of Wisdom/Knowledge; man is associated with mind/spirit and woman with the body/nature.

Given this philosophical heritage, it is not surprising that later philosophers should come to view 'Reason' in the same way. Reason and its attributes are contrasted with nature/body/matter. Moreover, Reason is understood as a masculine attribute most closely associated with the male, and nature is understood as a feminine attribute most closely associated with the female. Analysis of the works of Kant, Rousseau and Hegel illustrates this point. Descartes, the figure must closely associated with dualism, does not equate man with the mind and woman with nature. Paradoxically, philosophers who are highly critical of his dualistic interpretation of reality maintain an implicit dualism when considering the roles of men and women.[13]

Perusal of more recent philosophical writings reveals similar assumptions. J. R. Lucas notes that women are 'less likely' to be mathematically minded. He appears to reach this conclusion from the dearth of female practitioners in that 'purest of disciplines' maths and logic. The assumption seems to be that the higher forms of reasoning are out of woman's reach, not that there may be other factors which prevent women from entering certain disciplines.

The inability to recognize the way in which philosophical assumptions draw upon gender language and reinforce gender roles can lead to a distorted view of what constitutes 'proper' philosophy. Mary Warnock in her introduction to a collection of writings by 'women philosophers' shows the limitation of such an approach.[14] While offering a fascinating collection of philosophical writings by women, she admits to excluding feminist writings from her collection. The rationale for this omission lies in Warnock's understanding of philosophy. Philosophy, she claims, is concerned with generalizations and abstract ideas.[15] Furthermore, the 'true' philosopher is concerned with producing 'rational' arguments to support their case. On both grounds Warnock believes feminist philosophers fail to be properly philosophical. In examining feminist writings she sums up her feelings in the following way:

> There tends to be too much unexamined dogma in these writings, too much ill-concealed proselytizing, too little objective analysis, to allow them to qualify for inclusion among philosophical writing proper.[16]

Such a conclusion is problematic. Warnock omits discussion of the historical development of rationality and its implications for accounts of the sexes. As such, her work maintains masculinist ideals of rationality as abstraction and generalization, and reinforces the notion of mind as distinct from the physical world. Warnock's refusal to consider the societal and environmental factors which contribute to understandings of 'universal' truth-claims limits the success of her 'rediscovery' of women who were also philosophers.

This brief survey of the basic assumptions which support 'mainstream' philosophical works goes some way to exposing the problem facing feminists. An explicitly dualistic division of reality may have been challenged, but the hierarchies implicit in this way of thinking – and specifically the hierarchical account of male/female relationships – remain.

Feminist Philosophy and the Western Tradition

An immediate response to the problematic nature of philosophical methodology might be to reject the philosophical canon *in toto*. Once the connection between misogyny and philosophical frameworks is made, it seems difficult to use any aspect of the philosophers' thought to structure or inform a distinctively feminist philosophy. Alternatively, a selective use of the canon might be advocated, but this may prove problematic. In formulating her own account of autonomy, Mary Daly sees Nietzsche as a 'prophet' whose ideas were undermined by his misogyny.[17] If one broadens the discussion and considers Nietzsche's views on women (and indeed 'slaves'), it seems that to appropriate his critique of Christianity and his understanding of the individual is to ignore the overall thrust of his work towards hierarchical distinctions on the basis of sex and class. Arguably, his attitudes towards women and 'lesser males' is part and parcel of his understanding of the nature of reality. To separate one aspect of his thinking from the overall shape of his philosophy may be to miss the interconnections between the different aspects of his thought.

Some thoughts of Luce Irigaray have the potential to move the reader beyond this apparent impasse. In suggesting that women might 'have a fling' with the philosophers, Irigaray offers a radical way of approaching the philosophical canon. Simply rejecting the importance of these texts will not do. Selective readings are likewise inadequate. Instead, Irigaray suggests a radical subversion of the idea of mimicry. Rather than mimicking the good behaviour of a 'wife' in accepting the philosophers' ideas unthinkingly, the feminist philosopher should use this material to confront the philosopher with the unjust, inadequate and unbalanced nature of his writing. In Irigaray's words:

> To play with mimesis is thus, for a woman, to try to recover the place of her exploitation by discourse, without allowing herself to be simply reduced to it.[18]

The aim of playing with the discourse is 'to make "visible", by an effect of playful repetition, what was supposed to remain invisible'.[19] Irigaray suggests that we adopt the playful attitude of a 'mistress' towards the words and the concepts. In this way it is possible to expose the attitude to women present within the text. In approaching the discussion of woman and her 'nature', Irigaray offers the following advice:

> [Women] should not put [the issue], then, in the form 'What is woman?' but rather, repeating/interpreting the way in which, within discourse, the feminine finds itself defined as lack, deficiency, or as imitation and negative image of the subject, they should signify that with respect to this logic a disruptive excess is possible on the feminine side.[20]

In challenging the 'understanding' of women which dominates the western tradition, women open up the possibility of a new philosophy, one which is not hindered by the outmoded notions of 'masculine' and 'feminine' which have shaped political and social attitudes towards women and men. Divisive understandings of humanity which are accepted implicitly by philosophers can be made explicit and challenged. This act of revelation makes possible a new approach to the task of describing and commenting on all aspects of reality. The aim of this selection from the philosophers is to aid this end: to make what is invisible, visible, and then to move on, heralding, in Irigaray's powerful image, a 'new morning of the world'.[21]

PART I

THE GREEKS

1 Plato *c*.427–347 BCE

Introduction and Background

Plato's philosophy has dominated the discourse of the western tradition. A pupil of Socrates, Plato develops his philosophy through a series of dialogues between Socrates and his pupils. Central to this philosophy is a dualistic understanding of reality. For Plato, the physical world is a pale reflection of the 'Ideal World' of Absolutes, Forms and Ideas. Human beings are understood to combine features of both worlds; the body relates to the material world, the soul to the World of Ideas or Forms. The task of the philosopher is to attain true understanding of this higher dimension by resisting the desires of the physical world.

In recent years, attention has been given to Plato's account of women, and particularly the apparently 'feminist' content of some of his writings. At the heart of the case for a 'feminist Plato' lies the *Republic*. In Book V, Plato argues that women should receive the same education as men. If a woman is appropriately educated and shows leadership qualities, there is no reason why she should not be a 'Guardian' (or leader) of Plato's ideal state.

However, the claim that Plato is feminist has been much disputed. While parts of the *Republic* may suggest an egalitarian Plato, other aspects refute such a claim. The language Plato uses suggests that while in theory women might be leaders of his ideal society, in practice he expects men to take on this role. This is notably the case when he argues for the dissolution of the family. 'Wives and children' – not 'spouses and children' – are to be held in common. More explicitly, Plato accepts the argument that men tend to be better at all things than women. As Julia Annas points out, 'it is hardly a feminist argument to claim that women do not have a special sphere because men can outdo them at absolutely everything'.[1]

In other works, Plato argues for the innate inferiority of women. In the *Symposium* he argues that love of man for man is a higher form of love than love of man for woman. The latter form of love is purely connected with procreation; the love of man for man leads to the higher appreciation of the Good. In the *Timaeus*, a hierarchy of creation is advanced, for women are closer to animals than are men. This hierarchical account of creation is coupled with a dualistic view of reality which Plato adopts from Pythagoras.[2] For Pythagoras, bodiliness is associated with femaleness, and spirituality or higher reasoning with maleness. While Plato does not explicitly accept this distinction, implicitly this notion supports his understanding of men and women. In the *Laws*, a later work than the *Republic*, this notion comes to the fore.

Straightforward identifications of Plato's writings as 'feminist' seem without grounds. While aspects of his work are useful for those wishing to argue for the equality of woman, other aspects betray the thinking of an age where women's lives were very much in the hands of men.

REPUBLIC V (451–7)*

I suppose that I must retrace my steps and say what I perhaps ought to have said before in the proper place. The part of the men has been played out, and now properly enough comes the turn of the women. Of them I will proceed to speak, and the more readily since I am invited by you.

For men born and educated like our citizens, the only way, in my opinion, of arriving at a right conclusion about the possession and use of women and children is to follow the path on which we originally started, when we said that the men were to be the guardians and watchdogs of the herd.

True.

Let us further suppose the birth and education of our women to be subject to similar or nearly similar regulations; then we shall see whether the result accords with our design.

What do you mean?

What I mean may be put into the form of a question, I said: Are dogs divided into 'hes' and 'shes', or do they both share equally in hunting and in keeping watch and in the other duties of dogs? or do we entrust to the males the entire and exclusive care of the flocks, while we leave the females at home, under the idea that the bearing and suckling their puppies is labour enough for them?

No, he said, *they share alike; the only difference between them is that the males are stronger and the females weaker.*

But can you use different animals for the same purpose, unless they are bred and fed in the same way?

You cannot.

Then, if women are to have the same duties as men, they must have the same nurture and education?

Yes.

The education which was assigned to the men was music and gymnastic.

Yes.

Then women must be taught music and gymnastic and also the art of war, which they must practise like the men?

That is the inference, I suppose.

I should rather expect, I said, that several of our proposals, if they are carried out, being unusual, may appear ridiculous.

*Reprinted from *The Dialogues of Plato*, translated by Benjamin Jowett; reproduced by permission of Oxford University Press.

No doubt of it.

Yes, and the most ridiculous thing of all will be the sight of women naked in the palaestra,[1] exercising with the men, especially when they are no longer young; they certainly will not be a vision of beauty, any more than the enthusiastic old men who in spite of wrinkles and ugliness continue to frequent the gymnasia.

Yes, indeed, he said: *according to present notions the proposal would be thought ridiculous.*

But then, I said, as we have determined to speak our minds, we must not fear the jests of the wits which will be directed against this sort of innovation; how they will talk of women's attainments both in music and gymnastic, and above all about their wearing armour and riding upon horseback!

Very true, he replied.

Yet having begun we must go forward to the rough places of the law; at the same time begging of these gentlemen for once in their life to be serious. Not long ago, as we shall remind them, the Hellenes were of the opinion, which is still generally received among the barbarians, that the sight of a naked man was ridiculous and improper; and when first the Cretans and then the Lacedaemonians introduced the custom, the wits of that day might equally have ridiculed the innovation.

No doubt.

But when experience showed that to let all things be uncovered was far better than to cover them up, and the ludicrous effect to the outward eye vanished before the better principle which reason asserted, then the man was perceived to be a fool who directs the shafts of his ridicule at any other sight but that of folly and vice, or seriously inclines to weigh the beautiful by any other standard but that of the good.

Very true, he replied.

First, then, whether the question is to be put in jest or in earnest, let us come to an understanding about the nature of woman: Is she capable of sharing either wholly or partially in the actions of men, or not at all? And is the art of war one of those arts in which she can or cannot share? That will be the best way of commencing the enquiry, and will probably lead to the fairest conclusion.

That will be much the best way.

Shall we take the other side first and begin by arguing against ourselves; in this manner the adversary's position will not be undefended.

Why not? he said.

Then let us put a speech into the mouths of our opponents. They will say: 'Socrates and Glaucon, no adversary need convict you, for you yourselves, at the first foundation of the State, admitted the principle that everybody was to do the one work suited to his own nature.' And certainly, if I am not mistaken, such an admission was made by us. 'And do not the natures of men and women differ very much indeed?' And we shall reply: Of course they do. Then we shall be asked, 'Whether the tasks assigned to men and to women should not be different, and such as are agreeable to their different natures?' Certainly they should. 'But if so, have you not fallen into a serious inconsistency in saying that men and women, whose natures are so entirely different, ought to perform the same actions?' What defence will you make for us, my good Sir, against any one who offers these objections?

That is not an easy question to answer when asked suddenly; and I shall and I do beg of you to draw out the case on our side.

These are the objections, Glaucon, and there are many others of a like kind, which I foresaw long ago; they made me afraid and reluctant to take in hand any law about the possession and nurture of women and children.

By Zeus, he said, *the problem to be solved is anything but easy.*

Why yes, I said, but the fact is that when a man is out of his depth, whether he has fallen into a little swimming bath or into mid-ocean, he has to swim all the same . . . Well then, let us see if any way of escape can be found. We acknowledged – did we not? that different natures ought to have different pursuits, and that men's and women's natures are different. And now what are we saying? – that different natures ought to have the same pursuits – this is the inconsistency which is charged upon us.

Precisely.

Verily, Glaucon, I said, glorious is the power of the art of contradiction!

Why do you say so?

Because I think that many a man falls into the practice against his will. When he thinks that he is reasoning he is really disputing, just because he cannot define and divide, and so know that of which he is speaking; and he will pursue a merely verbal opposition in the spirit of contention and not of fair discussion.

Yes, he replied, *such is very often the case; but what has that to do with us and our argument?*

A great deal; for there is certainly a danger of our getting unintentionally into a verbal opposition.

In what way?

Why we valiantly and pugnaciously insist upon the verbal truth, that different natures ought to have different pursuits, but we never considered at all what was the meaning of sameness or difference of nature, or why we distinguished them when we assigned different pursuits to different natures and the same to the same natures.

Why, no, he said, *that was never considered by us*.

I said: Suppose that by way of illustration we were to ask the question whether there is not an opposition in nature between bald men and hairy men; and if this is admitted by us, then, if bald men are cobblers, we should forbid the hairy men to be cobblers, and conversely?

That would be a jest, he said.

Yes, I said, a jest; and why? because we never meant when we constructed the State, that the opposition of natures should extend to every difference, but only to those differences which affected the pursuit in which the individual is engaged; we should have argued, for example, that a physician and one who is in mind a physician may be said to have the same nature.

True.

Whereas the physician and the carpenter have different natures?

Certainly.

And if, I said, the male and female sex appear to differ in their fitness for any art or pursuit, we should say that such pursuit or art ought to be assigned to one or the other of them; but if the difference consists only in women bearing and men begetting children, this does not amount to a proof that a woman differs from a man in respect of the sort of education she should receive; and we shall therefore continue to maintain that our guardians and their wives ought to have the same pursuits.

Very true, he said.

Next, we shall ask our opponent how, in reference to any of the pursuits or arts of civic life, the nature of a woman differs from that of a man?

That will be quite fair.

And perhaps he, like yourself, will reply that to give a sufficient answer on the instant is not easy; but after a little reflection there is no difficulty.

Yes, perhaps.

Suppose then that we invite him to accompany us in the argument, and then we may hope to show him that there is nothing peculiar in the constitution of women which would affect them in the administration of the State.

By all means.

Let us say to him: Come now, and we will ask you a question: – when you spoke of a nature gifted or not gifted in any respect, did you mean to say that one man will acquire a thing easily, another with difficulty; a little learning will lead the one to discover a great deal; whereas the other, after much study and application, no sooner learns than he forgets; or again, did you mean, that the one has a body which is a good servant to his mind, while the body of the other is a hindrance to him? – would not these be the sort of differences which distinguish the man gifted by nature from the one who is ungifted?

No one will deny that.

And can you mention any pursuit of mankind in which the male sex has not all these gifts and qualities in a higher degree than the female? Need I waste time in speaking of the art of weaving, and the management of pancakes and preserves, in which womankind does really appear to be great, and in which for her to be beaten by a man is of all things the most absurd?

You are quite right, he replied, *in maintaining the general inferiority of the female sex: although many women are in many things superior to many men, yet on the whole what you say is true.*

And if so my friend, I said, there is no special faculty of administration in a state which a woman has because she is a woman, or which a man has by virtue of his sex, but the gifts of nature are alike diffused in both; all the pursuits of men are the pursuits of women also, but in all of them a woman is inferior to a man.

Very true.

Then are we to impose all our enactments on men and none of them on women?

That will never do.

One woman has a gift of healing, another not; one is a musician, and another has no music in her nature?

Very true.

And one woman has a turn for gymnastic and military exercises, and another is unwarlike and hates gymnastics?

Certainly.

And one woman is a philosopher, and another is an enemy of philosophy; one has spirit, and another is without spirit?

That is also true.

Then one woman will have the temper of a guardian, and another not. Was not the selection of the male guardians determined by differences of this sort?

Yes.

Men and women alike possess the qualities which make a guardian; they differ only in their comparative strength or weakness.

Obviously.

And those women who have such qualities are to be selected as the companions and colleagues of men who have similar qualities and whom they resemble in capacity and in character?

Very true.

And ought not the same natures to have the same pursuits?

They ought.

Then, as we were saying before, there is nothing unnatural in assigning music and gymnastic to the wives of the guardian – to that point we come round again.

Certainly not.

The law which we then enacted was agreeable to nature, and therefore not an impossibility or mere aspiration; and the contrary practice, which prevails at present, is in reality a violation of nature.

That appears to be true.

We had to consider, first, whether our proposals were possible, and secondly, whether they were the most beneficial?

Yes.

And the possibility has been acknowledged?

Yes.

The very great benefit has next to be established?

Quite so.

You will admit that the same education which makes a man a good guardian will make a woman a good guardian; for their original nature is the same?

Yes.

I should like to ask you a question.

What is it?

Would you say that all men are equal in excellence, or is one man better than another?

The latter.

And in the commonwealth which we were founding do you conceive the guardians who have been brought up on our model system to be more perfect men, or the cobblers whose education has been cobbling?

What a ridiculous question!

You have answered me, I replied: Well, and may we not further say that our guardians are the best of our citizens?

By far the best.

And will not their wives be the best women?

Yes, by far the best.

And can there be anything better for the interests of the State than that the men and women of a State should be as good as possible?

There can be nothing better.

And this is what the arts of music and gymnastic, when present in such manner as we have described, will accomplish?

Certainly.

Then we have made an enactment not only possible but in the highest degree beneficial to the State?

True.

Then let the wives of our guardians strip, for their virtue will be their robe, and let them share in the toils of war and the defence of their country; only in the distribution of labours the lighter are to be assigned to the women, who are the weaker natures, but in other respects their duties are to be the same. And as for the man who laughs at naked women exercising their bodies from the best of motives, in his laughter he is plucking 'A fruit of unripe wisdom,' and he himself is ignorant of what he is laughing at, or what he is about; for that is, and ever will be, the best of sayings, *That the useful is the noble and the hurtful is the base.*

Very true.

Here, then, is one difficulty in our law about women, which we may say that we have now escaped; the wave has not swallowed us up alive for enacting that the guardians of either sex should have all their pursuits in common; to the utility and also to the possibility of this arrangement the consistency of the argument with itself bears witness.

Yes, that was a mighty wave which you have escaped.

Yes, I said, but a greater is coming; you will not think much of this when you see the next.

Go on; let me see.

The law, I said, which is the sequel of this and of all that has preceded, is to the following effect, – 'that the wives of our guardians are to be common, and their children are to be common, and no parent is to know his own child, nor any child his parent'.

NOTE

1. [Ed.] *palaestra*: place in Greek cities where boys learnt the art of wrestling and gymnastics.

SYMPOSIUM (207–12)*

All this she taught me at various times when she spoke of love. And I remember her once saying to me, 'What is the cause, Socrates, of love, and the attendant desire? See you not how all animals, birds, as well as beasts, in their desire of procreation, are in agony when they take the infection of love, which begins with the desire of union; whereto is added the care of offspring, on whose behalf the weakest are ready to battle against the strongest even to the uttermost, and to die for them, and will let themselves be tormented with hunger or suffer anything in order to maintain their young. Man may be supposed to act thus from reason; but why should animals have these passionate feelings? Can you tell me why?' Again I replied that I did not know. She said to me: 'And do you expect ever to become a master in the art of love, if you do not know this?' 'But I have told you already, Diotima,[1] that my ignorance is the reason why I come to you; for I am conscious that I want a teacher; tell me then the cause of this and of the other mysteries of love.' 'Marvel not,' she said, 'if you believe that love is of the immortal, as we have several times acknowledged; for here again, and on the same principle too, the mortal nature is seeking as far as is possible to be everlasting and immortal: and this is only to be attained by generation, because generation always leaves behind a new existence in the place of the old. Nay even in the life of the same individual there is succession and not absolute unity: a man is called the same, and yet in the short interval which elapses between youth and age, and in which every animal is said to have life and identity, he is undergoing a perpetual process of loss and reparation – hair, flesh, bones, blood, and the whole body are always changing.

*Reprinted from *The Dialogues of Plato*, translated by Benjamin Jowett; reproduced by permission of Oxford University Press.

Which is true not only of the body, but also of the soul, whose habits, tempers, opinions, desires, pleasures, pains, fears, never remain the same in any one of us, but are always coming and going; and equally true of knowledge, and what is still more surprising to us mortals, not only do the sciences in general spring up and decay, so that in respect of them we are never the same; but each of them individually experiences a like change. For what is implied in the word "recollection", but the departure of knowledge, which is ever being forgotten, and is renewed and preserved by recollection, and appears to be the same although in reality new, according to that law of succession by which all mortal things are preserved, not absolutely the same, but by substitution, the old worn-out mortality leaving another new and similar existence behind – unlike the divine, which is always the same and not another? And in this way, Socrates, the mortal body, or mortal anything, partakes of immortality; but the immortal in another way. Marvel not then at the love which all men have of their offspring; for that universal love and interest is for the sake of immortality.'

I was astonished at her words, and said: 'Is this really true, O thou wise Diotima?' And she answered with all the authority of an accomplished sophist: 'Of that, Socrates, you may be assured; – think only of the ambition of men, and you will wonder at the senselessness of their ways, unless you consider how they are stirred by the love of an immortality of fame. They are ready to run all risks greater far than they would have run for their children, and to spend money and undergo any sort of toil, and even to die, for the sake of leaving behind them a name which shall be eternal. Do you imagine that Alcestis would have died to save Admetus,[2] or Achilles to avenge Patroclus[3] . . . if they had not imagined that the memory of their virtues, which still survives among us, would be immortal? Nay,' she said, 'I am persuaded that all men do all things, and the better they are the more they do them, in hope of the glorious fame of immortal virtue; for they desire the immortal.

'Those who are pregnant in the body only, betake themselves to women and beget children – this is the character of their love; their offspring, as they hope, will preserve their memory and give them the blessedness and immortality which they desire in the future. But souls which are pregnant – for there certainly are men who are more creative in their souls than in their bodies – conceive that which is proper for the soul to conceive or contain. And what are these conceptions? – wisdom and virtue in general.

And such creators are poets and all artists who are deserving of the name inventor. But the greatest and fairest sort of wisdom by far is that which is concerned with the ordering of states and families, and which is called temperance and justice. And he who in youth has the seed of these implanted in him and is himself inspired, when he comes to maturity desires to beget and generate. He wanders about seeking beauty that he may beget offspring – for in deformity he will beget nothing – and naturally embraces the beautiful rather than the deformed body; above all when he finds a fair and noble and well-nurtured soul, he embraces the two in one person, and to such an one he is full of speech about virtue and the nature and pursuits of a good man; and he tries to educate him; and at the touch of the beautiful which is ever present to his memory, even when absent, he brings forth that which he had conceived long before, and in company with him tends that which he brings forth; and they are married by a far nearer tie and have a closer friendship than those who beget mortal children for the children who are their common offspring are fairer and more immortal. Who, when he thinks of Homer and Hesiod[4] and other great poets, would not rather have their children than ordinary human ones? Who would not emulate them in the creation of children such as theirs, which have preserved their memory and given them everlasting glory? . . . There is Solon, too, who is the revered father of Athenian laws; and many others there are in many other places, both among Hellenes and barbarians, who have given to the world many noble works, and have been the parents of virtue of every kind; and many temples have been raised in their honour for the sake of children such as theirs; which were never raised in honour of any one, for the sake of his mortal children.

'These are the lesser mysteries of love, into which even you, Socrates, may enter; to the greater and more hidden ones which are the crown of these, and to which, if you pursue them in a right spirit, they will lead, I know not whether you will be able to attain. But I will do my utmost to inform you, and do you follow if you can. For he who would proceed aright in this matter should begin in youth to visit beautiful forms; and first, if he be guided by his instructor aright, to love one such form only – out of that he should create fair thoughts; and soon he will of himself perceive that the beauty of one form is akin to the beauty of another; and then if beauty of form in general is his pursuit, how foolish would he be not to recognize that the beauty in every form is one and the same! And when he perceives this he will abate his violent love of the one, which he will despise and deem a small thing, and will become a lover of all beautiful forms; in the next stage he will consider that the beauty of the mind is more honourable than the beauty of the outward form. So that if a virtuous soul have but a little comeliness, he will be content to love and tend him, and will search out and bring to the birth thoughts which may improve the young, until he is compelled to contemplate and see the beauty of institutions and laws, and to understand that the beauty of them all is of one family, and that personal beauty is a trifle; and after laws and institutions he will go on to the sciences, that he may see their beauty, being not like a servant in love with the beauty of one youth or man or institution, himself a slave mean and narrow-minded, but drawing towards and contemplating the vast sea of beauty, he will create many fair and noble thoughts and notions in boundless love of wisdom; until on that shore he grows and waxes strong, and at last the vision is revealed to him of a single science, which is the science of beauty everywhere. To this I will proceed; please to give me your very best attention:

'He who has been instructed thus far in the things of love, and who has learned to see the beautiful in due order and succession, when he comes toward the end will suddenly perceive a nature of wondrous beauty (and this, Socrates, is the final cause of all our former toils) – a nature which in the first place is everlasting, not growing and decaying, or waxing and waning; secondly, not fair in one point of view and foul in another, or at one time or in one relation or at one place fair, at another time or in another relation or at another place foul, as if fair to some and foul to others, or in the likeness of a face or hands or any other part of the bodily frame, or in any form of speech or knowledge, or existing in any other being, as for example, in an animal, or in heaven, or in earth, or in any other place; but beauty absolute, separate, simple, and everlasting, which without diminution and without increase, or any change, is imparted to the ever-growing and perishing beauties of all other things. He who from these ascending under the influence of true love, begins to perceive that beauty, is not far from the end. And the true order of going, or being led by another, to the things of love, is to begin from the beauties of earth and mount upwards for the sake of that other beauty, using these as steps only, and from one going on to two, and from two to all fair forms, and from fair forms to fair practices, and from fair practices to fair notions, until from fair notions he arrives at the notion of absolute beauty, and at last knows what the essence of beauty is. This, my dear Socrates,' said the stranger of Mantineia, 'is that life above all others which man should live, in the contemplation of beauty absolute; a beauty which if you once beheld, you would see not to be after the measure of gold, and garments, and fair boys and youths, whose presence now entrances you; and you and many a one would be content to live seeing them only and conversing with them without meat or drink, if that were possible – you only want to look at them and to be with them. But what if man had eyes to see the true beauty – the divine beauty, I mean, pure and clear and unalloyed, not clogged with the pollutions of mortality and all the colours and vanities of human life – thither looking, and holding converse with the true beauty simple and divine? Remember how in that communion only, beholding beauty with the eye of the mind, he will be enabled to bring forth, not images of beauty, but realities (for he has hold not of an image but of a reality), and bringing forth and nourishing true virtue to become the friend of God and be immortal, if mortal man may. Would that be an ignoble life?'

Such, Phaedrus – and I speak not only to you, but to all of you – were the words of Diotima; and I am persuaded of their truth. And being persuaded of them, I try to persuade others, that in the attainment of this end human nature will not easily find a helper better than love.

NOTES

1. [Ed.] *Diotima*: credited with the role of teacher to Socrates, there is doubt that such a woman philosopher ever existed. Walter Hamilton: 'It is almost universally and no doubt rightly held that Diotima is a fictitious personage, in spite of the apparently historical statements made about her by Socrates. It is not desirable here to go into the arguments in favour of this conclusion, but it may be noticed that this is not the only place in the Platonic dialogues where Socrates is made to ascribe the substance of what he has to say to others . . .' (from introduction to 1951 Penguin edition of *Symposium*, p. 19). Why are 'scholars' so keen to write her off as fictitious? For discussion of this point and an argument for her historicity, see M. E. Waithe, 'Diotima of Mantinea', in M. E. Waithe (ed.), *A History of Women Philosophers* (Dordrecht: Kluwer Academic Press, 1987).

2. [Ed.] *Alcestis . . . Admetus*: characters from Euripides' drama *Alcestis*. Alcestis dies for her husband Admetus, but is restored to life by Hercules.

3. [Ed.] *Achilles . . . Patroclus*: in the *Iliad*, Achilles dies avenging Patroclus' death at the hands of Hector.

4. [Ed.] *Homer and Hesiod*: (*c*.700 BCE) writers of epic Greek poetry.

TIMAEUS (90–2)*

And we should consider that God gave the sovereign part of the human soul to be the divinity of each one, being that part which, as we say, dwells at the top of the body, and inasmuch as we are a plant not of an earthly but of a heavenly growth, raises us from earth to our kindred who are in heaven. And in this we say truly; for the divine power suspended the head and root of us from that place where the generation of the soul first began, and thus made the whole body upright. When a man is always occupied with the cravings of desire and ambition, and is eagerly striving to satisfy them, all his thoughts must be mortal, and, as far as it is possible altogether to become such, he must be mortal every whit, because he has cherished the mortal part. But he who has been earnest in the love of knowledge and of true wisdom, and has exercised his intellect more than any other part of him, must have thoughts immortal and divine, if he attain truth, and in so far as human nature is capable of sharing in immortality, he must altogether be immortal; and since he is ever cherishing the divine power, and has the divinity within him in perfect order, he will be perfectly happy. Now there is only one way of taking care of things, and this is to give to each the food and motion which are natural to it. And the motions which are naturally akin to the divine principle within us are the thoughts and revolutions of the universe. These each man should follow, and correct the courses of the head which were corrupted at our birth, and by learning the harmonies and revolutions of the universe, should assimilate the thinking being to the thought, renewing his original nature, and having assimilated them should attain to that perfect life which the gods have set before mankind, both for the present and the future.

Thus our original design of discoursing about the universe down to the creation of man is nearly completed. A brief mention may be made of the generation of other animals, so far as the subject admits of brevity; in this manner our argument will best

*Reprinted from *The Dialogues of Plato*, translated by Benjamin Jowett; reproduced by permission of Oxford University Press.

attain a due proportion. On the subject of animals, then, the following remarks may be offered. Of the men who came into the world, those who were cowards or led unrighteous lives may with reason be supposed to have changed into the nature of women in the second generation. And this was the reason why at that time the gods created in us the desire of sexual intercourse, contriving in man one animated substance, and in woman another, which they formed respectively in the following manner. The outlet for drink by which liquids pass through the lung under the kidneys and into the bladder, which receives and then by the pressure of the air emits them, was so fashioned by them to penetrate also into the body of the marrow, which passes from the head along the neck and through the back, and which in the preceding discourse we have named the seed. And the seed having life, and becoming endowed with respiration, produces in that part in which it respires a lively desire of emission, and thus creates in us the love of procreation. Wherefore also in men the organ of generation becomes rebellious and masterful, like an animal disobedient to reason, and maddened with the sting of lust, seeks to gain absolute sway; and the same is the case with the so-called womb or matrix of women; the animal within them is desirous of procreating children, and when remaining unfruitful long beyond its proper time, gets discontented and angry, and wandering in every direction through the body, closes up the passages of breath, and, by obstructing respiration, drives them to extremity, causing all varieties of disease, until at length the desire and love of the man and the woman, bringing them together and as it were plucking the fruit from the tree, sow in the womb, as in a field, animals unseen by reason of their smallness and without form; these again are separated and matured within; they are then finally brought out into the light, and thus the generation of animals is completed.

Thus were created women and the female sex in general. But the race of birds was created out of innocent light-minded men, who, although their minds were directed toward heaven, imagined, in their simplicity, that the clearest demonstration of the things above was to be obtained by sight; these were remodelled and transformed into birds, and they grew feathers instead of hair. The race of wild pedestrian animals, again, came from those who had no philosophy in any of their thoughts, and never considered at all about the nature of the heavens, because they had ceased to use the courses of the head, but followed the guidance of those parts of the soul which are in the breast. In consequence of these habits of theirs they had their front-legs and their heads resting upon the earth to which they were drawn by natural affinity; and the crowns of their heads were elongated and of all sorts of shapes, into which the courses of the soul were crushed by reason of disuse. And this was the reason why they were created quadrupeds and polypods: God gave the more senseless of them the more support that they might be more attracted to the earth. And the most foolish of them, who trail their bodies entirely upon the ground and have no longer any need of feet, he made without feet to crawl upon the earth. The fourth class were the inhabitants of the water: these were made out of the most entirely senseless and ignorant of all, who the transformers did not think any longer worthy of pure respiration, because they possessed a soul which was made impure by all sorts of transgression; and instead of the subtle and pure medium of air, they gave them the deep and muddy sea to be their element of respiration; and hence arose the race of fishes and oysters, and other aquatic animals, which have received the most remote habitations as a punishment of their outlandish ignorance. These are the laws by which animals pass into one another, now, as ever, changing as they lose or gain wisdom and folly.

LAWS (781a–b)*

For with you, Cleinias and Megillus, the common tables of men are, as I said, a heaven-born and admirable institution, but you are mistaken in leaving the women unregulated by law. They have no similar institution of public tables in the light of day, and just that part of the human race which is by nature prone to secrecy and stealth on account of their weakness – I mean the female sex – has been left without regulation by the legislator, which is a great mistake. And, in consequence of this neglect, many things have grown lax among you, which might have been far better, if they had been only regulated by law; for the neglect of regulations about women may not only be regarded as a neglect of half the entire matter, but in proportion as woman's nature is inferior to that of men in capacity for virtue, in that

*Reprinted from *The Dialogues of Plato*, translated by Benjamin Jowett; reproduced by permission of Oxford University Press.

degree the consequence of such neglect is more than twice as important. The careful consideration of this matter, and the arranging and ordering on a common principle of all our institutions relating both to men and women, greatly conduces to the happiness of the state. But at present, such is the unfortunate condition of mankind, that no man of sense will even venture to speak of common tables in places and cities in which they have never been established at all; and how can any one avoid being utterly ridiculous, who attempts to compel women to show in public how much they eat and drink? There is nothing at which the sex is more likely to take offence. For women are accustomed to creep into dark places, and when dragged out into the light they will exert their utmost powers of resistance, and be far too much for the legislator. And therefore, as I said before, in most places they will not endure to have the truth spoken without raising a tremendous outcry, but in this state perhaps they may.

STUDY QUESTIONS

1. What evidence might be advanced for the claim that Plato was a 'feminist'? Why might such a view be challenged?
2. Why might the hierarchies advanced in the *Symposium* and the *Timaeus* suggest that Plato's views are detrimental to feminism?

SELECT BIBLIOGRAPHY

General

A. Flew, *An Introduction to Western Philosophy* (London: Thames & Hudson, 1989).

For feminist analysis

J. Annas, 'Plato's Republic and Feminism', *Philosophy*, vol. 51 (1976), pp. 307–21.

J. Grimshaw, *Feminist Philosophers* (Brighton: Harvester Wheatsheaf, 1986).

G. Jantzen, *Power, Gender and Christian Mysticism* (Cambridge: Cambridge University Press, 1995).

H. Lesser, 'Plato's Feminism', *Philosophy*, vol. 54 (1979), pp. 113–17 (a response to Annas).

G. Lloyd, *The Man of Reason* (London: Methuen, 1984).

S. M. Okin, *Women in Western Political Thought* (London: Virago, 1980).

E. Spelman, *Inessential Woman: Problems of Exclusion in Feminist Thought* (Boston: Beacon Press, 1988).
M. E. Waithe, 'Diotima of Mantinea', in M. E. Waithe (ed.), *A History of Women Philosophers*, vol. 1 (Dordrecht: Kluwer Academic Press, 1987), pp. 83–116.
J. K. Ward (ed.), *Feminism and Ancient Philosophy* (London: Routledge, 1996); especially S. B. Levin, 'Women's Nature and Role in the Ideal of the Polis: *Republic V* Revisited', pp. 13–30; and A.-M. Bowery, 'Diotima Tells Socrates a Story', pp. 175–94.

2 ARISTOTLE 384–322 BCE

Introduction and Background

A pupil of Plato, Aristotle was to become as influential as his tutor in defining the shape of western philosophy. Like Plato, Aristotle's main concern was to explore the question of how one should live in this world. However, Aristotle's discussion of this question takes place against a rather different understanding of reality. For Plato, this world of impressions is juxtaposed with the 'real' World of Ideas or Forms. In his writings, Aristotle gives this distinction a decidedly 'this-worldly' focus. While maintaining the platonic distinction between 'form' (or ideas) and 'matter', Aristotle argues that this distinction is to be found in *this* world.

This approach informs Aristotle's account of the meaningful human life, intimately connecting the individual with society. Human beings are 'zoon politikon' (political animals), and as such their meaning is to be found in community. In particular, each person will only find fulfilment if they find their correct place within the state. It is against this backdrop that his account of women unfolds.

Aristotle's understanding of women is more consistent than Plato's. In *On the Generation of Animals*, Aristotle grounds his misogyny in his 'scientific' reflections. In this work, Aristotle explores the process of reproduction in animals. Previous societies had identified the female with the process of fertility to such an extent that the male role in reproduction was not acknowledged.[1] Aristotle turns this account on its head: the male is the sole source of life.[2] It is through the male's sperm that generation takes place. The male is active, the female passive; he provides the shape – or form – life will take, she provides the raw matter for procreation. Indeed, Aristotle goes so far as to suggest that when there is a flaw in the process of reproduction, a female results, leading him to the conclusion that 'the female is, as it were, a mutilated male'.

If his 'scientific' enquiry into the process of reproduction leads Aristotle to the conclusion that females are inferior to males, his structuring of political life reinforces this attitude. In his *Politics*, Aristotle offers a hierarchical account of social structures. Central to his concept of the state is the patriarchal family. Within this structure, Aristotle argues for the submission of woman to man, for just as the soul (or mind) must rule the body, so the male must rule the female. Maleness is thus associated with reason, femaleness with nature and the body.

It is tempting to write off Aristotle's 'scientific' arguments on the grounds that they do not constitute good science.[3] However, such a response ignores the extent to which bad biology not only underpins Aristotle's attitude towards women, but also permeates the understanding of woman within the western tradition. The implication of Aristotle's discussion of the reproductive process seems to be that the male is more fully human than the female. The male is the active, animating force. The male gives form to the shapeless matter offered by the female.

This notion has dominated western reflections on reality. Reason has been opposed to 'nature'. Reason is to shape and conquer the natural world. Active reason has been equated with masculinity. Passive nature has been equated with femininity. This has had a direct bearing on the social relations between men and women. It has also affected the shape of philosophical discourse. If man is equatable with reason, and woman with nature, the philosopher will, of course, be male.[4]

*ON THE GENERATION OF ANIMALS**

From Book I:21 (729b)

At the same time the answer to the next question we have to investigate is clear from these considerations, I mean how it is that the male contributes to generation and how it is that the semen from the male is the cause of the offspring. Does it exist in the body of the embryo as a part of it from the first, mingling with the material which comes from the female? Or does the semen communicate nothing to the material body of the embryo but only to the power and movement in it? For this power is that which acts and makes, while that which is made and receives the form is the residue of the secretion in the female. Now the latter alternative appears to be the right one both *a priori* and in view of the facts. For, if we consider the question on general grounds, we find that, whenever one thing is made from two of which one is active and the other passive, the active agent does not exist in that which is made; and, still more generally, the same applies when one thing moves and another is moved; the moving thing does not exist in that which is moved. But the female, as female, is passive, and the male, as male, is active, and the principle of the movement comes from him. Therefore, if we take the highest

*Reprinted from *The Oxford Translation of Aristotle*, edited by W. D. Ross; reprinted by permission of Oxford University Press.

genera under which they each fall, the one being active and motive and the other passive and moved, that one thing which is produced comes from them only in the sense in which a bed comes into being from the carpenter and the wood, or in which a ball comes into being from the wax and the form. It is plain then that it is not necessary that anything at all should come away from the male, and if anything does come away it does not follow that this gives rise to the embryo as being in the embryo, but only as that which imparts the motion and as the form; so the medical art cures the patient.

From Book I:21 (730a)

What occurs in birds and oviparous fishes is the greatest proof that neither does the semen come from all parts of the male nor does he emit anything of such a nature as to exist within that which is generated, as part of the material embryo, but that he only makes a living creature by the power which resides in the semen (as we said in the case of those insects whose females insert a part of themselves into the male). For if a hen-bird is in process of producing wind-eggs and is then trodden by the cock before the egg has begun to whiten and while it is still yellow, then they become fertile instead of being wind-eggs. And if while it is still yellow she be trodden by another cock, the whole brood of chicks turn out like the second cock. Hence some of those who are anxious to rear fine birds act thus; they change the cocks for the first and second treading, not as if they thought that the semen is mingled with the egg or exists in it, or that it comes from all parts of the cock; for if it did it would have come from both cocks, so that the chick would have all its parts doubled. But it is by its force that the semen of the male gives a certain quality to the material and the nutriment in the female, for the second semen added to the first can produce this effect by heat and concoction, as the egg acquires nutriment so long as it is growing.

The same conclusion is to be drawn from the generation of oviparous fishes. When the female has laid her eggs, the male sprinkles the milt over them, and those eggs are fertilized which it reaches, but not the others; this shows that the male does not contribute anything to the quantity but only to the quality of the embryo.

From what has been said it is plain that the semen does not come from the whole of the body of the male in those animals which emit it, and that the contribution of the female to the generative product is not the same as that of the male, but the male contributes the principle of movement and the female the material. This is why the female does not produce offspring by herself, for she needs a principle, i.e. something to begin the movement in the embryo and to define the form it is to assume. Yet in some animals, as birds, the nature of the female unassisted can generate to a certain extent, for they do form something, only it is incomplete; I mean the so-called wind-eggs.

From Book I:22 (730b)

For the same reason the development of the embryo takes place in the female; neither the male himself nor the female emits semen into the male, but the female receives within herself the share contributed by both, because in the female is the material from which is made the resulting product. Not only must the mass of material exist there from which the embryo is formed in the first instance, but further material must constantly be added that it may increase in size. Therefore the birth must take place in the female. For the carpenter must keep in close connection with his timber and the potter with his clay, and generally all workmanship and the ultimate movement imparted to matter must be connected with the material concerned, as, for instance, architecture is *in* the buildings it makes.

From these considerations we may also gather how it is that the male contributes to generation. The male does not emit semen at all in some animals, and where he does this is no part of the resulting embryo; just so no material part comes from the carpenter to the material, i.e. the wood in which he works, nor does any part of the carpenter's art exist within what he makes, but the shape and the form are imparted from him to the material by means of the motion he sets up. It is his hands that move his tools, his tools that move the material; it is his knowledge of his art, and his soul, in which is the form, that move his hands or any other part of him with a motion of some definite kind, a motion varying with the varying nature of the object made. In like manner, in the male of those animals which emit semen, Nature uses the semen as a tool and as possessing motion in actuality, just as tools are used in the products of any art, for in them lies in a certain sense the motion of the art. Such, then, is the way in which these males contribute to generation. But when the male does not emit semen, but the female inserts some part of herself into the male, this is parallel to a case in which a man should carry the material to the workman. For by reason of weakness in such males Nature is not able to do anything by any secondary means, but the movements imparted to the material are scarcely strong enough when Nature herself watches over them. Thus here she resembles a modeller in clay rather than a carpenter, for she does not touch the work she is forming by means of tools, but, as it were, with her own hands.

Book II:3 (736a–37a)

The next question to raise and to answer is this. If, in the case of those animals which emit semen into the female, that which enters makes no part of the resulting embryo, where is the material part of it diverted if (as we have seen) it acts by means of the power residing in it? It is not only necessary to decide whether what is forming in the female receives anything material, or not, from that which has entered her, but also concerning the soul in virtue of which an animal is so called (and this is in virtue of the sensitive part of the soul) – does this exist originally in the semen and in the unfertilized embryo or not, and if it does whence does it come? For nobody would put down the unfertilized embryo as soulless or in every sense bereft of life (since both the semen and the embryo of an animal have every bit as much life as a plant), and it is productive up to a certain point. That then they possess the nutritive soul is plain (and plain is it from the discussions elsewhere about soul why this soul must be acquired first). As they develop they also acquire the sensitive soul in virtue of which an animal is an animal. For e.g. an animal does not become at the same time an animal and a man or a horse or any other particular animal. For the end is developed last, and the peculiar character of the species is the end of the generation in each individual. Hence arises a question of the greatest difficulty, which we must strive to solve to the best of our ability and as far as possible. When and how and whence is a share in reason acquired by those animals that participate in this principle? It is plain that the semen and unfertilized embryo, while still separate from each other, must be assumed to have the nutritive soul potentially, but not actually, except that (like those unfertilized embryos that are separated from the mother) it absorbs nourishment and performs the function of the nutritive soul. For at first all such embryos seem to live the life of a plant. And it is clear that we must be guided by this in speaking of the sensitive and the rational soul. For all three kinds of soul, not only the nutritive, must be possessed potentially before they are possessed in actuality. And it is necessary either (1) that they should all come into being in the embryo without existing previously outside it, or (2) that they should all exist previously, or (3) that some should so exist and others not. Again, it is necessary that they should either (1) come into being in the material supplied by the female without entering with the semen of the male, or (2) come from the male and be imparted to the material in the female. If the latter, then either all of them, or none, or some must come into being in the male from outside.

Now that it is impossible for them all to pre-exist is clear from this consideration. Plainly those principles whose activity is bodily cannot exist without a body, e.g. walking cannot exist without feet. For the same reason also they cannot enter from outside. For neither is it possible for them to enter by themselves, being inseparable from a body, nor yet in a body, for the semen is only a secretion of the nutriment in process of change. It remains, then, for the reason alone so to enter and alone to be divine, for no bodily activity has any connection with the faculty of reason.

Now it is true that the faculty of all kinds of soul seems to have a connection with a matter different from and more divine than the so-called elements; but as one soul differs from another in honour and dishonour, so differs also the nature of the corresponding matter. All have in their semen that which causes it to be productive; I mean what is called vital heat. This is not fire nor any such force, but it is the spiritus included in the semen and the foam-like, and the natural principle in the spiritus, being analogous to the element of the stars. Hence, whereas fire generates no animal and we do not find any living thing forming in either solids or liquids under the influence of fire, the heat of the sun and that of animals does generate them. Not only is this true of the heat that works through the semen, but whatever other residuum of the animal nature there may be, this also has still a vital principle in it. From such considerations it is clear that the heat in animals neither is fire nor derives its origin from fire.

Let us return to the material of the semen, in and with which comes away from the male the spiritus conveying the principle of soul. Of this principle there are two kinds; the one is not connected with matter, and belongs to those animals in which is included something divine (to wit, what is called reason), while the other is inseparable from matter. This material of the semen dissolves and evaporates because it has a liquid and watery nature. Therefore we ought not to expect it always to come out again from the female or to form any part of the embryo that has taken shape from it; the case resembles that of the fig-juice which curdles milk, for this too changes without becoming any part of the curdling masses.

It has been settled, then, in what sense the embryo and the semen have soul, and in what sense they have not; they have it potentially but not actually.

Now semen is a secretion and is moved with the same movement as that in virtue of which the body increases (this increase being due to subdivision of the nutriment in its last stage). When it has entered the uterus it puts into form the corresponding secretion of the female and moves it with the same movement wherewith it is moved itself. For the female's contribution also is a secretion, and has all the parts in it potentially though none of them actually; it has in it potentially even those parts which differentiate the female from the male, for just as the young of mutilated parents are sometimes born mutilated and sometimes not, so also the young born of a female are sometimes female and sometimes male instead. For the female is, as it were, a mutilated male, and the catamenia are semen, only not pure; for there is only one thing they have not in them, the principle of soul.

*POLITICS**

From Book I (1252a–60b)

1

Every state is a community of some kind, and every community is established with a view to some good; for mankind always act in order to obtain that which they think good. But, if all communities aim at some good, the state or political community,

*Reprinted from *The Oxford Translation of Aristotle*, edited by W. D. Ross; reprinted by permission of Oxford University Press.

which is the highest of all, and which embraces all the rest, aims at good in a greater degree than any other, and at the highest good.

Some people think that the qualifications of a statesman, king, householder, and master are the same, and that they differ, not in kind, but only in the number of their subjects. For example, the ruler over a few is called a master; over more, the manager of a household; over a still larger number, a statesman or king, as if there were no difference between a great household and a small state. The distinction which is made between the king and the statesman is as follows: When the government is personal, the ruler is a king; when, according to the rules of the political science, the citizens rule and are ruled in turn, then he is called a statesman.

But all this is a mistake; for governments differ in kind, as will be evident to any one who considers the matter according to the method which has hitherto guided us. As in other departments of science, so in politics, the compound should always be resolved into the simple elements or least parts of the whole. We must therefore look at the elements of which the state is composed, in order that we may see in what the different kinds of rule differ from one another, and whether any scientific result can be attained about each one of them.

2

He who thus considers things in their first growth and origin, whether a state or anything else, will obtain the clearest view of them. In the first place there must be a union of those who cannot exist without each other; namely, of male and female, that the race may continue (and this is a union which is formed, not of deliberate purpose, but because, in common with other animals and with plants, mankind have a natural desire to leave behind them an image of themselves), and of natural ruler and subject, that both may be preserved. For that which can foresee by the exercise of mind is by nature intended to be lord and master, and that which can with its body give effect to such foresight is a subject, and by nature a slave; hence master and slave have the same interest. Now nature has distinguished between the female and the slave. For she is not niggardly, like the smith who fashions the Delphian knife for many uses; she makes each thing for a single use, and every instrument is best made when intended for one and not for many uses. But among barbarians no distinction is made between women and slaves, because there is no natural ruler among them: they are a community of slaves, male and female. Wherefore the poets say,

> 'It is meet that Hellenes should rule over barbarians' (Euripedes),

as if they thought that the barbarian and the slave were by nature one.

Out of these two relationships between man and woman, master and slave, the first thing to arise is the family, and Hesiod is right when he says,

> 'First house and wife and an ox for the plough',

for the ox is the poor man's slave. The family is the association established by nature for the supply of men's everyday wants, and the members of it are called by Charondas 'companions of the cupboard', and by Epimenides the Cretan,[1] 'companions of the manger'. But when several families are united, and the association aims at something more than the supply of daily needs, the first society to be formed is the village. And the most natural form of the village appears to be that of a colony from the family, composed of the children and grandchildren, who are said to be 'suckled with the same milk'. And this is the reason why Hellenic states were under royal rule before they came together, as the barbarians still are. Every family is ruled by the eldest, and therefore in the colonies of the family the kingly form of government prevailed because they were of the same blood. As Homer says:

> 'Each one gives law to his children and to his wives.'

For they lived dispersedly, as was the manner in ancient times. Wherefore men say that the Gods have a king, because they themselves either are or were in ancient times under the rule of a king. For they imagine, not only the forms of the Gods, but their ways of life to be like their own.

When several villages are united in a single complete community, large enough to be nearly or quite self-sufficing, the state comes into existence, originating in the bare needs of life, and continuing in existence for the sake of a good life. And therefore, if the earlier forms of society are natural, so is the state, for it is the end of them, and the nature of a thing is its end. For what each thing is when fully developed, we call its nature, whether we are speaking of a man, a horse, or a family. Besides, the final cause and end of a thing is the best, and to be self-sufficing is the end and the best.

Hence it is evident that the state is a creation of nature, and that man is by nature a political animal. And he who by nature and not by mere accident is without a state, is either a bad man or above humanity; he is like the

'Tribeless, lawless, hearthless one,'

whom Homer [the *Odyssey* ix. 114] denounces – the natural outcast is forthwith a lover of war; he may be compared to an isolated piece at draughts.

Now, that man is more of a political animal than bees or any other gregarious animals is evident. Nature, as we often say, makes nothing in vain, and man is the only animal whom she has endowed with the gift of speech. And whereas mere voice is but an indication of pleasure or pain, and is therefore found in other animals (for their nature attains to the perception of pleasure and pain and the intimation of them one to another, and no further), the power of speech is intended to set forth the expedient and inexpedient, and therefore likewise the just and the unjust. And it is a characteristic of man that he alone has any sense of good and evil, of just and unjust, and the like, and the association of living beings who have this sense makes a family and a state.

Further, the state is by nature clearly prior to the family and to the individual, since the whole is of necessity prior to the part; for example, if the whole body be destroyed, there will be no foot or hand, except in an equivocal sense, as we might speak of a stone hand; for when destroyed the hand will be no better than that. But things are defined by their working and power; and we ought not to say that they are the same when they no longer have their proper quality, but only that they have the same name. The proof that the state is a creation of nature and prior to the individual is that the individual, when isolated, is not self-sufficing; and therefore he is like a part in relation to the whole. But he who is unable to live in society, or who has no need because he is sufficient for himself, must be either a beast or a god: he is no part of a state. A social instinct is implanted in all men by nature, and yet he who first founded the state was the greatest of benefactors. For man, when perfected, is the best of animals, but, when separated from law and justice, he is the worst of all; since armed injustice is the more dangerous, and he is equipped at birth with arms, meant to be used by intelligence and virtue, which he may use for the worst ends. Wherefore, if he have not virtue, he is the most unholy and the most savage of animals, and the most full of lust and gluttony. But justice is the bond of men in states, for the administration of justice, which is the determination of what is just, is the principle of order in political society.

3

Seeing then that the state is made up of households, before speaking of the state we must speak of the management of the household. The parts of household management correspond to the persons who compose the household, and a complete household consists of slaves and freemen. Now we should begin by examining everything in its fewest possible elements; and the first and fewest possible parts of a family are master and slave, husband and wife, father and children. . . .

5

And there are many kinds both of rulers and subjects (and that rule is the better which is exercised over better subjects – for example, to rule over men is better than to rule over wild beasts; for the work is better which is executed by better workmen, and where one man rules and another is ruled, they may be said to have a work); for in all things which form a composite whole and which are made up of parts, whether continuous or discrete, a distinction between the ruling and the subject element comes to light. Such a duality exists in living creatures, but not in them only; it originates in the constitution of the universe; even in things which have no life there is a ruling principle, as in a musical mode. But we are wandering from the subject. We will therefore restrict ourselves to the living creature, which, in the first place, consists of soul and body: and of these two, the one is by nature the ruler, and the other the subject. But then we must look for the intentions of nature in things which retain their nature, and not in things which are corrupted. And therefore we must study the man who is in the most perfect state both of body and soul, for in him we shall see the true relation of the two; although in bad or corrupted natures the body will often appear to rule over the soul, because they are in an evil and unnatural condition. At all events we may firstly observe in living creatures both a despotical and a constitutional rule; for the soul rules the body with a despotical rule, whereas the intellect rules the appetites with a constitutional and royal rule. And it is clear that the rule of the soul over the body, and of the mind and the rational element over the passionate, is natural and expedient; whereas the equality of the two or the rule of the inferior is always hurtful. The same holds good of animals in relation to men; for tame animals have a better nature than wild, and all tame animals are better off when they are ruled by man; for then they are preserved. Again, the male is by nature superior, and the female inferior; and the one rules, and the other is ruled; this principle, of necessity, extends to all mankind. Where then there is such a difference as between soul and body, or between man and animals (as in the case of those whose business is to use their body, and who can do nothing better), the lower sort are by nature slaves, and it is better for them as for all inferiors that they should be under the rule of a master. For he who can be, and therefore is, another's, and he who participates in rational principle enough to apprehend, but not to have, such a principle, is a slave by nature. Whereas the lower animals cannot even apprehend a principle, they obey their instincts. And indeed the use made of slaves and of tame animals is not very different; for both with their bodies minister to the needs of life. Nature would like to distinguish between the bodies of freemen and slaves, making the one strong for servile labour, the other upright, and although useless for such services, useful for political life in the arts both of war and peace. But the opposite often happens – that some have the souls and others have the bodies of freemen. And doubtless if men differed from one another in the mere forms of their bodies as much as the statues of the Gods do from men, all would acknowledge that the inferior class should be slaves of the superior. And if this is true of the body, how much more just that a similar distinction should exist in the soul? But the beauty of the body is seen, whereas the beauty of the soul is not seen. It is clear, then, that some men are by nature free, and others slaves, and that for these latter slavery is both expedient and right.

12

Of household management we have seen that there are three parts – one is the rule of a master over slaves, which has been discussed already [sections 1–7], another of a father, and the third of a husband. A husband and father, we saw, rules over wife and children, both free, but the rule differs, the rule over his children being a royal, over his wife a constitutional rule. For although there may be exceptions to the order of nature, the male is by nature fitter for command than the female, just as the elder and full-grown is superior to the younger and more immature. But in most constitutional states the citizens rule and are ruled by turns, for the idea of a constitutional state implies that the natures of the citizens are equal, and do not differ at all. Nevertheless, when one rules and the other is ruled we endeavour to create a difference of outward forms and names and titles of respect. . . . The relation of the male to the female is of this kind, but there the inequality is permanent. The rule of a father over his children is royal, for he rules by virtue both of love and of the respect due to age, exercising a kind of royal power. And therefore Homer has appropriately called Zeus 'father of Gods and men', because he is the king of them all. For a king is the natural superior of his subjects, but he should be of the same kin or kind with them, and such is the relation of elder and younger, of father and son.

. . . A question may indeed to raised, whether there is any excellence at all in a slave beyond and higher than merely instrumental and ministerial qualities – whether he can have the virtues of temperance, courage, justice, and the like; or whether slaves possess only bodily and ministerial qualities. And whichever way we answer the question, a difficulty arises; for, if they have virtue, in what will they differ from freemen? On the other hand, since they are men and share in rational principle, it seems absurd to say that they have no virtue. A similar question may be raised about women and children, whether they too have virtues: ought a woman to be temperate and brave and just, and is a child to be called temperate, and intemperate, or not? So in general we may ask about the natural ruler, and the natural subject, whether they have the same or different virtues. For if a noble nature is equally required in both, why should one of them always rule, and the other always be ruled? Nor can we say that this is a question of degree, for the difference between ruler and subject is a difference of kind, which the difference of more or less never is. Yet how strange is the supposition that the one ought, and the other ought not, to have virtue! For if the ruler is intemperate and unjust, how can he rule well? if the subject, how can he obey well? If he be licentious and cowardly, he will certainly not do his duty. It is evident, therefore, that both of them must have a share of virtue, but varying as natural subjects also vary among themselves. Here the very constitution of the soul has shown us the way; in it one part naturally rules, and the other is subject, and the virtue of the ruler we maintain to be different from that of the subject; – the one being the virtue of the rational, and the other of the irrational part. Now, it is obvious that the same principle applies generally, and therefore almost all things rule and are ruled according to nature. But the kind of rule differs; – the freeman rules over the slave after another manner from that in which the male rules over the female, or the man over the child; although the parts of the soul are present in all of them, they are present in different degrees. For the slave has no deliberative faculty at all; the woman has, but it is without authority, and the child has, but it is immature. So it must necessarily be supposed to be with the moral virtues also; all should partake of them, but only in such manner and degree as is required by each for the fulfilment of his duty. Hence the ruler ought to have moral virtue in perfection, for his function, taken absolutely, demands a master artificer, and rational principle is such an artificer; the subjects, on the other hand, require only that measure of virtue which is proper to each of them. Clearly, then, moral virtue belongs to all of them; but the temperance of a man and of a woman, of the courage and justice of a man and of a woman, are not, as Socrates maintained, the same; the courage of a man is shown in commanding, of a woman in obeying. And this holds of all other virtues, as will be more clearly seen if we look at them in detail, for those who say generally that virtue consists in a good disposition of the soul, or in doing rightly, or the like, only deceive themselves. Far better than such definitions is their mode of speaking, who, like Gorgias [Meno 71], enumerate their virtues. All classes must be deemed to have their special attributes; as the poet says of women,

> 'Silence is a woman's glory' [Sophocles],

but this is not equally the glory of man. The child is imperfect, and therefore obviously his virtue is not relative to himself alone, but to the perfect man and to his teacher, and in like manner the virtue of the slave is relative to a master. Now we determined that a slave is useful for the wants of life, and therefore he will obviously require only so much virtue as will prevent him from failing in his duty through cowardice or lack of self-control. . . .

So much for this subject; the relations of husband and wife, parent and child, their several virtues, what in their intercourse with one another is good, and what is evil, and how we may pursue the good and escape the evil, will have to be discussed when we speak of the different forms of government. For, inasmuch as every family is a part of a state, and these relationships are the parts of a family, and the virtue of the part must have regard to the virtue of the whole, women and children must be trained by education with an eye to the constitution, if the virtues of either of them are supposed to make any difference in the virtues of the state. And they must make a difference: for the children grow up to be citizens, and half the free persons in a state are women.

NOTE

1. [Ed.] *Epimenides*: legendary figure dated between 600 and 500 BCE. Poet, prophet and miracle man.

STUDY QUESTIONS

1. How does Aristotle's understanding of human biology affect his understanding of the nature of woman? What response might be made to his ideas?
2. What evidence is there for the claim that Aristotle associates the male with reason and the female with nature?

SELECT BIBLIOGRAPHY

General

M. J. Adler, *Aristotle for Everybody* (New York: Collier Macmillan, 1978).
A. MacIntyre, *After Virtue* (London: Duckworth, 1985).

For feminist analysis

J. Hughes, 'The Philosopher's Child', in *Feminist Perspectives in Philosophy*, edited by M. Griffiths and M. Whitford (Basingstoke: Macmillan, 1988), pp. 72–89.

J. Grimshaw, *Feminist Philosophers* (Brighton: Harvester Wheatsheaf, 1986), ch. 2.

R. Miles, *The Women's History of the World* (London: Paladin, 1992), chs 1, 3.

S. M. Okin, *Women in Western Political Thought* (London: Virago, 1980).

S. Pomeroy, *Goddesses, Whores, Wives, and Slaves* (London: Pimlico, 1975).

J. K. Ward (ed.), *Feminism and Ancient Philosophy* (London: Routledge, 1996); especially D. McGowan Tress, 'The Metaphysical Science of Aristotle's *Generation of Animals* and Its Feminist Critics', pp. 31–50; K. Cook, 'Sexual Inequality in Aristotle's Theories of Reproduction and Inheritance', pp. 51–67.

PART II

THE CHURCH FATHERS

3 Tertullian *c*.160–*c*.220 CE

Introduction and Background

Tertullian, one of the great 'Fathers' of the Latin Church, was an African, a citizen of what is now modern Tunisia. A formidable character, he was 'impetuous, hot-blooded, at times intellectually reckless'.[1] Indeed, his works betray precisely this fiery nature; even admirers such as Campenhausen note the way in which his work 'often violently exceeds the bounds of good taste'.[2]

This side of his character is particularly noticeable when his writings on women are considered. His *On Female Dress* contains material which is often cited by feminists drawing attention to the patriarchal roots of the Christian Church. Tertullian bears witness to, in Marina Warner's words, the 'undertow of misogyny in patristic thought'.[3] In this piece, Tertullian argues that women should dress 'as Eve mourning and repentant, in order that by every garb of penitence she might the more fully expiate that which she derives from Eve'. *All* women are thus identified with Eve, the Mother of all Women, and as it was Eve who tempted Adam in Eden, *all* women must share the blame for 'Paradise lost'. According to Tertullian, the effects of this loss are still felt today through the ultimate punishment for this original act of disobedience against God – death.

The most cited piece of this passage is Tertullian's description of woman as 'the devil's gateway', the creature whose act of betrayal secured the fall of 'God's image, man'. Writers as diverse as Marina Warner, Joan Smith, Elaine Pagels and Mary Daly refer to this passage. Commentators on Tertullian, by way of contrast, seem to ignore these strongly 'anti-woman' writings. Campenhausen refers to him as 'happily married'.[4] This seems rather odd, especially if one considers Tertullian's comments on the joy of chastity:

> How much better a man feels when he happens to be away from his wife.[5]

And again, Tertullian's chief objection to the 'heresy' of Gnosticism appears to lie in his outrage that Gnostic women are given the same rights as men:

> Those heretical women – how audacious they are! They have no modesty; they are bold enough to teach, to engage in argument, to enact exorcisms, to undertake cures, and, it may be, even to baptise.[6]

Tertullian's writings resonate with themes which reoccur throughout the western philosophical tradition. Feminine and masculine roles – and indeed fundamental natures – are fiercely juxtaposed. Woman is identified with sexuality; if she wishes to be redeemed, Tertullian demands that she deny this aspect of her nature. Man, by way of contrast, is equated explicitly with 'the image of God', reminding the reader of Aristotle's claim that it is in rationality that one finds that which differentiates 'Man' from the animals. Woman is treated with suspicion, as the cause of 'man's' fall from grace. The expressly Christian mythical framework which shapes Tertullian's writings does not explicitly dominate later philosophical ideas. However, these attitudes towards woman continue to shape discussion on the nature of the sexes. This is hardly surprising, for the scholastic methodologies of the Early Church Fathers have contributed to the general shape of philosophical methodology.

*ON FEMALE DRESS**

Book I

Chapter 1 [*In this section Tertullian introduces his central theme: that Christian women should dress modestly in memory of the introduction of sin into the world through a woman, Eve. According to Tertullian, those objects which serve to glamorize a woman's body would have been coveted by Eve; if the women he addresses are to renounce this heritage, they must renounce these objects as well.*]

If there dwelt upon earth a faith as great as is the reward of faith which is expected in the heavens, no one of you at all, best beloved sisters, from the time that she had first 'known the Lord', and learned the truth concerning her own (that is, woman's) condition, would have desired too gladsome (not to say too ostentatious) a style of dress; so as not rather to go about in humble garb, and rather to affect meanness of appearance, walking about as Eve mourning and repentant, in order that by every garb of penitence she might the more fully expiate that which she derives from Eve – the ignominy, I mean, of the first sin, and the odium attaching to her as the cause of human perdition. 'In pains and in anxieties dost thou bear children, woman; and toward thine husband is thy inclination, and he lords it over thee.' And do you not know that you are each an Eve? The sentence of God on this sex of yours lives in this age: the guilt must of necessity live too. *You* are the devil's gateway: *you* are the unsealer of that forbidden tree: *you* are the first deserter of the divine law: *you* are she who persuaded him whom the devil was not valiant enough to attack. *You* destroyed so easily God's image, man. On account of *your* desert – that is, death – even the Son of God had to die. And do you think about adorning yourself over and above your tunics of skins? Come, now; if from the beginning of the world the Milesians sheared sheep, and the Serians[1] spun trees, and the

* From *The Writings of Tertullian*, vol. 1, translated by Rev. S. Thelwall (Edinburgh: T. & T. Clark, 1869).

Tyrians dyed, and the Phrygians embroidered with the needle, and the Babylonians with the loom, and pearls gleamed, and onyx-stones flashed; if gold itself also had already issued, with the cupidity[2] which accompanies it, from the ground; if the mirror, too, already had licence to lie so largely, Eve, expelled from paradise, Eve already dead, would also have coveted *these* things, I imagine! No more, then, ought she *now* to crave, or be acquainted with (if she desires to live again), what, when she *was* living, she had neither had nor known. Accordingly these things are all the baggage of woman in her condemned and dead state, instituted as if to swell the pomp of her funeral.

Chapter 2 [*In this section, Tertullian traces the origin of female ornamentation back to the fallen angels, who he appears to conflate with the strange passage in Genesis 6 which describes the race of giants born from the couplings of angels with some human women. According to Tertullian, it is these fallen angels who taught women to beautify their bodies.*]

For they, withal, who instituted them are assigned, under condemnation, to the penalty of death – those angels, to wit, who rushed from heaven on the daughters of men; so that this ignominy also attaches to woman. For when to an age much more ignorant than ours they had disclosed certain well-concealed material substances, and several not well revealed scientific arts – if it is true that they had laid bare the operations of metallurgy, and had divulged the natural properties of herbs, and had promulgated the powers of enchantments, and had traced out every curious art, even to the interpretation of the stars – they conferred properly and as it were peculiarly upon women that instrumental mean of womanly ostentation, the radiances of jewels wherewith necklaces are variegated, and the circlets of gold wherewith the arms are compressed, and the medicaments of orchil[3] with which wools are coloured, and that black powder itself where with the eyelids and eyelashes are made prominent. What is the quality of these things may be declared meantime, even at this point, from the quality and condition of their teachers; in that sinners could never have either shown or supplied anything conducive to integrity, unlawful lovers anything conducive to chastity, renegade spirits anything conducive to the fear of God. If these things are to be called *teachings*, ill masters must of necessity have taught ill; if as *wages of lust*, there is nothing base of which the wages are honourable. But why was it of so much importance to show these things as well as to confer them? Was it that women, without material causes of splendour, and without ingenious contrivances of grace, could not please *men*, who, while still unadorned, and uncouth, and – so to say – crude and rude, had moved the mind of *angels*? Or was it that the lovers would appear sordid and – through gratuitous use – contumelious, if they had conferred no compensating gift on the women who had been enticed into connubial connection with them? But these questions admit of no calculation. Women who possessed angels as husbands could desire nothing more; they had, forsooth, made a grand match! Assuredly they who, of course, did sometimes think whence they had fallen, and, after the heated impulses of their lusts, looked up toward heaven, thus requited that very excellence of women, natural beauty, as having proved a cause of evil, in order that their good fortune might profit them nothing; but that, being turned from simplicity and sincerity, they, together with the angels themselves, might become offensive to God. Sure they were that all ostentation, and ambition, and love of pleasing by carnal means, was *dis*pleasing to God. And these are the angels whom we are destined to judge: these are the angels whom in baptism we renounce: these, of course, are the reasons why they have deserved to be judged by man. What business, then, have their *things* with their *judges*? What commerce have they who are to condemn with them who are to be condemned? The same, I take it, as Christ has with Belial.[4] With what consistency do we mount that future judgment-seat to pronounce sentence against those whose gifts we now seek after? For you too, women as you are, have the self-same angelic nature promised as your reward, the self-same sex as men: the self-same advancement to the dignity of judging, does the Lord promise you. Unless, then, we begin even here to *pre*judge, by precondemning their *things*, which we are hereafter to condemn in *themselves*, *they* will rather judge and condemn *us*.

Chapter 4 [*In this section, Tertullian equates female ornamentation with ambition and prostitution. These attitudes and activities are radically opposed to the qualities a Christian woman should foster – namely humility and chastity.*]

. . . Female habit carries with it a twofold idea – dress and ornament. By 'dress' we mean what they call 'womanly gracing'; by 'ornament', what is suitable should be called 'womanly *dis*gracing'. The former is accounted to consist in gold, and silver, and gems, and garments; the latter in care of the hair, and of the skin, and of those parts of the body which attract the eye. Against the one we lay the charge of ambition, against the other of prostitution; so that even from this early stage of our discussion you may look forward and see what, out of all these, is suitable, handmaid of God, to *your* discipline, inasmuch as you are assessed on different principles from other women – those, namely, of humility and chastity.

Book II

Chapter 1 [*Here, Tertullian argues that it is not enough to avoid actual sexual impropriety. There is no defence in saying that one's conduct has been correct, if one dresses as a woman of ill-repute! Moreover, it is important not to incite carnal lust in others. Woman is thus described as responsible for the reactions of others.*]

Handmaids of the living God, my fellow-servants and sisters, the right which I enjoy with you – I, the most meanest in that right of fellow-servantship and brotherhood – emboldens me to address to you a discourse, not, of course, of affection, but paving the way for affection in the cause of your salvation. That salvation – and not the salvation of women only, but likewise of men – consists in the exhibition principally of modesty. For since, by the introduction into and appropriation in us of the Holy Spirit, we are all 'the temple of God', Modesty is the sacristan[5] and priestess of that temple, who is to suffer nothing unclean or profane to be introduced into it, for fear that the God who inhabits it should be offended, and quite forsake the polluted abode. But on the present occasion we are to speak not about modesty, for the enjoining and exacting of which the divine precepts which press upon us on every side are sufficient; but about the matters which pertain to it, that is, the manner in which it behoves you to walk. For most women (which very thing I trust God may permit me, with a view, of course, to my own personal censure, to censure in all), either from simple ignorance or else from dissimulation, have the hardihood so to walk as if modesty consisted only in the bare integrity of the flesh, and in turning away from actual fornication; and there were no need for anything extrinsic to boot – in the matter

(I mean) of the arrangement of dress and ornament, the studied graces of form and brilliance – wearing in their gait the self-same appearance as the women of the nations, from whom the sense of *true* modesty is absent, because in those who know not God, the Guardian and Master of truth, there is *nothing* true. For if any modesty can be believed to exist in Gentiles, it is plain that it must be imperfect and undisciplined to such a degree that, although it be actively tenacious of itself in the *mind* up to a certain point, it yet allows itself to relax into licentious extravagances of attire; just in accordance with Gentile perversity, in craving after that of which it carefully shuns the effect. How many a one, in short, is there who does not earnestly desire even to look pleasing to strangers? Who does not on that very account take care to have herself painted out, and denies that she has ever been an object of carnal appetite? And yet, granting that even this is a practice familiar to Gentile modesty – namely, not actually *to commit* the sin, but still to be *willing* to do so; or even not to be *willing*, yet still not *quite* to refuse – what wonder? For all things which are not God's are perverse. Let those women therefore look to it, who, by not holding fast the *whole* good, easily mingle with evil even what they do hold fast. Necessary it is that *you* turn aside from them, as in all other things, so also in your gait; since you ought to be 'perfect, as is your Father who is in the heavens'.

Chapter 2 [*Tertullian continues the theme of the previous chapter. It is important that a Christian woman refrains from dressing in a manner which will incite lust in others. She must abstain not only from sin, but from leading others into temptation. This leads Tertullian not only to the rejection of those things which beautify women artificially; he argues that even 'natural beauty' must be concealed in order that others (that is, 'men') are not led astray.*]

You must know that in the eye of perfect, that is, Christian, modesty, carnal desire of one's self on the part of others is not only not to be desired, but even execrated, but you: first, because the study of making personal grace (which we know to be naturally the inviter of lust) a mean of pleasing does not spring from a sound conscience: why therefore excite toward yourself that evil passion? Why invite that to which you profess yourself a stranger? Secondly, because we ought not to open a way to temptations, which, by their instancy, sometimes achieve a wickedness which God expels from them who are His; or, at all events, put the spirit into a thorough tumult by presenting a stumbling block to it. . . .

. . . Since, therefore, both our own interest and that of others is implicated in the studious pursuit of most perilous outward comeliness, it is time for you to know that not merely must the pageantry of fictitious and elaborate beauty be rejected by you; but that of even natural grace must be obliterated by concealment and negligence, as equally dangerous to the glances of the beholder's eyes. . . .

Chapter 5 [*Tertullian develops his theme by outlining the theological implications of those actions which some women undertake to beautify themselves. He argues that such steps suggest a dissatisfaction with that which God ('the Divine Artificer') has given us. Indeed, he argues that trying to perfect the work of God is an outrageous act of rebellion which puts one in league with the devil.*]

These suggestions are not made to you, of course, to be developed into an entire crudity and wildness of appearance; nor are we seeking to persuade you of the good of squalor and slovenliness; but of the limit and norm and just measure of cultivation of the person. There must be no overstepping of that line to which simple and sufficient refinements limit their desires – that line which is pleasing to God. For they who rub their skin with medicaments, stain their cheeks with rouge, make their eyes prominent with antimony, sin against Him. To them, I suppose, the plastic skill of God is displeasing! In their own persons, I suppose, they convict, they censure, the Artificer of all things! For censure they do when they amend, when they add to, His work; taking these their additions, of course, from the adversary artificer. That adversary artificer is the devil. For who would show the way to change the *body*, but he who by wickedness transfigured man's *spirit*? He it is, undoubtedly, who adapted ingenious devices of this kind; that in your own persons it may be apparent that you do, in a certain sense, do violence to God. Whatever is *born* is the work of God. Whatever, then, is *plastered on* that, is the devil's work. To super induce on a divine work Satan's ingenuities, how criminal is it! Our servants borrow nothing from our personal enemies: soldiers eagerly desire nothing from the foes of their own general; for, to demand for your own use anything from the adversary of him in whose hand you are, is a transgression. Shall a Christian be assisted in anything by that evil one? If he do, I know not whether this name of 'Christian' will continue to belong to him; for he will be *his* in whose lore he eagerly desires to be instructed. But how alien from *your* schoolings and professions are these things, how unworthy the Christian name, to wear a fictitious face, you, on whom simplicity in every form is enjoined! To lie in your appearance, you, to whom lying with the tongue is not lawful! To seek after what is another's, you, to whom is delivered the precept of abstinence from what is another's! To practise adultery in your mien, you, who make modesty your study! Think, blessed sisters, how will you keep God's precepts if you shall not keep in your own persons His lineaments?

Chapter 13 [*Tertullian rejects the argument that if God knows us to be chaste, it does not matter what others think. It is not enough to* be *chaste; we must* seem *to be chaste to others. Writing at a time of persecution for the Christian Church, Tertullian is also concerned that the love of riches and a luxurious lifestyle will not prepare Christians for the possible hardships ahead of them.*]

Perhaps some woman will say: 'To me it is not necessary to be approved by men; for I do not require the testimony of men: God is the inspector of the heart.' That we all know; provided, however, we remember what the same God has said through the apostle: 'Let your probity appear before men.' For what purpose, except that malice may have no access at all to you, or that you may be an example and testimony to the evil? Else, what is that: 'Let your works shine?' Why, moreover, does the Lord call us the light of the world; why has He compared us to a city built upon a mountain; if we do not shine in the midst of darkness, and stand eminent amid them who are sunk down? If you hide your lamp beneath a bushel, you must necessarily be left quite in darkness, and be run against by many. The things which make us luminaries of the world are these – our good works. What is *good*, moreover, provided it be true and full, loves not darkness: it joys in being seen, and exults over the very pointings which are made at it. To Christian modesty it is not enough to *be* so but to *seem* so too. For so great ought its plenitude to be, that it may flow out from the mind to the garb, and burst out from the conscience to the outward appearance; so that even from the outside it may gaze, as it were, upon its own furniture – a furniture such as to be suited to retain faith as its inmate perpetually. For such delicacies as tend by their softness and effeminacy to unman the manliness of faith are to be discarded. Otherwise, I know not whether the wrist that has been wont to be surrounded with the palm leaf-like bracelet will endure till it grow into the numb hardness of its own chain! I know not whether the leg that has rejoiced in the anklet will suffer itself to be squeezed into the gyve![6] I fear the neck, beset with pearl and emerald nooses, will give no room to the broadsword! Wherefore, blessed sisters, let us meditate on hardships, and we shall not feel them; let us abandon luxuries, and we shall not regret them. Let us stand ready to endure every violence, having nothing which we may fear to leave behind. It is these things which are the bonds which retard our hope. Let us cast away earthly ornaments if we desire heavenly. Love not gold; in which one substance are branded all the sins of the people of Israel. You ought to *hate* what ruined your fathers; what was adored by them who were forsaking God. Even *then* we find gold is food for the fire. But Christians always, and now more than ever, pass their times not in gold but in iron; the stoles of martyrdom are now preparing: the angels who are to carry us are now being awaited! Do you go forth to meet them already arrayed in the cosmetics and ornaments of prophets and apostles; drawing your whiteness from simplicity, your ruddy hue from modesty; painting your eyes with bashfulness, and your mouth with silence; implanting in your ears the words of God; fitting on your necks the yoke of Christ. Submit your head to your husbands, and you will be enough adorned. Busy your hands with spinning; keep your feet at home; and you will 'please' better than by arraying yourselves in gold. Clothe yourselves with the silk of uprightness, the fine linen of holiness, the purple of modesty. Thus painted, you will have God as your Lover!

NOTES

1. [Ed.] *Serians*: Chinese.
2. [Ed.] *cupidity*: passionate desire or covetousness.
3. [Ed.] *orchil*: red or violet dye derived from lichen.
4. [Ed.] *Belial*: Satan.
5. [Ed.] *sacristan*: official charged with the custody of the sacred objects of a church.
6. [Ed.] *gyve*: a shackle for the leg; a fetter.

STUDY QUESTIONS

1. Tertullian describes woman as 'the devil's gateway'. In developing this image he claims that the devil chose Eve as 'the weaker vessel' through whom he could corrupt the creation. How might this idea of the weakness of woman parallel Aristotle's 'biological' theory of the sexes?
2. The predominant characteristic which Tertullian ascribes to woman is sexuality. Man, by way of contrast, is described as 'the image of God'. What does this suggest about Tertullian's understanding of the division of reality?
3. Tertullian claims that it is not enough for a woman to be chaste; she must also *appear* to be chaste. The idea that a woman is responsible for the lustful thoughts and actions of others continues to the present day. Joan Smith cites the example of a judge who draws similar conclusions to Tertullian about a woman's responsibility:

   > In January 1982 a motorist called John Allen was convicted of raping a 17-year-old girl who hitched a lift with him after finding herself stranded after a party. Fining Allen a paltry £1000 instead of gaoling him, Judge Bertrand Richards observed: 'The victim was guilty of a great deal of contributory negligence.' (Smith, *Misogynies*, p. 3)

   Can you find other examples (in the media or literature) which reiterate this suggestion that woman is responsible for the actions of man?

SELECT BIBLIOGRAPHY

General

P. Brown, *The Body and Society* (New York: Columbia University Press, 1988), ch. 3.
H. von Campenhausen, *The Fathers of the Latin Church* (London: A. & C. Black, 1964).
H. Chadwick, *The Early Church* (Harmondsworth: Penguin, 1967).
J. N. D. Kelly, *Early Christian Doctrines* (London: A. & C. Black, 1958).

For feminist analysis

M. Daly, *Beyond God the Father* (London: Women's Press, 1986).
M. French, *Beyond Power* (London: Cardinal Press, 1991).
E. Pagels, *The Gnostic Gospels* (Harmondsworth: Penguin, 1990).
J. Smith, *Misogynies* (London: Faber & Faber, 1989).
M. Warner, *Alone of All Her Sex* (London: Picador, 1990).

4 Augustine 354–430 ce

Introduction and Background

It is difficult to overestimate the impact that Augustine's thought has had upon the theological and philosophical frameworks of the western world. Influenced by classical forms of thought, his ideas helped to develop a connection between Christian notions of God and the philosophical theism derived from Plato and Aristotle.

The story of Augustine's conversion to Christianity is perhaps the best known aspect of his life and work. He gives a lively account of this in his extremely readable *Confessions*. In many ways, his story expresses the struggle between the pull of the ascetic life and the desires of the flesh. Before becoming a Christian he was attracted to Manichaeism, an ultra-ascetic sect founded by the 'prophet' Mani. The ascetic 'ideal' attracted the youthful Augustine intellectually. However, he retained a mistress, who was also the mother of his son, Adeodatus. This relationship came to an abrupt end when his ambitions took him to Milan. The end of this important relationship (traditionally attributed to the 'machinations' of his mother Monica) was to have a profound effect upon him. It was at this time that he came into contact with the neoplatonism of Plotinus, a philosophy which was to pave the way for his conversion to Christianity. On becoming a Christian he renounced sexual activity altogether. Eventually he became Bishop of Hippo, a post he held for over thirty years until his death in 430 ce.

Augustine's ideas are particularly interesting for the feminist scholar. It is difficult to form a conclusive understanding of his attitude towards women. Indeed, the complexity of his private life suggests that he held a rather ambivalent attitude towards women, and particularly towards the sexuality which they apparently represented. In the extracts that follow, he frequently challenges the negative attitudes towards women held by some of his contemporaries. Notably he rejects the idea that women are not made in the image of God. However, as Kim Power points out, the way he attempts to justify this position involves an account of the mind which ultimately supports patriarchal gender roles.[1] According to Augustine, the image of God is found in the mind, 'the highest faculty of the rational soul'.[2] Both sexes possess this faculty, leading to the conclusion that 'the mind has no sex'.

This identification of the *imago Dei* with the mind is not as straightforward as it at first appears. Augustine equates the image of God with 'Wisdom' (or *Sapientia*). He contrasts this faculty of the mind with *Scientia*, the part of the mind which is concerned with understanding temporal things. Departing from the tradition of using feminine language for Wisdom, Augustine defines *Sapientia* in masculine terms. In contrast, *Scientia* is described as feminine. While this could be understood as merely a linguistic distinction, the implications of this gendered understanding of the mind have ramifications for Augustine's account of the role of woman. Just as *Scientia* acts as a 'helpmate' for *Sapientia*, so woman must act as a helpmate for man. Despite Augustine's claims that woman must be understood as the *imago Dei*, the gendered language he employs when writing of the mind leaves the reader with the impression that just as *Scientia* has to be kept in check by

Sapientia, it is only through adopting an appropriately subordinate position to man that woman can truly be said to be made in the image of God.

Thus Augustine paves the way for an understanding of reason and rationality as fundamentally masculine attributes. Consideration of Augustine's writings are, then, likely to reveal another strand in the masculinizing of reason. If his writings support a hierarchical understanding of the relationship between men and women, he does go some way to challenging the idea that the creation is evil or that matter is inherently wicked. Yet the overriding impression is one of a man who finds sex degrading and physicality a hindrance to the knowledge of God.

*CONFESSIONS**

Book VI

Chapter 11 [*Augustine reflects upon his pre-conversion experiences. Issues concerning his sensuality predominate his reflections.*]

20 Whilst I talked of these things, and these winds veered about and tossed my heart hither and thither, the time passed on; but I was slow to turn to the Lord, and from day to day deferred to live in Thee, and deferred not daily to die in myself. Being enamoured of a happy life, I yet feared it in its own abode, and, fleeing from it, sought after it. I conceived that I should be too unhappy were I deprived of the embracements of a woman; and of Thy merciful medicine to cure that infirmity I thought not, not having tried it. As regards continency, I imagined it to be under the control of our own strength (though in myself I found it not), being so foolish as not to know what is written, that none can be continent unless Thou give it; and that Thou wouldst give it, if with heartfelt groaning I should knock at Thine ears, and should with firm faith cast my care upon thee.

Chapter 12 [*Augustine discusses celibacy with his friend Alypius. Alypius is content with a celibate life, but is drawn into the sensual world by Augustine's inability to refute the delights of the flesh.*]

21 It was in truth Alypius who prevented me from marrying, alleging that thus we could by no means live together, having so

*Reprinted from the translation by J. G. Pilkington (Edinburgh: T. & T. Clark, 1876).

much undistracted leisure in the love of wisdom, as we had long desired. For he himself was so chaste in this matter that it was wonderful – all the more, too, that in his early youth he had entered upon that path, but had not clung to it; rather had he, feeling sorrow and disgust at it, lived from that time to the present most continently. But I opposed him with the examples of those who as married men had loved wisdom, found favour with God, and walked faithfully and lovingly with their friends. From the greatness of whose spirit I fell far short, and, enthralled with the disease of the flesh and its deadly sweetness, dragged my chain along, fearing to be loosed, and, as if it pressed my wound, rejected his kind expostulations, as it were the hand of one who would unchain me. Moreover, it was by me that the serpent spake unto Alypius himself, weaving and laying in his path, by my tongue, pleasant snares, wherein his honourable and free feet might be entangled.

22 For when he wondered that I, for whom he had no slight esteem, stuck so fast in the bird-lime of that pleasure as to affirm whenever we discussed the matter that it would be impossible for me to lead a single life, and urged in my defence when I saw him wonder that there was a vast difference between the life that he had tried by stealth and snatches (of which he had now but a faint recollection, and might therefore, without regret, easily despise), and my sustained acquaintance with it, whereto if but the honourable name of marriage were added, he would not then be astonished at my inability to contemn that course – then began he also to wish to be married, not as if overpowered by the lust of such pleasure, but from curiosity. For, as he said, he was anxious to know what that could be without which my life, which was so pleasing to him, seemed to me not life but a penalty. For his mind, free from that chain, was astounded at my slavery, and through that astonishment was going on to a desire of trying it, and from it to the trial itself, and thence, perchance, to fall into that bondage whereat he was so astonished, seeing he was ready to enter into 'a covenant with death'; and he that loves danger shall fall into it. For whatever the conjugal honour be in the office of well-ordering a married life, and sustaining children, influenced us but slightly. But that which did for the most part afflict me, already made a slave to it, was the habit of satisfying an insatiable lust; him about to be enslaved did an admiring wonder draw on. In this state were we, until Thou, O most High, not forsaking

our lowliness, commiserating our misery, didst come to our rescue by wonderful and secret ways.

Chapter 32 [*Augustine praises the works of God. He also touches upon the relationship of man and woman. While he does not deny mind and reason to woman, he holds to a hierarchical understanding of human relationships. Woman is subject to man just as action is subject to reason.*]

47 Thanks to Thee, O Lord. We behold the heaven and the earth, whether the corporeal part, superior and inferior, or the spiritual and corporeal creature; and in the embellishment of these parts, whereof the universal mass of the world or the universal creation consisteth, we see light made, and divided from the darkness. We see the firmament of heaven, whether the primary body of the world between the spiritual upper waters and the corporeal lower waters, or – because this also is called heaven – this expanse of air, through which wander the fowls of heaven, between the waters which are in vapours borne above them, and which in clear nights drop down in dew, and those which being heavy flow along the earth. We behold the waters gathered together through the plains of the sea; and the dry land both void and formed, so as to be visible and compact, and the matter of herbs and trees. We behold the lights shining from above – the sun to serve the day, the moon and the stars to cheer the night; and that by all these, times should be marked and noted. We behold on every side a humid element, fruitful with fishes, beasts, and birds; because the density of the air, which bears up the flights of birds, is increased by the exhalation of the waters. We behold the face of the earth furnished with terrestrial creatures, and man, created after Thy image and likeness, in that very image and likeness of Thee (that is, the power of reason and understanding) on account of which he was set over all irrational creatures. And as in his soul there is one power which rules by directing, another made subject that it might obey, so also for the man was corporeally made a woman, who, in the mind of her rational understanding should also have a like nature, in the sex, however, of her body should be in like manner subject to the sex of her husband, as the appetite of action is subjected by reason of the mind, to conceive the skill of acting rightly. These things we behold, and they are severally good, and all very good.

*ON THE TRINITY**

Book XII

Chapter 7 [*In this section, Augustine explores the idea that 'man' is made in the image of God. Is woman also made in the image of God? While rejecting the notion that woman is not made in the image of God, he makes a distinction between the way in which the phrase applies to man and the way in which it applies to woman. For Augustine, man is completely in the image of God. Woman is only completely in the image of God when she is in partnership with her husband. In arguing this point, Augustine draws upon his distinction between 'Wisdom' (that 'which beholds and consults truth') and 'Scientia' (which deals 'with the lower things'). Any 'equality' which Augustine assigns to woman is spiritual. A woman should cover her head, not because she is the spiritual inferior of man, but because of her temporal inferiority – an inferiority which arises because of her sex.*]

9 We ought not therefore so to understand that man is made in the image of the supreme Trinity, that is, in the image of God, as that the same image should be understood to be in three human beings; especially when the apostle says that the man is the image of God, and on that account removes the covering from his head, which he warns the woman to use, speaking thus: 'For a man indeed ought not to cover his head, forasmuch as he is the image and glory of God; but the woman is the glory of the man.' What then shall we say to this? If the woman fills up the image of the trinity after the measure of her own person, why is the man still called that image after she has been taken out of his side? Or if even one person of a human being out of three can be called the image of God, as each person also is God in the supreme Trinity itself, why is the woman also not the image of God? For she is instructed for this very reason to cover her head, which he is forbidden to do because he is the image of God [1 Corinthians 11:5, 7].

10 But we must notice how that which the apostle says, that not the woman but the man is the image of God, is not contrary to that which is written in Genesis, 'God created man: in the image of God created He him; male and female created He them: and

*Reprinted from the translation by A. W. Hadden (Edinburgh: T. & T. Clark, 1873).

He blessed them.' For this text says that human nature itself, which is complete in both sexes, was made in the image of God; and it does not separate the woman from the image of God which it signifies. For after saying that God made man in the image of God, 'He created him,' it says, 'male and female,' or at any rate, stopping the words otherwise, 'male and female created He them'. How then did the apostle tell us that the man is the image of God, and therefore he is forbidden to cover his head; but that the woman is not so, and therefore is commanded to cover hers? Unless, forsooth, according to that which I have said already, when I was treating of the nature of the human mind, that the woman together with her own husband is the image of God, so that that whole substance may be one image; but when she is referred separately to her quality of help-meet, which regards the woman herself alone, then she is not the image of God; but as regards the man alone, he is the image of God as fully and completely as when the woman too is joined with him in one. As we said of the nature of the human mind, that both in the case when as a whole it contemplates the truth it is the image of God; and in the case when anything is divided from it, and diverted in purpose to the dealing with temporal things; nevertheless on that side on which it beholds and consults truth, here also it is the image of God, but on that side whereby it is directed to the dealing with the lower things, it is not the image of God. And since it is so much the more formed after the image of God, the more it has extended itself to that which is eternal, and is on that account not to be restrained, so as to withhold and refrain itself from thence; therefore the man ought not to cover his head. But because too great a progression towards inferior things is dangerous to that rational dealing, that is conversant with things corporeal and temporal; this ought to have power on its head, which the covering indicates, by which it is signified that it ought to be restrained. For a holy and pious meaning is pleasing to the holy angels. For God sees not after the way of time, neither does anything new take place in His vision and knowledge, when anything is done in time and transitorily, after the way in which such things affect the senses, whether the carnal senses of animals and men, or even the heavenly senses of the angels.

11 For that the Apostle Paul, when speaking outwardly of the sex of male and female, figured the mystery of some more hidden truth, may be understood from this, that when he says in another

place that she is a widow indeed who is desolate, without children and nephews, and yet that she ought to trust in God, and to continue in prayers night and day [1 Timothy 5:5], he here indicates, that the woman having been brought into the transgression by being deceived, is brought to salvation by child bearing; and then he has added, 'If they continue in faith, and charity, and holiness, with sobriety' [1 Timothy 2:15]. As if it could possibly hurt a good widow, if either she had not sons, or if those whom she had did not choose to continue in good works. But because those things which are called good works are, as it were, the sons of our life, according to that sense of life in which it answers to the question, 'What is a man's life?' that is, 'How does he act in these temporal things?' . . . ; and because these good works are chiefly performed in the way of offices of mercy, while works of mercy are of no profit, either to Pagans, or to Jews who do not believe in Christ, or to any heretics or schismatics whatsoever in whom faith and charity and sober holiness are not found: what the apostle meant to signify is plain, and in so far figuratively and mystically, because he was speaking of covering the head of the woman, which will remain mere empty words, unless referred to some hidden sacrament.

12 For, as not only most true reason but also the authority of the apostle himself declares, man was not made in the image of God according to the shape of his body, but according to his rational mind. For the thought is a debased and empty one, which holds God to be circumscribed and limited by the lineaments of bodily members. But further, does not the same blessed apostle say, 'Be renewed in the spirit of your mind, and put on the new man, which is created after God' [Ephesians 4:23, 24]; and in another place more clearly, 'Putting off the old man,' he says, 'with his deeds; put on the new man, which is renewed to the knowledge of God after the image of Him that created him' [Colossians 3:9, 10]? If, then, we are renewed in the spirit of our mind, and he is the new man who is renewed to the knowledge of God after the image of Him that created him; no one can doubt, that man was made after the image of Him that created him, not according to the body, nor indiscriminately according to any part of the mind, but according to the rational mind, wherein the knowledge of God can exist. And it is according to this renewal, also, that we are made sons of God by the baptism of Christ; and putting on the new man, certainly put on Christ through faith. Who is there, then, who will hold women to be

alien from this fellowship, whereas they are fellow-heirs of grace with us; and whereas in another place the same apostle says, 'For ye are all the children of God by faith in Christ Jesus; for as many as have been baptized into Christ have put on Christ: there is neither Jew nor Greek, there is neither bond nor free, there is neither male nor female; for ye are all one in Christ Jesus' [Galatians 3:26–28]? Pray, have faithful women then lost their bodily sex? But because they are there renewed after the image of God, where there is no sex; man is there made after the image of God, where there is no sex, that is, in the spirit of his mind. Why, then, is the man on that account not bound to cover his head, because he is the image and glory of God, while the woman is bound to do so, because she is the glory of the man; as though the woman were not renewed in the spirit of her mind, which spirit is renewed to the knowledge of God after the image of Him who created him? But because she differs from the man in bodily sex, it was possible rightly to figure under her bodily covering that part of the reason which is diverted to the government of temporal things; so that the image of God may not remain, except on that side of the mind of man on which it cleaves to the beholding or the consulting of the eternal reasons of things; and this, it is clear, not men only, but also women have.

Chapter 8 [*In this chapter and in Chapter 12, Augustine considers the way in which human beings turn aside from the image of God. For our purposes, what is interesting in this section is the use Augustine makes of language in maintaining his distinction between the 'masculine' and 'feminine' faculties of the mind. Moreover, a clear hierarchy is drawn between masculine Wisdom and the feminine part of the mind which deals with temporal things.*]

13 A common nature, therefore, is recognized in their minds, but in their bodies a division of that one mind itself is figured. As we ascend, then, by certain steps of thought within, along the succession of the parts of the mind, there where something first meets us, which is not common to our selves with the beasts, reason begins, so that here the inner man can now be recognized. And if this inner man himself, through that reason to which the administering of things temporal has been delegated, slips on too far by over-much progress into outward things, that which is his head moreover consenting, that is, the (so to call it) masculine

part which presides in the watch-tower of counsel not restraining or bridling it: then he waxeth old because of all his enemies, viz. the demons with their prince the devil, who are envious of virtue; and that vision of eternal things is withdrawn also from the head himself, eating with his spouse that which was forbidden, so that the light of his eyes is gone from him; and so both being naked from that enlightenment of truth, and with the eyes of their conscience opened to behold how they were left shameful and unseemly, like the leaves of sweet fruits, but without the fruits themselves, they so weave together good words without the fruit of good works, as while living wickedly to cover over their disgrace as it were by speaking well.

Chapter 12

17 Let us now complete, so far the Lord helps us, the discussion which we have undertaken, respecting that part of reason to which knowledge belongs, that is, the cognizance of things temporal and changeable, which is necessary for managing the affairs of this life. For as in the case of that visible wedlock of the two human beings who were made first, the serpent did not eat of the forbidden tree, but only persuaded them to eat of it; and the woman did not eat alone, but gave to her husband, and they eat together; although she alone spoke with the serpent, and she alone was led away by him: so also in the case of that hidden and secret kind of wedlock, which is transacted and discerned in a single human being, the carnal, or as I may say, since it is directed to the senses of the body, the sensuous movement of the soul, which is common to us with beasts, is shut off from the reason of wisdom. For certainly bodily things are perceived by the sense of the body; but spiritual things, which are eternal and unchangeable, are understood by the reason of wisdom. But the reason of knowledge has appetite very near to it: seeing that what is called the science or knowledge of actions, reasons of the bodily things themselves, which are perceived by the bodily sense; if well, in order that it may refer that knowledge to the end of the chief good; but if ill, in order that it may enjoy them as being such good things as those wherein it reposes with a false blessedness. Whenever, then, that carnal or animal sense introduces into this purpose of the mind, which is conversant in things temporal and corporeal, with a view to the offices of a man's actions, by the living force of reason, some inducement to enjoy itself, that is, to

enjoy itself as if it were some private good of its own, not as the public and common, which is the unchangeable, good; then, as it were, the serpent discourses with the woman. And to consent to this allurement, is to eat of the forbidden tree. But if that consent is satisfied by the pleasure of thought alone, but the members are so restrained by the authority of higher counsel that they are not yielded as instruments of unrighteousness unto sin; this, I think, is to be considered as if the woman alone should have eaten the forbidden food. But if, in this consent to use wickedly the things which are perceived through the senses of the body, any sin at all is so determined upon, that if there is the power, it is also fulfilled by the body; then that woman must be understood to have given the unlawful food to her husband with her, to be eaten together. For it is not possible for the mind to determine, that a sin is not only to be thought of with pleasure, but also effectually committed, unless also that intention of the mind yields, and serves the bad action, with which rests the chief power of applying the members to an outward act, or of restraining them from one.

Chapter 13 [*While equating the masculine with Wisdom/reason and the feminine with knowledge/skill and the perception of the temporal realm, Augustine goes on to refute the claim that the mind should be equated with human males, and the body with human females.*]

20 Nor does it escape me, that some who before us were eminent defenders of the Catholic faith and expounders of the word of God, while they looked for these two things in one human being, whose entire soul they perceived to be a sort of excellent paradise, asserted that the man was the mind, but that the woman was the bodily sense. And according to this distribution, by which the man is assumed to be the mind, but the woman the bodily sense, all things seem aptly to agree together if they are handled with due attention: unless that it is written, that in all the beasts and flying things there was not found for man an helpmate like to himself; and then the woman was made out of his side. And on this account I, for my part, have not thought that the bodily sense should be taken for the woman, which we see to be common to ourselves and to the beasts; but I have desired to find something which the beasts had not; and I have rather thought the bodily sense should be understood to be the serpent, whom we read to have been more subtle than all beasts of the field

[Genesis 3:1]. For in those natural good things which we see are common to ourselves and to the irrational animals, the sense excels by a kind of living power; not the sense of which it is written in the epistle addressed to the Hebrews, where we read, that 'strong meat belongeth to them that are of full age, even those who by reason of use have their senses exercised to discern both good and evil' [Hebrews 5:14]; for these 'senses' belong to the rational nature and pertain to the understanding; but that sense which is divided into five parts in the body, through which corporeal species and motion is perceived not only by our selves, but also by the beasts.

21 But whether that the apostle calls the man the image and glory of God, but the woman the glory of the man [1 Corinthians 6:7] is to be received in this, or that, or in any other way; yet it is clear, that when we live according to God, our mind which is intent on the invisible things of Him ought to be fashioned with proficiency from His eternity, truth, charity; but that something of our own reasonable purpose, that is, of the same mind, must be directed to the using of changeable and corporeal things, without which this life does not go on; not that we may be conformed to this world, by placing our end in such good things, and by forcing aside the desire of blessedness towards them, but that whatever we do rationally in the using of temporal things, we may do it with the contemplation of attaining eternal things, passing through the former, but cleaving to the latter.

*CITY OF GOD**

Book XXII

17 [*Augustine addresses the question of whether women will remain female in the afterlife. Rejecting the claim that all will be raised as men, he goes on to argue that the element which will be removed in the next world is lust. Thus 'the sex of woman' will be given a new beauty which will not incite lust, but praise in the wonder of God's creative power.*]

*Reprinted from the translation by M. Dods (Edinburgh: T. & T. Clark, 1871).

From the words, 'Till we all come to a perfect man, to the measure of the age of the fullness of Christ' [Ephesians 4:13], and from the words 'Conformed to the image of the Son of God' [Romans 8:29], some conclude that women shall not rise women, but that all shall be men, because God made man only of earth, and woman of the man. For my part, they seem to be wiser who make no doubt that both sexes shall rise. For there shall be no lust, which is now the cause of confusion. For before they sinned, the man and the woman were naked, and were not ashamed. From those bodies, then, vice shall be withdrawn, while nature shall be preserved. And the sex of woman is not a vice, but nature. It shall then indeed be superior to carnal intercourse and child-bearing; nevertheless the female members shall remain adapted not to the old uses, but to a new beauty, which, so far from provoking lust, now extinct, shall excite praise to the wisdom and clemency of God, who both made what was not and delivered from corruption what He made. For at the beginning of the human race the woman was made of a rib taken from the side of the man while he slept; for it seemed fit that even then Christ and His Church should be foreshadowed in this event. For that sleep of the man was the death of Christ, whose side, as He hung lifeless upon the cross, was pierced with a spear, and there flowed from it blood and water, and these we know to be the sacraments by which the Church is 'built up'. For Scripture used this very word, not saying 'He formed' or 'framed', but 'built her up into a woman' [Genesis 2:22]. . . . The woman, therefore, is a creature of God even as the man; but by her creation from man unity is commended; and the manner of her creation prefigured, as has been said, Christ and the Church. He, then, who created both sexes will restore both. Jesus Himself also, when asked by the Sadducees, who denied the resurrection, which of the seven brothers should have to wife the woman whom all in succession had taken to raise up seed to their brother, as the law enjoined, says, 'Ye do err, not knowing the Scriptures nor the power of God' [Matthew 22:29]. And though it was a fit opportunity for His saying, 'She about whom you make inquiries shall herself be a man, and not a woman', He said nothing of the kind; but 'In the resurrection they neither marry nor are given in marriage, but are as the angles of God in heaven' [Matthew 22:30]. They shall be equal to the angels in immortality and happiness, not in flesh, nor in resurrection, which the angels did not need, because they could not die. The Lord then denied that there would be in the resurrection, not women, but marriages; and He uttered this denial in circumstances in which the question mooted would have been more easily and speedily solved by denying that the female sex would exist, if this had in truth been foreknown by Him. But, indeed, He even affirmed that the sex should exist by saying, 'They shall not be given in marriage', which can only apply to females; 'Neither shall they marry', which applies to males. There shall therefore be those who are in this world accustomed to marry and be given in marriage, only they shall there make no such marriages.

24 [*Augustine considers the blessings which God has given the human race. He focuses upon procreation, a blessing marred by the curse which followed the Fall, but a blessing nevertheless. He praises the physical world, but it is within the faculty of reason that the divine image is located.*]

. . . God, then, so created man that He gave him what we may call fertility, whereby he might propagate other men, giving them a congenital capacity to propagate their kind, but not imposing on them any necessity to do so. This capacity God withdraws at pleasure from individuals, making them barren; but from the whole race He has not withdrawn the blessing of propagation once conferred. But though not withdrawn on account of sin, this power of propagation is not what it would have been had there been no sin. For since 'man placed in honour fell, he has become like the beasts' [Psalm 49:20], and generates as they do, though the little spark of reason, which was the image of God in him, has not been quite quenched. But if conformation were not added to propagation, there would be no reproduction of one's kind. For even though there were no such thing as copulation, and God wished to fill the earth with human inhabitants, He might create all these as He created one without the help of human generation. And, indeed, even as it is, those who copulate can generate nothing, save by the creative energy of God. As, therefore, in respect of that spiritual growth whereby a man is formed to piety and righteousness, the apostle says, 'Neither is he that planteth anything, neither he that watereth, but God that giveth the increase' [1 Corinthians 3:7], so also it must be said that it is not he that generates that is anything, but God that giveth the essential form; that it is not the mother who carries and nurses the fruit of her womb that is anything, but God that giveth the increase. For He alone, by that energy wherewith 'He worketh hitherto', causes the seed to develop, and to evolve from certain secret and invisible folds into the visible forms of beauty which we see. He alone, coupling and connecting in some wonderful fashion the spiritual and corporeal natures, the one to command, the other to obey, makes a living being. And this work of His is so great and wonderful, that not only man, who is a rational animal, and consequently more excellent than all other animals of the earth, but even the most diminutive insect, cannot be considered attentively without astonishment and without praising the Creator.

It is He, then, who has given to the human soul a mind, in which reason and understanding lie as it were asleep during infancy, and as if they were not, destined, however, to be awakened and exercised as years increase, so as to become capable of knowledge and of receiving instruction, fit to understand what is true and to love what is good. It is by this capacity the soul drinks in wisdom, and becomes endowed with those virtues by which, in prudence, fortitude, temperance, and righteousness, it makes war upon error and the other inborn vices, and conquers them by fixing its desires upon no other object than the supreme and unchangeable Good. And even though this be not uniformly the result, yet who can competently utter or even conceive the grandeur of this work of the Almighty, and the unspeakable boon He has conferred upon our rational nature, by giving us even the capacity of such attainment? For over and above those arts which are called virtues, and which teach us how we may spend our life well, and attain to endless happiness – arts which are given to the children of the promise and the kingdom by the sole grace of God which is in Christ – has not the genius of man invented and applied countless astonishing arts, partly the result of necessity, partly the result of exuberant invention, so that this vigour of mind, which is so active in the discovery not merely of superfluous but even of dangerous and destructive things, betokens an inexhaustible wealth in the nature which can invent, learn, or employ such arts? What wonderful – one might say stupefying – advances has human industry made in the arts of weaving and building, of agriculture and navigation! With what endless variety are designs in pottery, painting, and sculpture produced, and with what skill executed! What wonderful spectacles are exhibited in the theatres, which those who have not seen them cannot credit! How skilful the contrivances for catching, killing, or taming wild beasts! And for the injury of men, also, how many kinds of poisons, weapons, engines of destruction, have been invented, while for the preservation or restoration of health the appliances and remedies are infinite! . . .

Moreover, even in the body, though it dies like that of the beasts, and is in many ways weaker than theirs, what goodness of God, what providence of the great Creator, is apparent! The organs of sense and the rest of the members, are not they so placed, the appearance, and form, and stature of the body as a whole, is it not so fashioned as to indicate that it was made for the service of a reasonable soul? Man has not been created stooping towards the earth, like the irrational animals; but his bodily form, erect and looking heavenwards, admonishes him to mind the things that are above. Then the marvellous nimbleness which has been given to the tongue and the hands, fitting them to speak, and write, and execute so many duties, and practise so many arts, does it not prove the excellence of the soul for which such an assistant was provided? And even apart from its adaptation to the work required of it, there is such a symmetry in its various parts, and so beautiful a proportion maintained, that one is at a loss to decide whether, in creating the body, greater regard was paid to utility or to beauty. Assuredly no part of the body has been created for the sake of utility which does not also contribute something to its beauty. . . . There are some things, too, which have such a place in the body, that they obviously serve no useful purpose, but are solely for beauty, as e.g. the teats on a man's breast, or the beard on his face; for that this is for ornament, and not for protection, is proved by the bare faces of women, who ought rather, as the weaker sex, to enjoy such a defence. If, therefore, of all those members which are exposed to our view, there is certainly not one in which beauty is sacrificed to utility, while there are some which serve no purpose but only beauty, I think it can readily be concluded that in the creation of the human body comeliness was more regarded than necessity. In truth, necessity is a transitory thing; and the time is coming when we shall enjoy one another's beauty without any lust – a condition which will specially redound to the praise of the Creator, who, as it is said in the psalm, has 'put on praise and comeliness' [Psalm 104:1]. . . .

STUDY QUESTIONS

1. Genevieve Lloyd suggests that Augustine offers woman 'spiritual equality and natural subordination' (Lloyd, *The Man of Reason*, p. 28).

Which parts of Augustine's argument might be used to support this analysis of his work?

2. To what extent does Augustine challenge the idea that man is equated with reason (or the mind) and woman with nature?

SELECT BIBLIOGRAPHY

General

A. Blamires, *Woman Defamed and Woman Defended* (Oxford: Clarendon Press, 1992), for general context.
P. R. L. Brown, *Augustine of Hippo: A Biography* (Berkeley: University of California Press, 1969).
H. Chadwick, *The Early Church* (Harmondsworth: Penguin, 1967).
H. Chadwick, *Augustine* (Oxford: Oxford University Press, 1986).
G. Clark, *Women in Late Antiquity* (Oxford: Clarendon Press, 1993).

For feminist analysis

G. Lloyd, *The Man of Reason* (London: Methuen, 1984), ch. 2.
N. Noddings, *Women and Evil* (Berkeley: University of California Press, 1989), ch. 1.
E. Pagels, *Adam, Eve, and the Serpent* (Harmondsworth: Penguin, 1988).
K. Power, *Veiled Desire: Augustine's Writings on Women* (London: Darton, Longman & Todd, 1995).

5 Thomas Aquinas 1225–1274

Introduction and Background

The writings of Thomas Aquinas have a significance which goes far beyond the context in which they were written. A medieval theologian, Aquinas's ideas remain central to the development of Catholic theology. Moreover, his *Summa Theologiae* remains a classic text for the philosophical approach to theology. Aquinas was much influenced by Aristotelian categories of thought, and this is particularly evident when one considers his thinking on the nature and role of women.

In 1244, Aquinas became a Dominican friar, a decision which so enraged his family that they imprisoned him for over a year. During this time, an event took place which appears to have had a lasting effect upon his attitude to women. One night, his brothers sent a woman to his cell. Enraged, Thomas drove her from his room. Falling into a deep sleep, he dreamt that angels had bound his loins 'in token of perpetual chastity'.[1] Subsequently, Thomas was to avoid women 'as a man avoids snakes'.[2]

In approaching the question of the nature and role of woman, Aquinas builds upon Aristotle's idea of the innate inferiority of women. However, Aquinas develops these ideas within a Christian framework. When he discusses woman's 'subjection' to man, he views this as integral to God's plan for creation. Subjection in this sense is understood not as slavery, which involves the subjection of one person to another, but as part of a hierarchical structuring of human relations which is good for all members of society. Again, we see the influence of Aristotle. Indeed, Aquinas understands subjection in this sense as part of God's plan from the beginning. Had there been no primeval 'fall' from grace, woman would still have been subjected to man. Her subjection is inevitable because of the distinct natures of men and women; 'the power of rational discernment is by nature stronger in man', and thus he is the 'natural' ruler of woman. Woman is understood as man's helpmate; but as Genevieve Lloyd points out, this notion of 'helpmate' should only be understood in relation to the function of procreation. 'In areas of life other than generation, "man can be more efficiently helped by another man"'.[3]

Analysis of Aquinas's ideas on women reveals a significant development in the history of ideas. In defining woman, he draws upon the 'insights' of Aristotelian philosophy *and* Christian theology. Woman is not only a 'misbegotten male' (Aristotle), she is also associated with the weakness of the first woman, Eve (Tertullian). Philosophy and theology combine to create a damning picture of the nature of woman and the need for her subjection to the higher powers of man.

*SUMMA THEOLOGIAE**

Ia. 92, 1

Question 92 Man's Actual Production as Far as Woman is Concerned

Next we must consider the production of woman. There are four points of inquiry here:

1 whether woman ought to have been produced in that original production of things;
2 whether she ought to have been made from man;
3 whether from man's rib;
4 whether she was made directly by God.

* From *St Thomas Aquinas: Summa Theologiae*, XIII, translated by E. Hill (London: Blackfriars/Eyre & Spottiswoode, 1964), © Cambridge University Press.

Article 1 Should woman have been made in that original creation of things?

THE FIRST POINT:

1 It seems that woman ought not to have been produced in the original production of things. For the Philosopher says that the female is a male *manqué*. But nothing *manqué* or defective should have been produced in the first establishment of things; so woman ought not to have been produced then.

2 Again, subjection and inferiority are a result of sin; for it was after sin that woman was told, *Thou shalt be under the power of man*, and Gregory[1] says that where we have done no wrong, we are all equal. Yet woman is by nature of lower capacity and quality than man; for the active cause is always more honourable than the passive, as Augustine says. So woman ought not to have been produced in the original production of things before sin.

3 Again, occasions of sin should be eliminated. But God foresaw that woman would be an occasion of sin for man. So he ought not to have produced her.

ON THE OTHER HAND, there is Genesis: *It is not good for man to be alone; let us make him a help that is like himself.*

REPLY: It is absolutely necessary to make woman, for the reason Scripture mentions, as a help for man; not indeed to help him in any other work, as some have maintained, because where most work is concerned man can get help more conveniently from another man than from a woman; but to help him in the work of procreation. This may be more clearly appreciated if we consider the procreative pattern in living things. At the bottom of the scale there are some living things which have no active procreative power themselves, but are procreated by an agent of a different species; like those plants and animals which are generated without seed by the active force of heavenly bodies out of suitable matter.

Next there are some living things which have their active and passive procreative powers joined together, as, for example, those plants which are generated from seed. Plants have no nobler function than procreation; so it is proper that they should be procreating all the time, and have the active power of procreation continually joined to the passive.

Next up the scale are the perfect animals, which have the active power of procreation in the male sex and the passive in the female. And because animals are capable of a vital function which is nobler than that of procreation, a function which their life is chiefly directed to, the consequence is that in perfect animals the male and female sex are not continually joined together, but only at times of mating. So we may fancy, if we like, that in mating male and female constitute a whole or unity, rather like that of a plant in which the male and female principles are permanently joined together – though in some one is more dominant, in some the other.

But at the top of the scale is man, whose life is directed to a nobler function still, that of understanding things. And so there was more reason than ever in man for emphasizing the distinction between the sexes, which was done by producing the woman separately from the man, while at the same time joining them together in a union of the flesh for the work of procreation. And therefore immediately after the formation of the woman it goes on to say, *They shall be two in one flesh* [Genesis 2:24].

Hence:

1 Only as regards nature in the individual is the female something defective and *manqué*. For the active power in the seed of the male tends to produce something like itself, perfect in masculinity; but the procreation of a female is the result either of the debility of the active power, of some unsuitability of the material, or of some change effected by external influences, like the south wind, for example, which is damp, as we are told by Aristotle.

But with reference to nature in the species as a whole, the female is not something *manqué*, but is according to the tendency of nature, and is directed to the work of procreation. Now the tendency of the nature of a species as a whole derives from God, who is the general author of nature. And therefore when he established a nature, he brought into being not only the male but the female too.

2 Subjection is of two kinds; one is that of slavery, in which the ruler manages the subject for his own advantage, and this sort of subjection came in after sin. But the other kind of subjection is domestic or civil, in which the ruler manages his subjects for their advantage and benefit. And this sort of subjection would have obtained even before sin. For the human group would have

lacked the benefit of order had some of its members not been governed by others who were wiser. Such is the subjection in which woman is by nature subordinate to man, because the power of rational discernment is by nature stronger in man. Nor is inequality among men incompatible with the state of innocence, as we shall see later on.

3 If God had removed everything from the world in which man has found an occasion of sin, the universe would have remained incomplete. Nor should the general good be forgone in order to avoid a particular evil – especially as God is so powerful that he can turn any evil to good account.

Article 2 Should she have been made from man?

THE SECOND POINT:

1 It seems that woman should not have been made from man. For sex is common to man and the other animals. But in the case of the other animals the female was not made from the male. Therefore it should not have been so in the case of man.
2 Again, things of the same kind have the same material. Male and female are of the same kind. Therefore as man was made from the slime of the earth, woman should have been made from it too, and not from man.
3 Again, woman was made to help man in procreation. But too close a relationship makes a person unsuitable for this, which is why close relations are excluded from marrying each other, as is clear from Leviticus [18:6]. So woman should not have been made from man.

ON THE OTHER HAND, there is Ecclesiasticus [17:5]: *He created from him* – namely from the man – *a help for him* – namely the woman.

REPLY: It was right for woman to be formed from man in the original establishment of things, for reasons that do not apply to the other animals. In the first place this was desirable in order to maintain a certain style and dignity for the first man, by making him, in virtue of his likeness to God, the original of his whole kind, just as God is the original of the whole universe. So Paul says that God *made the whole of mankind from one* [Acts 17:26].

In the second place this was good in order to make the man

love the woman more and stick to her more inseparably, knowing that she had been brought forth from himself. So it says in Genesis [2:23], *She was taken from man; therefore a man shall leave father and mother and stick to his wife*. And this was specially necessary in the human species, in which male and female remain together all their lives, which does not happen in the case of other animals.

Thirdly, as Aristotle says, with man male and female are not only joined together for purposes of procreation, as with the other animals, but to establish a home life, in which man and woman work together at the same things, and in which the man is head of the woman. So the woman was rightly formed from the man, as her origin and chief.

The fourth reason is sacramental or typological; for this episode stands for the Church taking its origin from Christ. Thus the Apostle says, *But this is a great sacrament (mystery), I mean in Christ and the Church* [Ephesians 5:23].

And that should deal with the first objection. As for the others:

2 Material means what something is made from. Now created nature needs a prescribed starting-point to work from; and since it is determined to one prescribed result, it also has a prescribed process. So from prescribed material it produces something in a prescribed species. But the divine power, being infinite and quite unprescribed, can make things identical in kind from any material it likes – like man from the slime of the earth and woman from the man.

3 The close relationship which bars marriage is contracted through natural procreation and ancestry. But the woman was not brought forth from the man through natural procreation, but solely through divine power. So Eve is not called Adam's daughter, and so the argument does not follow.

Article 3 Should she have been made from man's rib?

THE THIRD POINT:

1 It seems the woman should not have been made from the man's rib. For the man's rib was much smaller than the woman's body. Now something bigger can only be made from something smaller, either by addition – and in this case the woman should be described as formed from the added material rather than from the rib – or else by thinning out or

rarefaction. As Augustine says, it is impossible for a body to grow unless it thins out. But there is no evidence that woman's body is less dense than man's – at least not in the ratio of a rib to Eve's body. So Eve was not formed from Adam's rib.

2 Again, there was no waste in the works of the original creation. Adam's rib therefore pertained to the completeness of his body. Take it away and his body would be incomplete; which seems to be most unsuitable.

3 Again, a man's rib cannot be removed from him without pain. But pain did not exist before sin. So a rib should not have been taken from the man to form a woman out of it.

ON THE OTHER HAND, there is Genesis [2:22]: *The Lord God built the rib which he had taken from Adam into a woman.*

REPLY: It was right and proper for the woman to be formed from the man's rib. First, in order to signify the companionship there should be between man and woman; the woman should neither *have authority over the man* [1 Timothy 2:12] – and therefore she was not formed from his head; nor should she be despised by the man, as though she were merely his slave – and so she was not formed from his feet.

Secondly, for a sacramental, typological reason; because from the side of Christ sleeping on the cross flowed the sacraments, that is the blood and water, by which the Church was established.

1a. 93, 4

Question 93 The Final Product Made to the Image of God

Article 4 Is God's image found in every man?

THE FOURTH POINT:

1 It seems that God's image is not to be found in every man. For the Apostle says that *the man is the image of God, while the woman is the image of the man* [1 Corinthians 11:7]. Since then the woman is an individual member of the human race, it follows that being God's image does not pertain to every individual.

2 Again, the Apostle says that those *whom God foreknew to be conformed to the image of his Son these he predestined* [Romans 8:29]. But not all men have been predestined, and so all do not have the conformity of image.

3 Again, 'likeness' is involved in the idea of 'image', as we have seen. But sin makes a man unlike God, and so by sin he loses God's image.

ON THE OTHER HAND, there is the Psalm [38:7]: *Yet man passes as an image.*

REPLY: Since man is said to be after God's image in virtue of his intelligent nature, it follows that he is most completely after God's image in that point in which such a nature can most completely imitate God. Now it does this in so far as it imitates God's understanding and loving of *himself*.

Thus God's image can be considered in man at three stages: the first stage is man's natural aptitude for understanding and loving God, an aptitude which consists in the very nature of the mind, which is common to all men. The next stage is where a man is actually or dispositively knowing and loving God, but still imperfectly; and here we have the image by conformity of grace. The third stage is where a man is actually knowing and loving God perfectly; and his is the image by likeness of glory. Thus on the text of the Psalm [4:7], *The light of thy countenance O Lord is sealed upon us*, the *Gloss* distinguishes a threefold image, namely the image *of creation, of re-creation, and of likeness*. The first stage of image then is found in all men, the second only in the just, and the third only in the blessed.

Hence:

1 God's image is found equally in both man and woman as regards that point in which the idea of 'image' is principally realized, namely an intelligent nature. Thus after saying in Genesis [1:27], *after God's image he created him*, i.e. man, it adds *male and female he created them*; and it put *them* in the plural, as Augustine says, in case it should be supposed that the sexes are combined in one individual.

But as regards a secondary point, God's image is found in man in a way in which it is not found in woman; for man is the beginning and end of woman, just as God is the beginning and end of all creation. Thus after saying that *the man is the image and glory of God, while the woman is the glory of the man*, the Apostle goes on to show why he says it, and adds: *for the man is not* from *the woman, but the woman* from *the man; and the man was not created* for *the woman, but the woman* for *the man*.

2 & 3 These arguments are valid for the stages of image where it means conformity of grace and of glory.

NOTE

1. [Ed.] *Gregory*: Pope Gregory the Great (590–604). Aquinas cites his *Moralia in Job* XXI. 15.

STUDY QUESTIONS

1. Why might Aquinas be understood as bringing together philosophical and Christian theological ideas about the nature of woman? How does the information from these disciplines shape his understanding of woman?
2. 'For man is the beginning and end of woman, just as God is the beginning and end of all creation.' What might this comment suggest about the relationship between ideals of masculinity and ideas of God?

SELECT BIBLIOGRAPHY

General

A. Blamires (ed.), *Woman Defamed and Woman Defended* (Oxford: Clarendon Press, 1992).
A. Kenny, *Aquinas* (Oxford: Oxford University Press, 1980).

For feminist analysis

G. Lloyd, *The Man of Reason* (London: Methuen, 1984), ch. 2.
E. McLaughlin, 'Equality of Souls, Inequality of Sexes: Woman in Medieval Theology', in *Religion and Sexism*, ed. R. Ruether (New York: Simon & Schuster, 1974), pp. 213–66.
U. Ranke-Heinemann, *Eunuchs for the Kingdom of Heaven* (Harmondsworth: Penguin, 1991), ch. XVI.

6 Heinrich Kramer and James Sprenger 1486

Introduction and Background

The *Malleus Maleficarum* (or 'The Hammer of Witches') is best understood against the backdrop of the 'witchcraze' of the sixteenth century. During this period it is estimated that between thirty thousand and nine million women were condemned as witches, consorts of the devil.[1] Written by the Dominican fathers Heinrich Kramer and James Sprenger, the *Malleus* was to become 'the bible of witch-hunting'.[2] In this work, Kramer and Sprenger made the relatively new step of equating witchcraft with the worship of Satan. Papal approval was sought and given to their methods for identifying occult practices.[3] In particular, the use of torture was approved as a means of exposing and eradicating witchcraft.

Feminist writers have found in the *Malleus* a disturbing record of medieval misogyny.[4] Kramer and Sprenger identified witchcraft primarily with the acts of women. Drawing upon biblical and classical sources, they argued that women were more susceptible to the machinations of the devil. This susceptibility they located in woman's sexuality. Women, they claimed, were more carnal than men; so much so, that women would even resort to fulfilling their sexual urges with demons.

It is this identification of women with the demonic that has led some feminist writers, such as Mary Daly, to view the witch hunts as direct acts against women.[5] Arguing that 'the witchcraze focused predominantly upon women who had rejected marriage (spinsters) and women who had survived it (widows)',[6] she claims that women who refused to live within the parameters of patriarchal society were the primary target for the witchfinders. Thus witches were 'women living outside the control of the patriarchal family, women who presented an option – an option of "eccentricity", and of "indigestibility"'.[7]

Daly's assessment has not gone unchallenged. Keith Thomas claims that the sex of the suspected witch was of less importance than her/his position in society.[8] The suspected witch was likely to be 'in a socially or economically inferior position to her supposed victim'.[9] This assessment need not undermine the feminist analysis of the cause of the witchcraze. The position ascribed to women in a society dominated by men and masculine values is suggestive of a 'socially or economically inferior position'. As such, it seems likely that more witches will be female than male.

While the *Malleus* can tell us much about medieval attitudes towards women, consideration of the way in which twentieth-century commentators assess the *Malleus* can illuminate modern attitudes towards women. In the introduction to Montague Summers's 1928 edition of the *Malleus*, Summers uses the witchcraze as a paradigm for his own age. The witches are likened to the threat posed by the bolshevik movement to monarchy, private property, marriage, order, and religion.[10] In such times, dramatic measures are necessary to safeguard the structures of society:

> It was against this that the Inquisition had to fight, and who can be surprised if, when faced with so vast a conspiracy, the methods employed by the Holy Office may not seem – if the terrible conditions are conveniently forgotten – a little drastic, a little severe? There can be no doubt that had this most excellent tribunal continued to enjoy its full prerogative and the full exercise of its salutary powers, the world at large would be in a far happier and far more orderly position to-day.[11]

For Summers, the torture of thousands of women and men is excused in the name of preserving civic order. The preservation of woman's traditionally subordinate role is vital if the fundamental order of society is to be maintained:

> Possibly what will seem even more amazing to modern readers is the misogynic trend of various passages, and these not of the briefest nor least pointed. However, exaggerated as these may be, I am not altogether certain that they will not prove a wholesome and needful antidote in this feministic age, when the sexes seem confounded, and it appears to be the chief object of many females to ape the man, an indecorum by which they not only divest themselves of such charm as they might boast, but lay themselves open to the sternest reprobation in the name of sanity and common-sense.[12]

Summers' appropriation of a fifteenth-century text to criticize the twentieth-century movements of bolshevism and feminism is noteworthy, specifically because it suggests that the worldview of the late fifteenth century is applicable to the twentieth century. Fifteenth-century understandings of the subordinate female role remain relevant. Woman is the Eternal Female, and no amount of feminist theorizing or political agitation will ever change her fundamental nature:

> It is a work which must irresistibly capture the attention of all men who think, all who see, or are endeavouring to see, the ultimate reality beyond the accidents of matter, time and space.
>
> The *Malleus Maleficarum* is one of the world's few books written *sub specie aeternitatis*.[13]

THE *MALLEUS MALEFICARUM**

Part I

Question VI Why Superstition is chiefly found in Women

As for the first question, why a greater number of witches is found in the fragile feminine sex than among men; it is indeed a fact that it were idle to contradict, since it is accredited by actual

* From the translation by Montague Summers (New York: Dover Publications, 1971).

experience, apart from the verbal testimony of credible witnesses. And without in any way detracting from a sex in which God has always taken great glory that His might should be spread abroad, let us say that various men have assigned various reasons for this fact, which nevertheless agree in principle. Wherefore it is good, for the admonition of women, to speak of this matter; and it has often been proved by experience that they are eager to hear of it, so long as it is set forth with discretion.

For some learned men propound this reason; that there are three things in nature, the Tongue, an Ecclesiastic, and a Woman, which know no moderation in goodness or vice; and when they exceed the bounds of their condition they reach the greatest heights and the lowest depths of goodness and vice. When they are governed by a good spirit, they are most excellent in virtue; but when they are governed by an evil spirit, they indulge the worst possible vices.

This is clear in the case of the tongue, since by its ministry most of the kingdoms have been brought into the faith of Christ; and the Holy Ghost appeared over the Apostles of Christ in tongues of fire. Other learned preachers also have had as it were the tongues of dogs, licking the wounds and sores of the dying Lazarus. As it is said: 'With the tongues of dogs ye save your souls from the enemy.' . . .

But concerning an evil tongue you will find in *Ecclesiasticus* xxviii: 'A backbiting tongue hath disquieted many, and driven them from nation to nation: strong cities hath it pulled down, and overthrown the houses of great men.' And by a backbiting tongue it means a third party who rashly or spitefully interferes between two contending parties.

Secondly, concerning Ecclesiastics, that is to say, clerics and religious of either sex, St John Chrysostom[1] speaks on the text, 'He cast out them that bought and sold from the temple.' From the priesthood arises everything good, and everything evil. . . .

Now the wickedness of women is spoken of in *Ecclesiasticus* xxv: 'There is no head above the head of a serpent: and there is no wrath above the wrath of a woman. I had rather dwell with a lion and a dragon than to keep house with a wicked woman.' And among much which in that place precedes and follows about a wicked woman, he concludes: 'All wickedness is but little to the wickedness of a woman.' Wherefore St John Chrysostom says on the text, 'It is not good to marry' (S. *Matthew* xix): 'What else is woman but a foe to friendship, an unescapable punishment, a necessary evil, a natural temptation, a desirable calamity, a domestic danger, a delectable detriment, an evil of nature, painted with fair colours! Therefore if it be a sin to divorce her when she ought to be kept, it is indeed a necessary torture; for either we commit adultery by divorcing her, or we must endure daily strife.' Cicero[2] in his second book of *The Rhetorics* says: 'The many lusts of men lead them into one sin, but the one lust of women leads them into all sins; for the root of all woman's vices is avarice.' And Seneca[3] says in his *Tragedies*: 'A woman either loves or hates; there is no third grade. And the tears of a woman are a deception, for they may spring from true grief, or they may be a snare. When a woman thinks alone, she thinks evil.'

But for good women there is so much praise, that we read that they have brought beatitude to men, and have saved nations, lands, and cities; as is clear in the case of Judith,[4] Debbora,[5] and Esther.[6] See also I *Corinthians* vii: 'If a woman hath a husband that believeth not, and he be pleased to dwell with her, let her not leave him. For the unbelieving husband is sanctified by the believing wife.' And *Ecclesiasticus* xxvi: 'Blessed is the man who has a virtuous wife, for the number of his days shall be doubled.' And throughout that chapter much high praise is spoken of the excellence of good women; as also in the last chapter of *Proverbs* concerning a virtuous woman. . . .

Others again have propounded other reasons why there are more superstitious women found than men. And the first is, that they are more credulous; and since the chief aim of the devil is to corrupt faith, therefore he rather attacks them. See *Ecclesiasticus* xix: 'He that is quick to believe is light-minded, and shall be diminished.' The second reason is, that women are naturally more impressionable, and more ready to receive the influence of a disembodied spirit; and that when they use this quality well they are very good, but when they use it ill they are very evil.

The third reason is that they have slippery tongues, and are unable to conceal from their fellow-women those things which by evil arts they know; and, since they are weak, they find an easy and secret manner of vindicating themselves by witchcraft. See *Ecclesiasticus* as quoted above: 'I had rather dwell with a lion and a dragon than to keep house with a wicked woman. All wickedness is but little to the wickedness of a woman.' And to this may be added that, as they are very impressionable, they act accordingly.

There are also others who bring forward yet other reasons, of which preachers should be very careful how they make use. For it is true that in the Old Testament the Scriptures have much that is evil to say about women, and this because of the first temptress, Eve, and her imitators; yet afterwards in the New Testament we find a change of name, as from Eva to Ave (as St Jerome[7] says), and the whole sin of Eve taken away by the benediction of Mary. Therefore preachers should always say as much praise of them as possible.

But because in these times this perfidy is more often found in women than in men, as we learn by actual experience, if anyone is curious as to the reason, we may add to what has already been said the following: that since they are feebler both in mind and body, it is not surprising that they should come more under the spell of witchcraft.

For as regards intellect, or the understanding of spiritual things, they seem to be of a different nature from men; a fact which is vouched for by the logic of the authorities, backed by various examples from the Scriptures. Terence[8] says: 'Women are intellectually like children.' And Lactantius[9] (*Institutiones*, III): 'No woman understood philosophy except Temeste.' And *Proverbs* xi, as it were describing a woman, says: 'As a jewel of gold in a swine's snout, so is a fair woman which is without discretion.'

But the natural reason is that she is more carnal than a man, as is clear from her many carnal abominations. And it should be noted that there was a defect in the formation of the first woman, since she was formed from a bent rib, that is, a rib of the breast, which is bent as it were in a contrary direction to a man. And since through this defect she is an imperfect animal, she always deceives. For Cato[10] says: 'When a woman weeps she weaves snares.' And again: 'When a woman weeps, she labours to deceive a man.' And this is shown by Samson's wife,[11] who coaxed him to tell her the riddle he had propounded to the Philistines, and told them the answer, and so deceived him. And it is clear in the case of the first woman that she had little faith; for when the serpent asked why they did not eat of every tree in Paradise, she answered: 'Of every tree, etc. – lest perchance we die.' Thereby she showed that she doubted, and had little faith in the word of God. And all this is indicated by the etymology of the word; for *Femina* comes from *Fe* and *Minus*, since she is ever weaker to hold and preserve the faith. And this as regards faith is of her very nature; although both by grace and nature faith never failed in the Blessed Virgin, even at the time of Christ's Passion, when it failed in all men.

Therefore a wicked woman is by her nature quicker to waver in her faith, and consequently quicker to abjure the faith, which is the root of witchcraft.

And as to her other mental quality, that is, her natural will; when she hates someone whom she formerly loved, then she seethes with anger and impatience in her whole soul, just as the tides of the sea are always heaving and boiling. . . .

. . . And truly the most powerful cause which contributes to the increase of witches is the woeful rivalry between married folk and unmarried women and men. This is so even among holy women, so what must it be among the others? For you see in *Genesis* xxi how impatient and envious Sarah was of Hagar when she conceived: how jealous Rachel was of Leah because she had no children (*Genesis* xxx): and Hannah, who was barren, of the fruitful Peninnah (I *Kings* i): and how Miriam (*Numbers* xii) murmured and spoke ill of Moses, and was therefore stricken with leprosy: and how Martha was jealous of Mary Magdalen, because she was busy and Mary was sitting down (*Luke* x). To this point is *Ecclesiasticus* xxxvii: 'Neither consult with a woman touching her of whom she is jealous.' Meaning that it is useless to consult with her, since there is always jealousy, that is, envy, in a wicked woman. And if women behave thus to each other, how much more will they do so to men.

Valerius Maximus[12] tells how, when Phoroneus, the king of the Greeks, was dying, he said to his brother Leontius that there would have been nothing lacking to him of complete happiness if a wife had always been lacking to him. . . . And when the philosopher Socrates was asked if one should marry a wife, he answered: 'If you do not, you are lonely, your family dies out, and a stranger inherits; if you do, you suffer perpetual anxiety, querulous complaints, reproaches concerning the marriage portion, the heavy displeasure of your relations, the garrulousness of a mother-in-law, cuckoldom, and no certain arrival of an heir.' This he said as one who knew. For St Jerome in his *Contre Iouinianum* says: 'This Socrates had two wives, whom he endured with much patience, but could not be rid of their contumelies and clamorous vituperations. So one day when they were complaining against him, he went out of the house to escape their plaguing, and sat down before the house; and the women then threw filthy water over him. But the philosopher was not disturbed by this, saying, "I knew that the rain would come after the thunder."' . . .

And indeed, just as through the first defect in their intelligence they are more prone to abjure the faith; so through their second defect of inordinate affections and passions they search for, brood over, and inflict various vengeances, either by witchcraft, or by some other means. Wherefore it is no wonder that so great a number of witches exist in this sex. . . .

If we inquire, we find that nearly all the kingdoms of the world have been overthrown by women. Troy, which was a prosperous kingdom, was, for the rape of one woman, Helen, destroyed, and many thousands of Greeks slain. The kingdom of the Jews suffered much misfortune and destruction through the accursed Jezebel, and her daughter Athaliah,[13] Queen of Judah, who caused her son's sons to be killed, that on their death she might reign herself; yet each of them was slain. The kingdom of the Romans endured much evil through Cleopatra, Queen of Egypt, that worst of women. And so with others. Therefore it is no wonder if the world now suffers through the malice of women.

And now let us examine the carnal desires of the body itself, whence has arisen unconscionable harm to human life. Justly may we say with Cato of Utica:[14] 'If the world could be rid of women, we should not be without God in our intercourse.' For truly, without the wickedness of women, to say nothing of witchcraft, the world would still remain proof against innumerable dangers. . . .

'And I have found a woman more bitter than death, who is the hunter's snare, and her heart is a net, and her hands are bands' [Ecclesiastes VII, 26]. He that pleaseth God shall escape from her; but he that is a sinner shall be caught by her. More bitter than death, that is, than the devil: *Apocalypse* vi, 8, 'His name was Death.' For though the devil tempted Eve to sin, yet Eve seduced Adam. And as the sin of Eve would not have brought death to our soul and body unless the sin had afterwards passed on to Adam, to which he was tempted by Eve, not by the devil, therefore she is more bitter than death.

More bitter than death, again, because that is natural and destroys only the body; but the sin which arose from woman destroys the soul by depriving it of grace, and delivers the body up to the punishment for sin.

More bitter than death, again, because bodily death is an open and terrible enemy, but woman is a wheedling and secret enemy.

And that she is more perilous than a snare does not speak of the snare of hunters, but of devils. For men are caught not only through their carnal desires, when they see and hear women: for

St Bernard[15] says: 'Their face is a burning wind, and their voice the hissing of serpents: but they also cast wicked spells on countless men and animals.' And when it is said that her heart is a net, it speaks of the inscrutable malice which reigns in their hearts. And her hands are as bands for binding; for when they place their hands on a creature to bewitch it, then with the help of the devil they perform their design.

To conclude. All witchcraft comes from carnal lust, which is in women insatiable. See *Proverbs* xxx: 'There are three things that are never satisfied, yea, a fourth thing which says not, It is enough; that is, the mouth of the womb.' Wherefore for the sake of fulfilling their lusts they consort even with devils. More such reasons could be brought forward, but to the understanding it is sufficiently clear that it is no matter for wonder that there are more women than men found infected with the heresy of witchcraft. And in consequence of this, it is better called the heresy of witches than of wizards, since the name is taken from the more powerful party. And blessed be the Highest Who has so far preserved the male sex from so great a crime: for since He was willing to be born and to suffer for us, therefore He has granted to men this privilege.

NOTES

1. [Ed.] *St John Chrysostom*: a leading theologian (347–407 CE) of the patristic period, he was an advocate of celibacy and a renowned misogynist.
2. [Ed.] Marcus Tullius *Cicero*: (106–43 BCE) Roman statesman and orator. His ideas were particularly influential during the European Enlightenment.
3. [Ed.] Lucius Amaeus *Seneca*: (4 BCE–65 CE) Roman statesman, Stoic and playwright.
4. [Ed.] *Judith*: Jewish heroine who gives her name to the Apocryphal book, Judith was a citizen of Bethulia when it was captured by Holofernes, Nebuchadnezzar's general. Holofernes was captivated by her beauty, but, when he was drunk, she killed him, inspiring her people to overthrow the oppressors.
5. [Ed.] *Debbora*: (or Deborah) Judge of Israel, she rallied the Israelite tribes to defeat the Canaanite general Sisera.
6. [Ed.] *Esther*: Jewish heroine who gives her name to the biblical book. Queen of the Persian king Xerxes, she defeats the machinations of Haman to save her people.
7. [Ed.] *St Jerome*: (347–420 CE) Latin 'father' of the Church. Advocate of celibacy who viewed all sexual intercourse – even that taking

place within marriage – as unclean (see E. Pagels, *Adam, Eve and the Serpent* (Harmondsworth: Penguin, 1988), ch. 4, for a review of his ideas).

8. [Ed.] Publius Terentius *Terence*: Roman comic writer who died around 159 BCE. His plays offer realistic dialogue, and were well known in the Middle Ages.

9. [Ed.] Lucius Caecilius Firmianus *Lactantius*: (*c*.245–325 CE) Latin writer and Christian apologist. In the *Institutiones*, he offers a defence of Christian doctrine, arguing for the rational nature of its major doctrines.

10. [Ed.] Marcus Porcius *Cato*: (234–149 BCE) Roman statesman and writer. *Dicta Catonis* (the sayings of Cato) was a popular collection of his moral maxims in the Middle Ages.

11. [Ed.] *Samson's wife*: Delilah. For their story, see Judges 16.

12. [Ed.] *Valerius Maximus*: first-century compiler of anecdotes.

13. [Ed.] *Jezebel and Athaliah*: wife of King Ahab, Jezebel is a villain whose name continues to be used to describe 'wicked women'. Her story is told in 1 and 2 Kings, where she plays a key role in the Elijah stories. After her mother's gruesome death (cf. 2 Kings 9:30–7), Athaliah seized power and ruled Judah.

14. [Ed.] *Cato of Utica*: (95–46 BCE) Roman Praetor and Stoic. Grandson of Marcus Cato.

15. [Ed.] *St Bernard* of Clairvaux: (1090–1153) leading figure in the Cistercian monastic order, his negative views on women are well documented.

STUDY QUESTIONS

1. What evidence do Kramer and Sprenger offer for their claim that women are more likely to be drawn to witchcraft than men? Why might this 'evidence' be viewed with suspicion?
2. What might the examples used suggest about the way in which the Christian tradition can be applied to support misogyny?
3. 'And blessed be the Highest Who has so far preserved the male sex from so great a crime: for since He was willing to be born and to suffer for us, therefore He has granted to men this privilege.' Why might this quote suggest that Christian doctrines have supported misogyny?

SELECT BIBLIOGRAPHY

General reading

R. Cavendish, *The Powers of Evil* (London: Routledge & Kegan Paul, 1975).

K. Thomas, *Religion and the Decline of Magic* (Harmondsworth: Penguin, 1971).

For feminist analysis

M. Daly, *Gyn/Ecology* (London: Women's Press, 1991).
U. Ranke-Heinemann, *Eunuchs for the Kingdom of Heaven* (Harmondsworth: Penguin, 1991), ch. XIX.
J. Smith, *Misogynies* (London: Faber & Faber, 1989).
N. Tuana, *The Less Noble Sex* (Indianapolis: Indiana University Press, 1993).

PART III

EARLY MODERN PHILOSOPHERS

7 René Descartes 1596–1650

Introduction and Background

Descartes's ideas on the nature of the self have profoundly shaped the philosophy and culture of the western world. While critical of Aristotle's philosophy, his understanding of the self reflects the dualistic structure of reality which can be traced to both Aristotle and Plato. Just as Aristotle opposed form to matter, and Plato juxtaposed this world with the World of Ideas, so Descartes argues that the human being is composed of two radically different substances – mind and body. For Descartes, the essential self is located not in the mutable body, but in the transcendent mind. And this conclusion can be established by following his method of 'radical doubt'. In doubting all that we have previously held to be true, we can attain with absolute certainty the 'fact' that we are thinking things.

An analysis of Descartes's ideas poses some problems for the feminist philosopher. Descartes's thought cannot be straightforwardly dismissed as misogynistic. Indeed, his philosophy seems to have been egalitarian in intent. For Descartes, the mind has no sex. In the *Discourse on Method* he argues that the ability to reason is common to all; what he offers is a method which will help all who are so inclined to attain clear reasoning. Moreover, his ideas found a considerable following amongst the men *and* women of his time. As Erica Harth notes in her study of the women who followed Descartes's method, the term *cartésienne* was coined specifically for these female followers of Descartes.[1] Descartes gained much from his female followers. In particular, he corresponded with two women, Princess Elisabeth of Bohemia and Queen Christina of Sweden.[2] The intellectual depth and rigour of this correspondence suggests that he took seriously his belief that all could be trained to reason – even women. By claiming that the life of reason, the life of the philosopher, could take place anywhere, Descartes opened up the traditional realm of women to the same intellectual status as the academy.

Despite his claims for the universality of rationality, Descartes's views have been challenged; not only by feminists studying the history of ideas, but also by some of his female contemporaries. Margaret Cavendish (1623–73) was highly critical of his distinction between mind and body.[3] More recently, Genevieve Lloyd has continued this attack upon cartesian dualism. The body is defined as non-rational, and is thus inferior to the mind. Human life is viewed as a struggle between these two aspects of the individual. In similar vein, Jane Fox writes that Descartes's ideas betray a 'desperate attempt to escape from the body, sexuality and the wiles of the Unconscious'.[4] According to Lloyd and Fox, Descartes's apparently radical methodology remains ensnared within the prevalent framework of western Christendom. The body is evil, a hindrance, to be spurned and subdued. A further connection can be made. Historically the body and matter have been linked with women; if Lloyd and Fox's analysis is accepted, does Descartes's understanding of the body betray a subconscious misogyny?

Descartes's correspondence with Elisabeth of Bohemia suggests something of the ambiguity inherent in his thinking. Elisabeth appears to have been something of a natural academic. Her sister Sophie commented that 'her great learning made her a bit absent-minded and often made us laugh'.[5] If her family found her desire for knowledge and learning a cause for amusement, Descartes found in her the perfect intellectual equal. He claimed that he had never met anyone with as good an understanding of his work as Elisabeth. Elisabeth appears to have gained much from Descartes's philosophical method. She applied his critical method to all that she encountered. However, her letters suggest that Descartes's philosophical method springs from a male perspective on and experience of life. She writes of her problems and responsibilities; problems and responsibilities which stem from the roles allotted to her as a woman. These duties hinder her philosophical studies:

> The life that I am constrained to lead does not allow me enough free time to acquire a habit of meditation in accordance with your rules. Sometimes the interests of my household, which I must not neglect, sometimes conversations and civilities I cannot eschew, so thoroughly deject this weak mind with annoyances or boredom that it remains, for a long time afterward, useless for anything else.[6]

This moving comment leads to the heart of the problem with Descartes's method for philosophical reasoning. As Harth puts it, Elisabeth 'did not enjoy Descartes's male prerogative of roaming about alone, relatively free from domestic care'.[7] The constraints placed upon her as a woman are not appreciated by Descartes, who experiences the freedom of a man in a masculinist society. The universality of Descartes's method is revealed to be a false universality. Descartes's attempt to show the similarity of the male and female mind fails to expose the problems posed by an unjust society.

Yet Descartes's ideas represent a significant movement away from the negative picture of woman commonly held by western philosophers. His methodology suggests a denial of the claim that man embodies reason, woman nature. A further development needs to be made which exposes the injustice of a society that undermines the attempts of women to explore their world by ascribing to them a particular role.

THE *DISCOURSE ON METHOD**

Part One

Good sense is of all things in the world the most equally distributed, for everybody thinks himself so abundantly provided with it, that even those most difficult to please in all other matters do not commonly desire more of it than they already possess. It is

* From R. Descartes, *Philosophical Works*, vol. 1, edited by E. S. Haldane and G. R. T. Ross (Cambridge: Cambridge University Press, 1911).

unlikely that this is an error on their part; it seems rather to be evidence in support of the view that the power of forming a good judgment and of distinguishing the true from the false, which is properly speaking what is called Good sense or Reason, is by nature equal in all men. Hence too it will show that the diversity of our opinions does not proceed from some men being more rational than others, but solely from the fact that our thoughts pass through diverse channels and the same objects are not considered by all. For to be possessed of good mental powers is not sufficient; the principal matter is to apply them well. The greatest minds are capable of the greatest vices as well as of the greatest virtues, and those who proceed very slowly may, provided they always follow the straight road, really advance much faster than those who, though they run, forsake it.

For myself I have never ventured to presume that my mind was in any way more perfect than that of the ordinary man; I have even longed to possess thought as quick, or an imagination as accurate and distinct, or a memory as comprehensive or ready, as some others. And besides these I do not know any other qualities that make for the perfection of the human mind. For as to reason or sense, inasmuch as it is the only thing that constitutes us men and distinguishes us from the brutes, I would fain believe that it is to be found complete in each individual. . . .

But I shall not hesitate to say that I have had great good fortune from my youth up, in lighting upon and pursuing certain paths which have conducted me to considerations and maxims from which I have formed a Method, by whose assistance it appears to me I have the means of gradually increasing my knowledge and of little by little raising it to the highest possible point which the mediocrity of my talents and the brief duration of my life can permit me to reach. For I have already reaped from it fruits of such a nature that, even though I always try in the judgments I make on myself to lean to the side of self-depreciation rather than to that of arrogance, and though, looking with the eye of a philosopher on the diverse actions and enterprises of all mankind, I find scarcely any which do not seem to me vain and useless, I do not cease to receive extreme satisfaction in the progress which I seem to have already made in the search after truth, and to form such hopes for the future as to venture to believe that, if amongst the occupations of men, simply as men, there is some one in particular that is excellent and important, that is the one which I have selected.

It must always be recollected, however, that possibly I deceive myself, and that what I take to be gold and diamonds is perhaps no more than copper and glass. I know how subject we are to delusion in whatever touches ourselves, and also how much the judgments of our friends ought to be suspected when they are in our favour. But in this Discourse I shall be very happy to show the paths I have followed, and to set forth my life as in a picture, so that everyone may judge of it for himself; and thus in learning from the common talk what are the opinions which are held of it, a new means of obtaining self-instruction will be reached, which I shall add to those which I have been in the habit of using.

Thus my design is not here to teach the Method which everyone should follow in order to promote the good conduct of his Reason, but only to show in what manner I have endeavoured to conduct my own. Those who set about giving precepts must esteem themselves more skilful than those to whom they advance them, and if they fall short in the smallest matter they must of course take the blame for it. But regarding this Treatise simply as a history, or, if you prefer it, a fable in which, amongst certain things which may be imitated, there are possibly others also which it would not be right to follow, I hope that it will be of use to some without being hurtful to any, and that all will thank me for my frankness.

I have been nourished on letters since my childhood, and since I was given to believe that by their means a clear and certain knowledge could be obtained of all that is useful in life, I had an extreme desire to acquire instruction. But so soon as I had achieved the entire course of study at the close of which one is usually received into the ranks of the learned, I entirely changed my opinion. For I found myself embarrassed with so many doubts and errors that it seemed to me that the effort to instruct myself had no effect other than the increasing discovery of my own ignorance. And yet I was studying at one of the most celebrated Schools in Europe, where I thought that there must be men of learning if they were to be found anywhere in the world. I learned there all that others learned; and not being satisfied with the sciences that we were taught, I even read through all the books which fell into my hands, treating of what is considered most curious and rare. Along with this I knew the judgments that others had formed of me, and I did not feel that I was esteemed inferior to my fellow-students, although there were amongst them some destined to fill the places of our masters. And finally our century seemed to me as flourishing, and as fertile in great minds, as any which had preceded. And this made me take the liberty of judging all others by myself and of coming to the conclusion that there was no learning in the world such as I was formerly led to believe it to be. . . .

As soon as age permitted me to emerge from the control of my tutors, I entirely quitted the study of letters. And resolving to seek no other science than that which could be found in myself, or at least in the great book of the world, I employed the rest of my youth in travel, in seeing courts and armies, in intercourse with men of diverse temperaments and conditions, in collecting varied experiences, in proving myself in the various predicaments in which I was placed by fortune, and under all circumstances bringing my mind to bear on the things which came before it, so that I might derive some profit from my experience. For it seemed to me that I might meet with much more truth in the reasonings that each man makes on the matters that specially concern him, and the issue of which would very soon punish him if he made a wrong judgment, than in the case of those made by a man of letters in his study touching speculations which lead to no result, and which bring about no other consequences to himself excepting that he will be all the more vain the more they are removed from common sense, since in this case it proves him to have employed so much the more ingenuity and skill in trying to make them seem probable. And I always had an excessive desire to learn to distinguish the true from the false, in order to see clearly in my actions and to walk with confidence in this life.

It is true that while I only considered the manners of other men I found in them nothing to give me settled convictions; and I remarked in them almost as much diversity as I had formerly seen in the opinions of philosophers. So much was this the case that the greatest profit which I derived from their study was that, in seeing many things which, although they seem to us very extravagant and ridiculous, were yet commonly received and approved by other great nations, I learned to believe nothing too certainly of which I had only been convinced by example and custom. Thus little by little I was delivered from many errors which might have obscured our natural vision and rendered us less capable of listening to Reason. But after I had employed several years in thus studying the book of the world and trying to acquire some experience, I one day formed the resolution of also making myself an object of study and of employing all the strength of my mind in choosing the road I should follow. This succeeded much better, it appeared to me, than if I had never departed either from my country or my books.

Part Two

I was then in Germany, to which country I had been attracted by the wars which are not yet at an end. And as I was returning from the coronation of the Emperor to join the army, the setting in of winter detained me in a quarter where, since I found no society to divert me, while fortunately I had also no cares or passions to trouble me, I remained the whole day shut up alone in a stove-heated room, where I had complete leisure to occupy myself with my own thoughts. One of the first of the considerations that occurred to me was that there is very often less perfection in works composed of several portions, and carried out by the hands of various masters, than in those on which one individual alone has worked. Thus we see that buildings planned and carried out by one architect alone are usually more beautiful and better proportioned than those which many have tried to put in order and improve, making use of old walls which were built with other ends in view. . . . And similarly I thought that the sciences found in books – in those at least whose reasonings are only probable and which have no demonstrations, composed as they are of the gradually accumulated opinions of many different individuals – do not approach so near to the truth as the simple reasoning which a man of common sense can quite naturally carry out respecting the things which come immediately before him. Again I thought that since we have all been children before being men, and since it has for long fallen to us to be governed by our appetites and by our teachers (who often enough contradicted one another, and none of whom perhaps counselled us always for the best), it is almost impossible that our judgments should be so excellent or solid as they should have been had we had complete use of our reason since our birth, and had we been guided by its means alone.

It is true that we do not find that all the houses in a town are rased to the ground for the sole reason that the town is to be rebuilt in another fashion, with streets made more beautiful; but at the same time we see that many people cause their own houses to be knocked down in order to rebuild them, and that sometimes they are forced so to do where there is danger of the houses falling of themselves, and where the foundations are not secure. From such examples I argued to myself that there was no plausibility in the claim of any private individual to reform a state by altering everything, and by overturning it throughout, in order to set it right again. Nor is it likewise probable that the whole body of the Sciences, or the order of teaching established by the Schools should be reformed. But as regards all the opinions which up to this time I had embraced, I thought I could not do better than endeavour once for all to sweep them completely away, so that they might later on be replaced, either by others which were better, or by the same, when I had made them conform to the uniformity of a rational scheme. . . .

This is the reason why I cannot in any way approve of those turbulent and unrestful spirits who, being called neither by birth nor fortune to the management of public affairs, never fail to have always in their minds some new reforms. And if I thought that in this treatise there was contained the smallest justification for this folly, I should be very sorry to allow it to be published. My design has never extended beyond trying to reform my own opinion and to build on a foundation which is entirely my own. If my work has given me a certain satisfaction, so that I here present to you a draft of it, I do not so do because I wish to advise anybody to imitate it. Those to whom God has been most beneficent in the bestowal of His graces will perhaps form designs which are more elevated; but I fear much that this particular one will seem too venturesome for many. The simple resolve to strip oneself of all opinions and beliefs formerly received is not to be regarded as an example that each man should follow, and the world may be said to be mainly composed of two classes of minds neither of which could prudently adopt it. There are those who, believing themselves to be cleverer than they are, cannot restrain themselves from being precipitate in judgment and have not sufficient patience to arrange their thoughts in proper order; hence, once a man of this description had taken the liberty of doubting the principles he formerly accepted, and had deviated from the beaten track, he would never be able to maintain the path which must be followed to reach the appointed end more quickly, and he would hence remain wandering astray all through his life. Secondly, there are those who having reason or modesty enough to judge that they are less capable of distinguishing truth from falsehood than some others from whom instruction might be obtained, are right in contenting themselves with following the opinions of these others rather than in searching better ones for themselves. . . .

I believed that I should find the four [laws] which I shall state quite sufficient, provided that I adhered to a firm and constant resolve never on any single occasion to fail in their observance.

The first of these was to accept nothing as true which I did not clearly recognise to be so: that is to say, carefully to avoid precipitation and prejudice in judgments, and to accept in them nothing more than what was presented to my mind so clearly and distinctly that I could have no occasion to doubt it.

The second was to divide up each of the difficulties which I examined into as many parts as possible, and as seemed requisite in order that it might be resolved in the best manner possible.

The third was to carry on my reflections in due order, commencing with objects that were the most simple and easy to understand, in order to rise little by little, or by degrees, to knowledge of the most complex, assuming an order, even if a fictitious one, among those which do not follow a natural sequence relatively to one another.

The last was in all cases to make enumerations so complete and reviews so general that I should be certain of having omitted nothing. . . .

What pleased me most in this Method was that I was certain by its means of exercising my reason in all things, if not perfectly, at least as well as was in my power. . . .

Part Three

And finally, as it is not sufficient, before commencing to rebuild the house which we inhabit, to pull it down and provide materials and an architect (or to act in this capacity ourselves, and make a careful drawing of its design), unless we have also provided ourselves with some other house where we can be comfortably lodged during the time of rebuilding, so in order that I should not remain irresolute in my actions while reason obliged me to be so in my judgments, and that I might not omit to carry on my life as happily as I could, I formed for myself a code of morals for the time being which did not consist of more than three or four maxims, which maxims I should like to enumerate to you.

The first was to obey the laws and customs of my country, adhering constantly to the religion in which by God's grace I had been instructed since my childhood, and in all other things directing my conduct by opinions the most moderate in nature, and the farthest removed from excess in all those which are commonly received and acted on by the most judicious of those with whom I might come in contact. . . . And amongst many opinions all equally received, I chose only the most moderate, both because these are always most suited for putting into practice, and probably the best (for all excess has a tendency to be bad), and also because I should have in a less degree turned aside from the right path, supposing that I was wrong, than if, having chosen an extreme course, I found that I had chosen amiss. . . .

My second maxim was that of being as firm and resolute in my actions as I could be, and not to follow less faithfully opinions the most dubious, when my mind was once made up regarding them, than if these had been beyond doubt. In this I should be following the example of travellers, who, finding themselves lost in a forest, know that they ought not to wander first to one side and then to the other, nor, still less, to stop in one place, but understand that they should continue to walk as straight as they can in one direction, not diverging for any slight reason, even though it was possibly chance alone that first determined them in their choice. By this means if they do not go exactly where they wish, they will at least arrive somewhere at the end, where probably they will be better off than in the middle of a forest. . . .

My third maxim was to try always to conquer myself rather than fortune, and to alter my desires rather than change the order of the world, and generally to accustom myself to believe that there is nothing entirely within our power but our own thoughts: so that after we have done our best in regard to the things that are without us, our ill-success cannot possibly be failure on our part. And this alone seemed to me sufficient to prevent my desiring anything in the future beyond what I could actually obtain, hence rendering me content; for since our will does not naturally induce us to desire anything but what our understanding represents to it as in some way possible of attainment, it is certain that if we consider all good things which are outside of us as equally outside of our power, we should not have more regret in resigning those goods which appear to pertain to our birth, when we are deprived of them for no fault of our own, than we have in not possessing the kingdoms of China or Mexico. In the same way, making what is called a virtue out of a necessity, we should no more desire to be well if ill, or free, if in prison, than we now do to have our bodies formed of a substance as little corruptible as diamonds, or to have wings to fly with like birds. I allow, however, that to accustom oneself to regard all things from this point of view requires long exercise and meditation often repeated; and I believe that it is principally in this that is to be found the secret of those philosophers who, in ancient times, were able to free themselves from the empire of fortune, or, despite suffering or poverty, to rival their gods in their happiness. For, ceaselessly occupying themselves in considering the limits which were prescribed to them by nature, they persuaded themselves so completely that nothing was within their own power but their thoughts, that this conviction alone was sufficient to prevent their having any longing for other things. And they had so absolute a mastery over their thoughts that they had some reason for esteeming themselves as more rich and more powerful, and more free and more happy than other men, who, however favoured by nature or fortune they might be, if devoid of this philosophy, never could arrive at all at which they aim.

And last of all, to conclude this moral code, I felt it incumbent on me to make a review of the various occupations of men in this life in order to try to choose out the best; and without wishing to say anything of the employment of others I thought that I could not do better than continue in the one in which I found myself engaged, that is to say, in occupying my whole life in cultivating my Reason, and in advancing myself as much as possible in the knowledge of the truth in accordance with the method which I had prescribed myself. . . .

Having thus assured myself of these maxims, and having set them on one side along with the truths of religion which have always taken the first place in my creed, I judged that as far as the rest of my opinions were concerned, I could safely undertake to rid myself of them. And inasmuch as I hoped to be able to reach my end more successfully in converse with man than in living longer shut up in the warm room where these reflections had come to me, I hardly awaited the end of winter before I once more set myself to travel. And in all the nine following years I did nought but roam hither and thither, trying to be a spectator rather than an actor in all the comedies the world displays. More especially did I reflect in each matter that came before me as to anything which could make it subject to suspicion or doubt, and give occasion for mistake, and I rooted out of my mind all the errors which might have formerly crept in. . . .

These nine years thus passed away before I had taken any definite part in regard to the difficulties as to which the learned are in the habit of disputing, or had commenced to seek the foundation of any philosophy more certain than the vulgar. . . . And it is just eight years ago that this desire made me resolve to remove myself from all places where any acquaintances were possible, and to retire to a country such as this, where the long-continued war has caused such order to be established that the armies which are maintained seem only to be of use in allowing the inhabitants to enjoy the fruits of peace with so much the more security; and where, in the crowded throng of a great and very active nation, which is more concerned with its own affairs than curious about those of others, without missing any of the conveniences of the most populous towns, I can live as solitary and retired as in deserts the most remote.

STUDY QUESTIONS

1. How might Descartes's ideas on the universality of reason relate to women?
2. 'My third maxim was to try always to conquer myself rather than fortune, and to alter my desires rather than change the order of the world, and generally to accustom myself to believe that there is nothing entirely within our power but our own thoughts . . .' Why might this passage be problematic for women who wish to confront the injustice of social systems?
3. In the final paragraph of Part Three Descartes claims that the pursuit of reason can take place anywhere. How might this relate to Elisabeth of Bohemia's complaints about the demands of her lifestyle?

SELECT BIBLIOGRAPHY

General

J. Cottingham, *Descartes* (Oxford: Blackwell, 1986).
B. Williams, *Descartes* (Harmondsworth: Penguin, 1978).

For feminist analysis

S. Åkerman, 'Kristina Wasa, Queen of Sweden', in M. E. Waithe (ed.), *A History of Women Philosophers*, vol. 3 (Dordrecht: Kluwer Academic Press, 1991), pp. 21–40.
J. Grimshaw, *Feminist Philosophers* (Brighton: Harvester Wheatsheaf, 1986).

E. Harth, *Cartesian Women* (Ithaca: Cornell, 1992).
L. Irigaray, 'The Eye of a Man Recently Dead', in *Speculum of the Other Woman*, translated by G. Gill (Ithaca: Cornell, 1985), pp. 180–90.
G. Lloyd, *The Man of Reason* (London: Methuen, 1984).
A. Nye, 'Polity and Prudence: The Ethics of Elisabeth, Princess Palatine', in L. L. McAlister (ed.), *Hypatia's Daughters: Fifteen Hundred Years of Women Philosophers* (Indianapolis: Indiana University Press, 1996), pp. 68–91.
L. Schiebinger, 'Margaret Cavendish, Duchess of Newcastle', in M. E. Waithe (ed.), *A History of Women Philosophers*, vol. 3 (Dordrecht: Kluwer Academic Publishers, 1991), pp. 1–20.

8 Thomas Hobbes 1588–1679

Background and Introduction

Hobbes's political ideas were shaped to a large extent by the political context of his day. Living through the English Civil War, his political thought is dominated by the need to resist the 'anarchy' which arises from social disorder.

Central to Hobbes's philosophy is the belief that everything is material. Thus he is opposed to the mind/body dualism of his contemporary Descartes.[1] For Hobbes, the notion of the self as an incorporeal soul is incoherent. Instead, he understands God and the soul as 'invisible physical objects'.[2] The apparent materialism of his thought did little to endear him to either the Royalists or the Parliamentarians of his time. Politically, Hobbes was a Royalist, but Royalists were wary of his purely secular justification of monarchy. According to Hobbes, the sovereign rules by contract with 'his' people, *not* by divine right (although Hobbes understands the sovereign to act in place of God). In rejecting the claim that supernatural support can be given to the idea of monarchy, Hobbes anticipates the later theories of Feuerbach and Marx. Religion is understood in purely human terms; human fear leads to the desire for some kind of divine power. Hobbes replaces the supernatural, omnipotent God with the State, which he believes assures human security.

Accordingly, the state (or 'Leviathan') creates a barrier which prevents human beings from 'lapsing into the unpleasantness of the state of nature'.[3] Nature for Hobbes is a negative concept, associated with war. Humanity is a prey to destructive impulses, and a strong power – Leviathan – is necessary if these impulses are to be kept in check.[4]

Having defined nature so negatively, it is not surprising that Hobbes should write of the state in exalted terms. Leviathan is understood as protector. In using this almost parental image, Hobbes goes to extreme lengths to support the power of the state. He is convinced that 'the worst tyrannies of Leviathan are unlikely to be worse than the anarchy of the state of nature, so rebellion against Leviathan is only justified if he fails in his duty to protect his citizens'.[5] Thus, as F. C. Hood notes, 'the whole purpose of Leviathan is to show that violation of the laws cannot be justified by any pretext'.[6]

Hobbes's understanding of the state is paralleled in his account of the family. For Hobbes, the family can be equated with 'a little commonwealth'.[7] In the family, the father rules the children just as the master rules the servants. Hobbes is at pains to deny that paternal dominion should be derived from biological parenthood; were that the case, father *and* mother would have an equal right to dominion over the child. He does not, however, argue that dominion should be given to fathers on the grounds that men are 'the most excellent sex'; on the contrary, in 'the state of nature' men and women are equals. Rather, he claims that civil law demands this patriarchal structure as historically commonwealths have been erected by fathers, not mothers.

Hobbes's thought is informative, as he not only equates the structure of society with the shape of the patriarchal family, but he also relates the structure of society to his understanding of God. Hobbes conceives God as incomprehensible, and absolutely sovereign. The hierarchical society which he advocates thus reflects the distinction between God and human beings. As such, patriarchal notions of power govern his account of the relationships between God and humanity, State and Citizen, man and woman.

*LEVIATHAN**

Chapter XX: Of Dominion Paternal, and Despotical

Dominion is acquired in two ways: by generation, and by conquest. The right of dominion by generation is that which the parent hath over his children, and is called PATERNAL; and is not so derived from the generation, as if, therefore, the parent had dominion over his child because he begat him, but from the child's consent, either express, or by other sufficient arguments declared. For, as to the generation, God hath ordained to man a helper; and there be always two that are equally parents. The dominion, therefore, over the child, should belong equally to both; and he be equally subject to both, which is impossible, for no man can obey two masters. And whereas some have attributed the dominion to the man only, as being of the more excellent sex, they misreckon in it. For there is not always that difference of strength, or prudence between the man and the woman, as that the right can be determined without war. In commonwealths,

* From *The Second Part, Of Commonwealth* (London, 1651), edited by Robert Lindsey.

this controversy is decided by the civil law; and for the most part (but not always), the sentence is in favour of the father, because, for the most part, commonwealths have been erected by the fathers, not by the mothers of families. But the question lieth now in the state of mere nature where there are supposed no laws of matrimony, no laws for the education of children, but the law of nature, and the natural inclination of the sexes, one to another, and to their children. In this condition of mere nature, either the parents between themselves dispose of the dominion over the child by contract, or do not dispose thereof at all. If they dispose thereof, the right passeth according to the contract. We find in history that the Amazons[1] contracted with the men of the neighbouring countries, to whom they had recourse for issue, that the issue male should be sent back, but the female remain with themselves, so that the dominion of the females was in the mother.

If there be no contract, the dominion is in the mother. For in the condition of mere nature, where there are no matrimonial laws, it cannot be known who is the father unless it be declared by the mother: and therefore the right of dominion over the child dependeth on her will, and is consequently hers. Again, seeing the infant is first in the power of the mother, so as she may either nourish or expose it. If she nourish it, it oweth its life to the mother, and is therefore obliged to obey her rather than any other; and by consequence the dominion over it is hers. But if she expose it, and another find and nourish it, the dominion is in him that nourisheth it. For it ought to obey him by whom it is preserved; because preservation of life being the end, for which one man becomes subject to another, every man is supposed to promise obedience to him in whose power it is to save or destroy him.

If the mother be the father's subject, the child is in the father's power. And if the father be the mother's subject (as when a sovereign queen marrieth one of her subjects), the child is subject to the mother because the father also is her subject.

If a man and woman, monarchs of two several kingdoms, have a child and contract concerning who shall have the dominion of him, the right of the dominion passeth by the contract. If they contract not, the dominion followeth the dominion of the place of his residence. For the sovereign of each country hath dominion over all that reside therein.

He that hath the dominion over the child, hath dominion also over the children of the child, and over their children's children. For he that hath dominion over the person of a man, hath dominion over all that is his, without which, dominion were but a title without the effect. . . .

The master of the servant, is master also of all he hath, and may exact the use thereof; that is to say, of his goods, of his labour, of his servants, and of his children, as often as he shall think fit. For he holdeth his life of his master by the covenant of obedience; that is, of owning, and authorizing whatsoever the master shall do. And in case the master, if he refuse, kill him, or cast him into bonds, or otherwise punish him for his disobedience, he is himself the author of the same, and cannot accuse him of injury.

In sum, the rights and consequences of both paternal and despotical dominion are the very same with those of a sovereign by institution; and for the same reasons, which reasons are set down in the precedent chapter. So that for a man that is monarch of divers[2] nations, whereof he hath, in one the sovereignty by institution of the people assembled, and in another by conquest, that is by the submission of each particular, to avoid death or bonds; to demand of one nation more than of the other, from the title of conquest, as being a conquered nation, is an act of ignorance of the rights of sovereignty. For the sovereign is absolute over both alike, or else there is no sovereignty at all. And so every man may lawfully protect himself, if he can, with his own sword, which is the condition of war.

By this it appears that a great family, if it be not part of some commonwealth, is of itself, as to the rights of sovereignty, a little monarchy. Whether that family consist of a man and his children, or of a man and his servants, or of a man and his children, and servants together; wherein the father or master is the sovereign. But yet a family is not properly a commonwealth unless it be of that power by its own number, or by other opportunities as not to be subdued without the hazard of war. For where a number of men are manifestly too weak to defend themselves united, every one may use his own reason in time of danger to save his own life, either by flight, or by submission to the enemy, as he shall think best. In the same manner as a very small company of soldiers, surprised by an army, may cast down their arms and demand quarter, or run away rather than be put to the sword. And thus much shall suffice concerning what I find by speculation and deduction, of sovereign rights, from the nature, need, and designs of men, in erecting of commonwealths, and putting themselves under monarchs or assemblies, entrusted with power enough for their protection.

Let us now consider what the Scripture teacheth in the same point. . . . For obedience of servants St Paul saith: 'Servants obey your masters in all things' (Colossians 3:22), and, 'children obey your parents in all things' (Colossians 3:20). There is simple obedience in those that are subject to paternal or despotical dominion. . . .

To these places may be added also that of Genesis, 'Ye shall be as gods, knowing good and evil' (3:5). And, 'Who told thee that thou wast naked? Hast thou eaten of the tree, of which I commanded thee thou shouldest not eat?' (Genesis 3:11). For the cognizance or judicature of Good and Evil, being forbidden by the name of the fruit of the tree of knowledge, as a trial of Adam's obedience; the Devil to inflame the ambition of the woman, to whom that fruit already seemed beautiful, told her that, by tasting it, they should be as gods, knowing Good and Evil. Whereupon, having both eaten, they did indeed take upon them God's office, which is Judicature of Good and Evil, but acquired no new ability to distinguish between them aright. And whereas it is said, that having eaten, they saw they were naked, no man hath so interpreted that place as if they had been formerly blind and saw not their own skins. The meaning is plain: that it was then they first judged their nakedness (wherein it was God's will to create them) to be uncomely; and by being ashamed, did tacitly censure God himself. And thereupon, God saith, 'Hast thou eaten, etc.', as if he should say, doest thou that owest me obedience, take upon thee to judge of my Commandments? Whereby, it is clearly, though allegorically, signified that the commands of them that have the right to command are not by their subjects to be censured nor disputed.

So that it appeareth plainly, to my understanding, both from reason and Scripture, that the sovereign power, whether placed in one man, as in monarchy, or one assembly of men, as in popular, and aristocratical commonwealths, is as great as possibly men can be imagined to make it. And though of so unlimited a power, men may fancy many evil consequences; yet the consequences of the want of it, which is perpetual war of man against his neighbour, are much worse. The condition of man in this life shall never be without inconveniences; but there happeneth in no commonwealth any great inconvenience but what proceeds from the subjects' disobedience, and breach of those covenants, from which the commonwealth hath its being. And whosoever thinking sovereign power too great, will seek to make it less, must subject himself to the power that can limit it – that is to say, to a greater.

The greatest objection is that of the practice when men ask, where, and when, such power has, by subjects, been acknowledged. But one may ask them again, when, or where has there been a kingdom long free from sedition and civil war? In those nations, whose commonwealths have been long-lived, and not been destroyed but by foreign war, the subjects never did dispute of the sovereign power. But howsoever, an argument from the practice of men, that have not sifted to the bottom, and with exact reason weighed the causes and nature of commonwealths, and suffer daily those miseries that proceed from the ignorance thereof, is invalid. For though in all places of the world, men should lay the foundation of their houses on the sand, it could not thence be inferred that so it ought to be. The skill of making and maintaining commonwealths, consisteth in certain rules, as doth arithmetic and geometry, not, as tennis-play, on practice only; which rules, neither poor men have the leisure, nor men that have had the leisure, have hitherto had the curiosity, or the method to find out.

NOTES

1. [Ed.] *Amazons*: according to Greek legend, tribe of female warriers from north-east Asia. Name derived from 'breastless', as they would cut off the right breast to make it easier to use weapons in battle.
2. [Ed.] *divers*: various.

STUDY QUESTIONS

1. To what extent can Hobbes's distinction between the natural state of humanity and the Commonwealth/State be seen to support the historical equations between woman/nature, and man/reason?
2. Hobbes argues for the absolute rights of 'Leviathan'. If the family is understood as 'a little monarchy', what might this claim suggest about his understanding of the relationship between men and women?

SELECT BIBLIOGRAPHY

General

F. C. Hood, *The Divine Politics of Thomas Hobbes* (Oxford: Clarendon Press, 1964).

S. Priest, *The British Empiricists* (Harmondsworth: Penguin, 1990).
R. S. Woolhouse, *The Empiricists* (Oxford: Oxford University Press, 1988).

For feminist analysis

K. Green, *The Woman of Reason* (Cambridge: Polity Press, 1995).
A. Jaggar, *Feminist Politics and Human Nature* (Brighton: Harvester Press, 1983).
C. Pateman, *The Sexual Contract* (Cambridge: Polity Press, 1988).

9 John Locke 1632–1704

Introduction and Background

Heralded by some as the 'inventor of liberalism',[1] John Locke builds upon the empiricism of Hobbes, but with significant differences. Central to Locke's philosophy is the claim that 'man' is fundamentally a rational being. The chief obstacle to the attainment of reason is 'our feeble passionate nature'.[2] As such, he rejects Hobbes's materialism for a mind/body dualism similar to that proffered by Descartes.

The connection between Locke's thought and that of Hobbes is evident in Locke's belief that firm government is needed to avoid a return to the undesirable state of nature. Unlike Hobbes, however, Locke does not equate 'nature' with war. In the state of nature, people are perfectly free and equal. But people's natural rights to 'life, liberty, health and goods' cannot be preserved without an appropriate form of government. Consequently, political power takes precedence over nature.

While Hobbes argued for an all-powerful State, Locke argues that all government must be dependent on the *consent* of the governed. Government without consent is slavery and every citizen has the right to rebel against this. If a ruler fails to act for the good of all, the cititzens need feel no obligation to the ruler.

Locke's analysis of family relationships at times appears to offer an egalitarian approach to human relationships. Gordon Schochet notes that when Locke discusses the sources of paternal power, he places familial authority upon mothers as well as fathers.[3] A mother, afterall, has nourished the child in her own body. Locke even concludes that paternal power might 'more properly [be] called *Parental Power*' (2 Treatises, Book II, §52). Tellingly, he later ignores this conclusion and reverts to the phrase 'Paternal Power' (2 Treatises, Book II, §69).

For all this apparent equality, Locke views the husband as the superior party in the marriage relationship, for he is 'abler and stronger'. Ultimately, a hierarchical structure regulates his account of human social structures. The patriarchal family forms the basis for society. The distinction between man and wife, which led to that between parents and children, ultimately leads to master–servant distinctions. When political society was formed, the father could easily be transformed into a prince. Yet while he makes this connection, Locke does not suggest that this is 'right'. Rather, his concern is to illuminate the origins of government. As he puts it, 'an Argument from what has been, to what should of right be, has no great force' (2 Treatises, Book II, §103).

For all that, feminist critics have suggested that Locke's ideas have contributed to the suppression of women. Karen Green argues that it is through Locke's philosophy that 'the public/private distinction [comes] into political thought'.[4] While suggesting the connections between the structure of the family and the structure of the state, Locke makes a clear distinction between paternal and political power. Green suggests that if this is recognized, it is difficult to identify Locke's political philosophy as egalitarian. While Locke recognizes 'maternal' power, he also argues that women are not suited to political rule. Therefore the right to dominion cannot derive from parenthood, for women have as much parental authority as men. In giving women 'power' in the family, Locke denies them the same power in the political realm. Women's liberty is within the private, not the public, realm. As an aside, it is worth noting that one of his first commentators was Mary Astell. Moreover, Locke exchanged letters with Catharine Trotter Cockburn, and discussed his philosophy with Damaris Cudworth Masham.[5] It seems that for Locke, the 'private woman' could still engage in philosophy.

*TWO TREATISES OF GOVERNMENT**

Chapter V: Of Adam's Title to Sovereignty by the Subjection of Eve

47 Further, it is to be noted, that these words here of Genesis 3:16, which our author calls 'the original grant of government', were not spoken to Adam, neither, indeed, was there any grant in them made to Adam, but a punishment laid upon Eve; and if we will take them as they were directed in particular to her, or in her, as a representative, to all other women, they will at most concern the female sex only, and import no more but that subjection they should ordinarily be in to their husbands; but there is here no more law to oblige a woman to such a subjection, if the circumstances either of her condition or contract with her husband should exempt her from it, than there is that she should bring forth her

* From *First Treatise, 'An Essay Concerning Certain False Principles'* (London, 1690), edited by Robert Lindsey.

children in sorrow and pain if there could be found a remedy for it, which is also a part of the same curse upon her, for the whole verse runs thus: 'Unto the woman He said, I will greatly multiply thy sorrow and thy conception; in sorrow thou shalt bring forth children, and thy desire shall be to thy husband, and he shall rule over thee.' 'Twould, I think, have been a hard matter for anybody but our author to have found out a grant of 'monarchical government to Adam' in these words, which were neither spoke to, nor of him. Neither will any one, I suppose, by these words think the weaker sex, as by a law so subjected to the curse contained in them, that 'tis their duty not to endeavour to avoid it. And will any one say that Eve, or any other woman, sinned if she were brought to bed without those multiplied pains God threatens her here with, or that either of our Queens, Mary or Elizabeth, had they married any of their subjects, had been by this text put into a political subjection to him, or that he thereby should have had 'monarchical rule' over her? God in this text gives not, that I see, any authority to Adam over Eve, or men over their wives, but only foretells what should be the woman's lot, how by His Providence He would order it so that she should be subject to her husband, as we see that generally the laws of mankind and customs of nations have ordered it so, and there is, I grant, a foundation in Nature for it.

48 Thus when God says of Jacob and Esau that 'the elder should serve the younger' (Genesis 25:23), nobody supposes that God hereby made Jacob Esau's sovereign, but foretold what should, *de facto*, come to pass.

But if these words here spoke to Eve must needs be understood as a law to bind her and all other women to subjection, it can be no other subjection than what every wife owes her husband, and then if this be the 'original grant of government' and the 'foundation of monarchical power', there will be as many monarchs as there are husbands. If, therefore, these words give any power to Adam, it can be only a conjugal power, not political, the power that every husband hath to order the things of private concernment in his family, as proprietor of the goods and land there, and to have his will take place in all things of their common concernment before that of his wife; but not a political power of life and death over her, much less over anybody else.

*TWO TREATISES OF GOVERNMENT**

Chapter VI: Of Paternal Power

52 It may perhaps be censured an impertinent criticism in a discourse of this nature to find fault with words and names that have obtained in the world. And yet possibly it may not be amiss to offer new ones when the old are apt to lead men into mistakes, as this of paternal power probably has done, which seems so to place the power of parents over their children wholly in the father, as if the mother had no share in it; whereas if we consult reason or revelation, we shall find she has an equal title, which may give one reason to ask whether this might not be more properly called parental power? For whatever obligation Nature and the right of generation lays on children, it must certainly bind them equal to both the concurrent causes of it. And accordingly we see the positive law of God everywhere joins them together without distinction, when it commands the obedience of children: 'Honour thy father and thy mother' (Exodus 20:12); 'Whosoever curseth his father or his mother' (Leviticus 20:9); 'Ye shall fear every man his mother and his father' (Leviticus 19:3); 'Children, obey your parents' (Ephesians 6:1) etc., is the style of the Old and New Testament.

53 Had but this one thing been well considered without looking any deeper into the matter, it might perhaps have kept men from running into those gross mistakes they have made about this power of parents, which however it might, without any great harshness, bear the name of absolute dominion and regal authority, when under the title of 'paternal' power, it seemed appropriated to the father; would yet have sounded but oddly, and in the very name shown the absurdity, if this supposed absolute power over children had been called parental, and thereby discovered that it belonged to the mother too. For it will but very ill serve the turn of those men who contend so much for the absolute power and authority of the fatherhood, as they call it, that the mother should have any share in it. And it would have but ill supported the monarchy they contend for, when by the very name it appeared, that that fundamental authority from whence

* From *Second Treatise*, '*An Essay Concerning the True Origin, Extent and End of Civil Government*' (London, 1690), edited by Robert Lindsey.

they would derive their government of a single person only was not placed in one, but two persons jointly. But to let this of names pass.

54 Though I have said above 'That all men by nature are equal', I cannot be supposed to understand all sorts of 'equality'. Age or virtue may give men a just precedency. Excellency of parts and merit may place others above the common level. Birth may subject some, and alliance or benefits others, to pay an observance to those to whom Nature, gratitude, or other respects, may have made it due; and yet all this consists with the equality which all men are in, in respect of jurisdiction or dominion one over another, which was the equality I there spoke of, as proper to the business in hand, being that equal right that every man hath to his natural freedom, without being subjected to the will or authority of any other man.

55 Children, I confess, are not born in this full state of equality, though they are born to it. Their parents have a sort of rule and jurisdiction over them when they come into the world, and for some time after, but it is but a temporary one. The bonds of this subjection are like the swaddling clothes they are wrapped up in and supported by in the weakness of their infancy. Age and reason as they grow up, loosen them till at length they drop quite off, and leave a man at his own free disposal.

56 Adam was created a perfect man, his body and mind in full possession of their strength and reason, and so was capable, from the first instance of his being, to provide for his own support and preservation, and govern his actions according to the dictates of the law of reason God had implanted in him. From him the world is peopled with his descendants, who are all born infants, weak and helpless, without knowledge or understanding. But to supply the defects of this imperfect state till the improvement of growth and age had removed them, Adam and Eve, and after them all parents were, by the law of Nature, under an obligation to preserve, nourish and educate the children they had begotten, not as their own workmanship, but the workmanship of their own Maker, the Almighty, to whom they were to be accountable for them.

57 The law that was to govern Adam was the same that was to govern all his posterity, the law of reason. But his offspring

having another way of entrance into the world, different from him, by a natural birth, that produced them ignorant, and without the use of reason, they were not presently under that law. For nobody can be under a law that is not promulgated to him; and this law being promulgated or made known by reason only, he that is not come to the use of his reason cannot be said to be under this law. And Adam's children being not presently as soon as born under this law of reason, were not presently free. For law, in its true notion, is not so much the limitation as the direction of a free and intelligent agent to his proper interest, and prescribes no farther than is for the general good of those under that law. Could they be happier without it, the law, as an useless thing, would of itself vanish; and that ill deserves the name of confinement, which hedges us in only from bogs and precipices. So that however it may be mistaken, the end of law is not to abolish or restrain, but to preserve and enlarge freedom. For in all the states of created beings, capable of laws, where there is no law there is no freedom. For liberty is to be free from restraint and violence from others, which cannot be where there is no law; and is not, as we are told, 'A liberty for every man to do what he lists.'[1] For who could be free, when every other man's humour[2] might domineer over him? But a liberty to dispose and order freely as he lists his person, actions, possessions, and his whole property within the allowance of those laws under which he is, and therein not to be subject to the arbitrary will of another, but freely follow his own.

58 The power, then, that parents have over their children, arises from that duty which is incumbent on them, to take care of their offspring during the imperfect state of childhood. To inform the mind, and govern the actions of their yet ignorant nonage,[3] till reason shall take its place and ease them of that trouble, is what the children want, and the parents are bound to. For God having given man an understanding to direct his actions, has allowed him a freedom of will and liberty of acting, as properly belonging thereunto, within the bounds of that law he is under. But whilst he is in an estate wherein he has no understanding of his own to direct his will, he is not to have any will of his own to follow. He that understands for him must will for him too; he must prescribe to his will, and regulate his actions; but when he comes to the estate that made his father a free man, the son is a free man too. . . .

61 Thus we are born free as we are born rational; not that we have actually the exercise of either: age that brings one, brings with it the other too. And thus we see how natural freedom and subjection to parents may consist together, and are both founded on the same principle. A child is free by his father's title, by his father's understanding, which is to govern him till he hath it of his own. The freedom of a man at years of discretion, and the subjection of a child to his parents, whilst yet short of it, are so consistent and so distinguishable, that the most blinded contenders for monarchy, 'by right of fatherhood', cannot miss of it; the most obstinate cannot but allow of it. For were their doctrine all true, were the right heir of Adam now known, and by that title, settled a monarch in his throne, invested with all the absolute, unlimited power Sir Robert Filmer[4] talks of, if he should die as soon as his heir were born, must not the child, notwithstanding he were never so free, never so much sovereign, be in subjection to his mother and nurse, to tutors and governors, till age and education brought him reason and ability to govern himself and others? The necessities of his life, the health of his body, and the information of his mind would require him to be directed by the will of others and not his own. And yet will any one think that this restraint and subjection were inconsistent with, or spoiled him of, that liberty or sovereignty he had a right to, or gave away his empire to those who had the government of his nonage? This government over him only prepared him the better and sooner for it. If anybody should ask me when my son is of age to be free, I shall answer, just when his monarch is of age to govern. 'But at what time', says the judicious Hooker,[5] 'a man may be said to have attained so far forth the use of reason as sufficeth to make him capable of those laws whereby he is then bound to guide his actions; this is a great deal more easy for sense to discern than for any one, by skill and learning, to determine' (*The Law of Ecclesiastical Polity*, Book I, §6). . . .

64 But what reason can hence advance this care of the parents due to their offspring, into an absolute, arbitrary dominion of the father, whose power reaches no farther than by such a discipline as he finds most effectual to give such strength and health to their bodies, such vigour and rectitude to their minds, as may best fit his children to be most useful to themselves and others. And, if it be necessary to his condition, to make them work when they are

able for their own subsistence. But in this power the mother, too, has her share with the father.

65 Nay, this power so little belongs to the father by any peculiar right of Nature, but only as he is guardian of his children, that when he quits his care of them he loses his power over them, which goes along with their nourishment and education, to which it is inseparably annexed, and belongs as much to the foster-father of an exposed child as to the natural father of another. So little power does the bare act of begetting give a man over his issue, if all his care ends there, and this be all the title he hath to the name and authority of a father. And what will become of this paternal power in that part of the world where one woman hath more than one husband at a time? Or in those parts of America where, when the husband and wife part, which happens frequently, the children are all left to the mother, follow her, and are wholly under her care and provision? And if the father die whilst the children are young, do they not naturally everywhere owe the same obedience to their mother, during their minority, as to their father, were he alive? And will any one say that the mother hath a legislative power over her children that she can make standing rules which shall be of perpetual obligation, by which they ought to regulate all the concerns of their property, and bound their liberty all the course of their lives, and enforce the observation of them with capital punishments? For this is the proper power of the magistrate, of which the father hath not so much as the shadow. His command over his children is but temporary, and reaches not their life or property. It is but a help to the weakness and imperfection of their nonage; a discipline necessary to their education. And though a father may dispose of his own possessions as he pleases when his children are out of danger of perishing for want; yet his power extends not to the lives or goods which either their own industry, or another's bounty, has made theirs, nor to their liberty neither, when they are once arrived to the enfranchisement of the years of discretion. The father's empire then ceases, and he can from thenceforwards no more dispose of the liberty of his son than that of any other man. And it must be far from an absolute or perpetual jurisdiction from which a man may withdraw himself, having licence from Divine authority to 'leave father and mother and cleave to his wife'. . . .

67 The subjection of a minor, places in the father, a temporary government which terminates with the minority of the child. And the honour due from a child places in the parents a perpetual right to respect, reverence, support and compliance, to more or less, as the father's care, cost, and kindness in his education has been, more or less. And this ends not with minority, but holds in all parts and conditions of a man's life. The want of distinguishing these two powers which the father hath in the right of tuition, during minority, and the right of honour all his life, may perhaps have caused a great part of the mistakes about this matter. For, to speak properly of them, the first of these is rather the privilege of children and duty of parents, than any prerogative of paternal power. The nourishment and education of their children is a charge so incumbent on parents for their children's good, that nothing can absolve them from taking care of it. And though the power of commanding and chastising them go along with it, yet God hath woven into the principles of human nature such a tenderness for their offspring, that there is little fear that parents should use their power with too much rigour; the excess is seldom on the severe side, the strong bias of nature drawing the other way. And therefore God Almighty, when He would express His gentle dealing with the Israelites, He tells them that though He chastened them, 'He chastened them as a man chastens his son' (Deuteronomy 8:5), i.e. with tenderness and affection, and kept them under no severer discipline than what was absolutely best for them, and had been less kindness to have slackened. This is that power to which children are commanded obedience, that the pains and care of their parents may not be increased or ill-rewarded. . . .

69 The first part, then, of paternal power, or rather duty, which is education, belongs so to the father that it terminates at a certain season. When the business of education is over it ceases of itself, and is also alienable before. For a man may put the tuition of his son in other hands; and he that has made his son an apprentice to another has discharged him, during that time, of a great part of his obedience, both to himself and to his mother. But all the duty of honour, the other part, remains nevertheless entire to them; nothing can cancel that. It is so inseparable from them both, that the father's authority cannot dispossess the mother of this right, nor can any man discharge his son from honouring her that bore him. But both these are very far from a power to make laws, and enforcing them with penalties that may reach

estate, liberty, limbs and life. The power of commanding ends with nonage; and though after that, honour and respect, support and defence, and whatsoever gratitude can oblige a man to, for the highest benefits he is naturally capable of, be always due from a son to his parents. Yet all this puts no sceptre into the father's hand, no sovereign power of commanding. He has no dominion over his son's property or actions, nor any right that his will should prescribe to his son's in all things. However, it may become his son in many things, not very inconvenient to him and his family, to pay a deference to it.

70 A man may owe honour and respect to an ancient or wise man, defence to his child or friend, relief and support to the distressed, and gratitude to a benefactor, to such a degree that all he has, all he can do, cannot sufficiently pay it. But all these give no authority, no right of making laws to any one over him from whom they are owing. And 'tis plain, all this is due, not to the bare title of father; not only because, as has been said, it is owing to the mother too, but because these obligations to parents, and the degrees of what is required of children, may be varied by the different care and kindness, trouble and expense, is often employed upon one child more than another.

71 This shows the reason how it comes to pass that parents in societies, where they themselves are subjects, retain a power over their children, and have as much right to their subjection as those who are in the state of Nature, which could not possibly be, if all political power were only paternal, and that, in truth, they were one and the same thing: for then, all paternal power being in the prince, the subject could naturally have none of it. But these two powers, political and paternal, are so perfectly distinct and separate, and built upon so different foundations, and given to so different ends, that every subject that is a father, has as much a paternal power over his children as the prince has over his. And every prince that has parents, owes them as much filial duty and obedience as the meanest of his subjects do to theirs, and can therefore contain not any part or degree of that kind of dominion which a prince or magistrate has over his subject.

72 Though the obligation on the parents to bring up their children, and the obligation on children to honour their parents, contain all the power, on the one hand, and submission on the

other, which are proper to this relation; yet there is another power, ordinarily, in the father, whereby he has a tie on the obedience of his children, which, though it be common to him with other men, yet the occasions of showing it, almost constantly happening to fathers in their private families, and in instances of it elsewhere being rare, and less taken notice of, it passes in the world for a part of 'paternal jurisdiction'. And this is the power men generally have to bestow their estates on those who please them best. The possession of the father, being the expectation and inheritance of the children ordinarily, in certain proportions, according to the law and custom of each country; yet it is commonly in the father's power to bestow it with a more sparing or liberal hand, according as the behaviour of this or that child hath comported[6] with his will and humour. . . .

74 To conclude, then, though the father's power of commanding extends no farther than the minority of his children, and to a degree only fit for the discipline and government of that age; and though that honour and respect, and all that which the Latins called piety, which they indispensably owe to their parents all their lifetimes, and in all estates, with all that support and defence, is due to them, gives the father no power of governing, i.e. making laws and exacting penalties on his children. Though by this he has no dominion over the property or actions of his son, yet 'tis obvious to conceive how easy it was, in the first ages of the world, and in places still where the thinness of people gives families leave to separate into unpossessed quarters, and they have room to remove and plant themselves in yet vacant habitations, for the father of the family to become the prince of it. He had been a ruler from the beginning of the infancy of his children; and when they were grown up, since without some government it would be hard for them to live together, it was likeliest it should, by the express or tacit consent of the children, be in the father, where it seemed, without any change, barely to continue. And when, indeed, nothing more was required to it than the permitting the father to exercise alone in his family that executive power of the law of Nature which every free man naturally hath, and by that permission resigning up to him a monarchical power whilst they remained in it. But that this was not by any paternal right, but only by the consent of his children, is evident from hence, that nobody doubts but if a stranger, whom chance or business had brought to his family, had there killed any of his children, or committed any other fact,[7] he might condemn and

put him to death, or otherwise have punished him as well as any of his children, which was impossible he should do by virtue of any paternal authority over one who was not his child, but by virtue of that executive power of the law of Nature which, as a man, he had a right to; and he alone could punish him in his family, where the respect of his children had laid by the exercise of such a power, to give way to the dignity and authority they were willing should remain in him above the rest of his family.

75 Thus 'twas easy and almost natural for children, by a tacit and almost natural consent, to make way for the father's authority and government. They had been accustomed in their childhood to follow his direction, and to refer their little differences to him; and when they were men, who was fitter to rule them? Their little properties and less covetousness seldom afforded greater controversies; and when any should arise, where could they have a fitter umpire than he, by whose care they had every one been sustained and brought up, and who had a tenderness for them all? 'Tis no wonder that they made no distinction betwixt minority and full age, nor looked after one and twenty, or any other age, that might make them the free disposers of themselves and fortunes, when they could have no desire to be out of their pupilage. The government they had been under during it continued still to be more their protection than restraint, and they could nowhere find a greater security to their peace, liberties, and fortunes, than in the rule of a father.

76 Thus the natural fathers of families, by an insensible change, became the politic monarchs of them too; and as they chanced to live long, and leave able and worthy heirs for several successions or otherwise, so they laid the foundations of hereditary or elective kingdoms under several constitutions and manors, according as chance, contrivance, or occasions happened to mould them. But if princes have their titles in the father's right, and it be a sufficient proof of the natural right of fathers to political authority, because they commonly were those in whose hands we find, *de facto*, the exercise of government. I say, if this argument be good, it will as strongly prove that all princes, nay, princes only, ought to be priests, since it is as certain that in the beginning 'the father of the family was priest, as that he was ruler in his own household'.

Chapter VII: Of Political or Civil Society

77 God, having made man such a creature that, in His own judgement, it was not good for him to be alone, put him under strong obligations of necessity, convenience, and inclination, to drive him into society, as well as fitted him with understanding and language to continue and enjoy it. The first society was between man and wife, which gave beginning to that between parents and children; to which, in time, that between master and servant came to be added. And though all these might, and commonly did meet together, and make up but one family, wherein, the master or mistress of it had some sort of rule, proper to a family; each of these, or all together, came short of 'political society', as we shall see if we consider the different ends, ties, and bounds of each of these.

78 Conjugal society is made by a voluntary compact between man and woman, and though it consist chiefly in such a communion and right in one another's bodies as is necessary to its chief end, procreation; yet it draws with it mutual support and assistance, and a communion of interests too, as necessary not only to unite their care and affection, but also necessary to their common offspring, who have a right to be nourished and maintained by them, till they are able to provide for themselves.

79 For the end of conjunction between male and female being not barely procreation, but the continuation of the species, this conjunction betwixt male and female ought to last, even after procreation, so long as is necessary to the nourishment and support of the young ones, who are to be sustained by those that got them, till they are able to shift and provide for themselves. This rule, which the infinite wise Maker hath set to the works of His hands, we find, the inferior creatures steadily obey. In those vivaporous[8] animals which feed on grass, the conjunction between male and female lasts no longer than the very act of copulation, because the teat of the dam being sufficient to nourish the young till it be able to feed on grass. The male only begets, but concerns not himself for the female or young, to whose sustenance he can contribute nothing. But in beasts of prey, the conjunction lasts longer because the dam, not being able well to subsist herself and nourish her numerous offspring by her own prey alone, a more laborious as well as more dangerous way of living than by feeding on grass, the assistance of the male is

necessary to the maintenance of their common family, which cannot subsist, till they are able to prey for themselves, but by the joint care of male and female. The same is observed in all birds (except some domestic ones, where plenty of food excuses the cock from feeding, and taking care of the young brood), whose young, needing food in the nest, the cock and hen continue mates till the young are able to use their wing and provide for themselves.

80 And herein, I think, lies the chief, if not the only reason, why the male and female in mankind are tied to a longer conjunction than other creatures; viz., because the female is capable of conceiving, and, *de facto*, is commonly with child again, and brings forth too a new birth, long before the former is out of a dependency for support on his parents' help and able to shift for himself, and has all the assistance due to him from his parents, whereby the father, who is bound to take care for those he hath begot, is under an obligation to continue in conjugal society with the same woman longer than other creatures, whose young, being able to subsist of themselves before the time of procreation returns again, the conjugal bond dissolves of itself, and they are at liberty till Hymen,[9] at his usual anniversary season, summons them again to choose new mates. Wherein one cannot but admire the wisdom of the great Creator, who, having given to man an ability to lay up for the future, as well as supply the present necessity, hath made it necessary that society of man and wife should be more lasting than of male and female amongst other creatures, that so their industry might be encouraged, and their interest better united, to make provision and lay up goods for their common issue, which uncertain mixture, or easy and frequent solutions of conjugal society would mightily disturb.

81 But though these are ties upon mankind which make the conjugal bonds more firm and lasting in a man than the other species of animals, yet it would give one reason to inquire why this compact, where procreation and education are secured and inheritance taken care for, may not be made determinable, either by consent, or at a certain time, or upon certain conditions, as well as any other voluntary compacts; there being no necessity, in the nature of the thing, nor to the ends of it, that it should always be for life – I mean, to such as are under no restraint of any positive law which ordains all such contracts to be perpetual.

82 But the husband and wife, though they have but one common concern, yet having different understandings, will, unavoidably, sometimes have different wills too. It therefore being necessary that the last determination (i.e. the rule), should be placed somewhere, it naturally falls to the man's share as the abler and the stronger. But this, reaching but to the things of their common interest and property, leaves the wife in the full and true possession of what, by contract, is her peculiar right; and at least gives the husband no more power over her than she has over his life. The power of the husband being so far from that of absolute monarch, that the wife has, in many cases, a liberty to separate from him where natural right or their contract allows it, whether that contract be made by themselves in the state of Nature or by the customs or laws of the country they live in, and the children, upon such separation, fall to the father or mother's lot as such contract does determine.

83 For all the ends of marriage being to be obtained under politic government, as well as in the state of Nature, the civil magistrate doth not abridge the right or power of either, naturally necessary to those ends; viz., procreation and mutual support and assistance whilst they are together, but only decides any controversy that may arise between man and wife about them. If it were otherwise, and that absolute sovereignty and power of life and death naturally belonged to the husband, and were necessary to the society between man and wife, there could be no matrimony in any of these countries, where the husband is allowed no such absolute authority; but the ends of matrimony requiring no such power in the husband, it was not at all necessary to it. The condition of conjugal society put it not in him, but whatsoever might consist with procreation and support of the children till they could shift for themselves: mutual assistance, comfort, and maintenance might be varied and regulated by that contract which first united them in that society; nothing being necessary to any society that is not necessary to the ends for which it is made.

84 The society betwixt parents and children, and the distinct rights and powers belonging respectively to them, I have treated of so largely in the foregoing chapter that I shall not here need to say anything of it; and I think it is plain that it is far different from a politic society.

85 Master and servant are names as old as history, but given to those of far different condition; for a free man makes himself a servant to another by selling him for a certain time the service he undertakes to do in exchange for wages he is to receive. And though this commonly puts him into the family of his master, and under the ordinary discipline thereof, yet it gives the master but a temporary power over him, and no greater than what is contained in the contract between them. But there is another sort of servants, which by a peculiar name we call slaves, who being captives, taken in a just war, are, by the right of Nature, subjected to the absolute dominion, and arbitrary power of their masters. These men having, as I say, forfeited their lives and, with it, their liberties, and lost their estates, and being in the state of slavery, not capable of any property, cannot in that state be considered as any part of civil society; the chief end whereof is the preservation of property.

86 Let us therefore consider a master of a family with all these subordinate relations of wife, children, servants and slaves, united under the domestic rule of a family, with what resemblance soever it may have in its order, offices, and number too, with a little commonwealth, yet is very far from it, both in its constitution, power, and end; or if it must be thought a monarchy, and the paterfamilias,[10] the absolute monarch in it, absolute monarchy will have but a very shattered and short power, when 'tis plain by what has been said before, that the master of the family has a very distinct and differently limited power, both as to time and extent, over those several persons that are in it; for excepting the slave (and the family is as much a family, and his power as paterfamilias as great, whether there be any slaves in his family or no) he has no legislative power of life and death over any of them, and none too but what a mistress of a family may have as well as he. And he certainly can have no absolute power over the whole family who has but a very limited one over every individual in it. But how a family, or any other society of men, differ from that which is properly political society, we shall best see by considering wherein political society itself consists.

87 Man being born, as has been proved, with a title to perfect freedom and an uncontrolled enjoyment of all the rights and privileges of the law of Nature, equally with any other man, or

number of men in the world, hath by nature a power not only to preserve his property, that is, his life, liberty and estate, against the injuries and attempts of other men, but to judge of and punish the breaches of that law in others, as he is persuaded the offence deserves, even with death itself, in crimes where the heinousness of the fact, in his opinion, requires it. But because no political society can be, nor subsist, without having in itself the power to preserve the property, and in order thereunto punish the offences of all those of that society, there, and there only, is political society, where every one of the members hath quitted this natural power, resigned it up into the hands of the community in all cases that exclude him not from appealing for protection to the law established by it. And thus all private judgement of every particular member being excluded, the community comes to be umpire; and by understanding indifferent rules and men authorized by the community for their execution, decides all the differences that may happen between any members of that society concerning any matter of right, and punishes those offences which any member hath committed against the society with such penalties as the law has established, whereby it is easy to discern who are, and are not, in political society together. Those who are united into one body, and have a common established law and judicature to appeal to, with authority to decide controversies between them and punish offenders, are in civil society one with another; but those who have no such common appeal, I mean on earth, are still in the state of Nature, each being where there is no other, judge for himself and executioner; which is, as I have before showed it, the perfect state of Nature. . . .

89 Wherever, therefore, any number of men so unite into one society as to quit everyone his executive power of the law of Nature, and to resign it to the public, there and there only is a political or civil society. And this is done wherever any number of men, in the state of Nature, enter into society to make one people one body politic under one supreme government; or else when any one joins himself to, and incorporates with any government already made. For hereby he authorizes the society, or which is all one, the legislative thereof, to make laws for him as the public good of the society shall require, to the execution whereof his own assistance (as to his own decrees) is due. And this puts men out of a state of Nature into that of a commonwealth, by setting up a judge on earth with authority to determine all

the controversies, and redress the injuries that may happen to any member of the commonwealth, which judge is the legislative or magistrates appointed by it. And wherever there are any number of men, however associated, that have no such decisive power to appeal to, there they are still in the state of Nature. . . .

94 But, whatever flatterers may talk to amuse people's understandings, it never hinders men from feeling; and when they perceive that any man, in what station soever, is out of the bounds of the civil society they are of, and that they have no appeal, on earth, against any harm they may receive from him, they are apt to think themselves in the state of Nature, in respect of him whom they find to be so; and to take care, as soon as they can, to have that safety and security, in civil society, for which it was first instituted, and for which only they entered into it. And therefore, though perhaps at first, as shall be showed more at large hereafter, in the following part of this discourse, some one good and excellent man having got a pre-eminency amongst the rest, had this deference paid to his goodness and virtue, as to a kind of natural authority, that the chief rule, with arbitration of their differences, by a tacit consent devolved into his hands, without any other caution but the assurance they had of his uprightness and wisdom; yet when time giving authority, and, as some men would persuade us, sacredness to customs, which the negligent and unforeseeing innocence of the first ages began, had brought in successors of another stamp, the people finding their properties not secure under the government as then it was (whereas government has no other end but the preservation of property), could never be safe, nor at rest, nor think themselves in civil society, till the legislative was so placed in collective bodies of men, call them senate, parliament, or what you please, by which means every single person became subject equally, with other the meanest men, to those laws, which he himself, as part of the legislative, had established; nor could any one, by his own authority, avoid the force of the law, when once made, nor by any pretence of superiority plead exemption, thereby to license his own, or the miscarriages of any of his dependants. No man in civil society can be exempted from the laws of it. For if any man may do what he thinks fit and there be no appeal on earth for redress or security against any harm he shall do, I ask whether he be not perfectly still in the state of Nature, and so can be no part or member of that civil society, unless any one

will say the state of Nature and civil society are one and the same thing, which I have never yet found any one so great a patron of anarchy as to affirm.

NOTES

1. [Ed.] *lists*: desires.
2. [Ed.] *humour*: in ancient physiology, it was believed that the human disposition was determined by the four humours, or fluids (blood, phlegm, choler and melancholy).
3. [Ed.] *nonage*: the state of being a minor.
4. [Ed.] *Sir Robert Filmer*: (1588–1653) best known for his *Patriarcha* (1630), in which he makes a direct correlation between the rule of kings and the rule of fathers. Locke's *Treatise* is a vehement response to this view.
5. [Ed.] Richard *Hooker*: (*c*.1554–1600) theologian. Best known for his *Treatise on the Laws of Ecclesiastical Polity* (1594), which stressed the importance of reason as well as criticizing the literal interpretation of the Bible by puritans.
6. [Ed.] *comported*: from comport: to behave oneself.
7. [Ed.] *fact*: act, deed.
8. [Ed.] *vivaporous*: those animals which can reproduce live young.
9. [Ed.] *Hymen*: Greek god of marriage.
10. [Ed.] *paterfamilias*: (Latin) in Roman law, the male head of a family or household.

STUDY QUESTIONS

1. Why might the distinction which Locke makes between the public and the private sphere be detrimental to women?
2. To what extent is Locke's account of reason connected to his account of the distinction between nature and state?
3. 'So little power does the bare act of begetting give a man over his issue . . .' (Section 65). What might this claim suggest about the limited power given to woman in Locke's philosophy?

SELECT BIBLIOGRAPHY

General

H. Aarsleff, 'The State of Nature and the Nature of Man in Locke', in *John Locke: Problems and Perspectives*, edited by J. W. Yolton (Cambridge: Cambridge University Press, 1969).

J. Dunn, *Locke* (Oxford: Oxford University Press, 1984).

S. Priest, *The British Empiricists* (Harmondsworth: Penguin, 1990).

G. J. Schochet, 'The Family and the Origins of the State in Locke's Political Philosophy', in *John Locke: Problems and Perspectives*, edited by J. W. Yolton (Cambridge: Cambridge University Press, 1969).

R. S. Woolhouse, *The Empiricists* (Oxford: Oxford University Press, 1988).

For feminist analysis

M. Astell, *An Essay in Defence of the Female Sex* (London: C. Hitch and R. Akenhead, 1694).

M. Butler, 'Early Liberal Roots of Feminism: John Locke and the Attack on Patriarchy', in *Feminist Interpretations and Political Theory*, edited by M. Lyndon Shaney and C. Pateman (Oxford: Blackwell, 1991).

D. H. Coole, *Women in Political Theory* (Brighton: Harvester Wheatsheaf, 1988), ch. 4.

L. Frankel, 'Damaris Cudworth Masham', in M. E. Waithe (ed.), *A History of Women Philosophers*, vol. 3 (Dordrecht: Kluwer Academic Publishers, 1991), pp. 73–86.

K. Green, *The Woman of Reason* (Cambridge: Polity, 1995).

K. Squadrito, 'Mary Astell', in M. E. Waithe (ed.), *A History of Women Philosophers*, vol. 3 (Dordrecht: Kluwer Academic Publishers, 1991), pp. 87–99.

M. E. Waithe, 'Catharine Trotter Cockburn', in M. E. Waithe (ed.), *A History of Women Philosophers*, vol. 3 (Dordrecht: Kluwer Academic Publishers, 1991), pp. 101–25.

PART IV
THE ENLIGHTENMENT

10 David Hume 1711–1776

Introduction and Background

David Hume is arguably the greatest of British philosophers. One of the foremost exponents of empiricism, Hume's philosophy starts with the premise that the only knowledge human beings can have of the world is that which is derived from experience. With human experience as the benchmark for what can reasonably be said, Hume has little time for the supernatural claims of religion.

While this apparent radicalism has been adopted by philosophers who wish to challenge 'supernaturalist' accounts of religion,[1] there is a more reactionary element to Hume's thinking. This is apparent in his account of 'justice'. Justice, according to Hume, is an artificial concept crucial to the creation of society; it should not be understood as an ideal which transcends the human realm. On the contrary, the notion of justice has evolved from human self-interest – notably from the desire to protect one's property. As such, justice is necessary if the structures of society are to be protected.

This might suggest something about the way in which Hume will approach the 'question' of woman's nature. Politically, he appears to have accepted conventional ideas about the propriety of certain social roles for maintaining good civic order. This acceptance extends to gender roles when in the *Treatise of Human Nature* he turns his attention to the question 'of chastity and modesty'. Here, he considers a problem which re-emerges in Rousseau's thinking. A man can never know with certainty that he is the father of his own child. In order to eradicate such doubts, society must stress the importance of chastity for women. To do this effectively, social pressures must be exerted which convince women that unchaste behaviour is shameful. Conventional morality is thus employed to control women's behaviour.

Hume's discussion of the nature of woman leads him to conclusions which are far from flattering. In the *Treatise* woman is defined in terms of her sexuality. At the mercy of her sexual desires, she is weaker than the male, who can resist the pull of sensuality. The essay 'Of Love and Marriage', withdrawn by Hume on the grounds that it was 'frivolous', continues this theme. Hume writes of the danger of 'power-crazed' women; somewhat odd when one considers the lack of political or public opportunities available for women of his time.

Hume's own assessment of the essay on love and marriage suggests that we should be wary of attributing the views in this piece to their author. To what extent is he being humorous rather than advocating a particular position on the status of women? Consideration of his relationships with women suggests a complex attitude to the female sex. Mme de Boufflers, a celebrated *salonnière*, was the object of his attentions whilst in Paris during the 1760s. The letters which passed between the two suggest a passionate relationship hindered by Hume's knowledge that she was a married woman as well as mistress of the Prince de Conti. In later life he considered marrying Nancy Orde, a woman much younger than himself, but this came to nothing. More darkly, his departure from Scotland in 1734 as a young man was apparently precipitated by allegations that he was the father of a servant girl's illegitimate child.

Hume's views on women suggest a conservatism dictated by conventional understandings of sexual and social roles. His friend Alison Cockburn noted that he referred to women as 'the weak pious sex',[2] a comment which suggests that the man who was considered by some to be a threat to the religious structures of his time ultimately adhered to an understanding of woman grounded in the thought forms of Christianity.

'OF CHASTITY AND MODESTY'*

If any difficulty attend this system concerning the laws of nature and nations, 'twill be with regard to the universal approbation or blame which follows their observance or transgression, and which some may not think sufficiently explained from the general interests of society. To remove, as far as possible, all scruples of this kind, I shall here consider another set of duties, viz. the modesty and chastity which belong to the fair sex. And I doubt not but these virtues will be found to be still more conspicuous instances of the operation of those principles which I have insisted on.

There are some philosophers who attack the female virtues with great vehemence and fancy; they have gone very far in detecting popular errors, when they can show that there is no foundation in nature for all that exterior modesty, which we require in the expressions and dress, and behaviour of the fair sex. I believe I may spare myself the trouble of insisting on so obvious a subject, and may proceed, without further preparation, to examine after what manner such notions arise from education, from the voluntary conventions of men, and from the interest of society.

Whoever considers the length and feebleness of human infancy with the concern which both sexes naturally have for their offspring, will easily perceive that there must be an union of male and female for the education of the young, and that this union must be of considerable duration. But in order to induce the men to impose on themselves this restraint, and undergo cheerfully all the fatigues and expenses to which it subjects them, they must believe that the children are their own, and that their natural instinct is not directed to a wrong object when they give a loose to love and tenderness. Now if we examine the structure of the

*From *A Treatise of Human Nature*, vol. III, Part II, Section XII (Edinburgh, 1740), edited by Robert Lindsey.

human body, we shall find that this security is very difficult to be attained on our part; and that since, in the copulation of the sexes, the principle of generation goes from the man to the woman, an error may easily take place on the side of the former, though it be utterly impossible with regard to the latter. From this trivial and anatomical observation is derived that vast difference betwixt the education and duties of the two sexes.

Were a philosopher to examine the matter *a priori*, he would reason after the following manner: Men are induced to labour for the maintenance and education of their children by the persuasion that they are really their own; and therefore, 'tis reasonable and even necessary, to give them some security in this particular. This security cannot consist entirely in the imposing of severe punishments on any transgressions of conjugal fidelity on the part of the wife; since these public punishments cannot be inflicted without legal proof, which 'tis difficult to meet with in this subject. What restraint, therefore, shall we impose on women in order to counterbalance so strong a temptation as they have to infidelity? There seems to be no restraint possible, but in the punishment of bad fame or reputation; a punishment which has a mighty influence on the human mind, and at the same time is inflicted by the world upon surmises and conjectures, and proofs, that would never be received in any court of judicature. In order, therefore, to impose a due restraint on the female sex, we must attach a peculiar degree of shame to their infidelity above what arises merely from its injustice, and must bestow proportionable praises on their chastity.

But though this be a very strong motive to fidelity, our philosopher would quickly discover, that it would not alone be sufficient to that purpose. All human creatures, especially of the female sex, are apt to overlook remote motives in favour of any present temptation. The temptation is here the strongest imaginable. Its approaches are insensible and seducing: and a woman easily finds, or flatters herself she shall find, certain means of securing her reputation and preventing all the pernicious consequences of her pleasures. 'Tis necessary, therefore, that, beside the infamy attending such licences, there should be some preceding backwardness or dread which may prevent their first approaches, and may give the female sex a repugnance to all expressions and postures, and liberties that have an immediate relation to that enjoyment.

Such would be the reasonings of our speculative philosopher. But I am persuaded, that if he had not a perfect knowledge of human nature, he would be apt to regard them as mere chimerical[1] speculations, and would consider the infamy attending infidelity, and backwardness to all its approaches, as principles that were rather to be wished than hoped for in the world. For what means, would he say, of persuading mankind that the transgressions of conjugal duty are more infamous than any other kind of injustice, when 'tis evident they are more excusable upon account of the greatness of the temptation? And what possibility of giving a backwardness to the approaches of a pleasure to which nature has inspired so strong a propensity; and a propensity that 'tis absolutely necessary in the end to comply with for the support of the species?

But speculative reasonings which cost so much pains to philosophers, are often formed by the world naturally and without reflection: as difficulties which seem insurmountable in theory, are easily got over in practice. Those who have an interest in the fidelity of women, naturally disapprove of their infidelity and all the approaches to it. Those who have no interest are carried along with the stream. Education takes possession of the ductile[2] minds of the fair sex in their infancy. And when a general rule of this kind is once established, men are apt to extend it beyond those principles from which it first arose. Thus batchelors, however debauched, cannot choose but be shocked with any instance of lewdness or impudence in women. And though all these maxims have a plain reference to generation, yet women past child-bearing have no more privilege in this respect than those who are in the flower of their youth and beauty. Men have undoubtedly an implicit notion that all those ideas of modesty and decency have a regard to generation; since they impose not the same laws, with the same force on the male sex, where that reason takes not place. The exception is there obvious and extensive, and founded on a remarkable difference, which produces a clear separation and disjunction of ideas. But as the case is not the same with regard to the different ages of women, for this reason, though men know, that these notions are founded on the public interest, yet the general rule carries us beyond the original principle and makes us extend the notions of modesty over the whole sex from their earliest infancy to their extremest old-age and infirmity.

Courage, which is the point of honour among men, derives its merit in a great measure from artifice, as well as the chastity of women; though it has also some foundation in nature, as we shall see afterwards.

As to the obligations which the male sex lie under with regard to chastity, we may observe that according to the general notions of the world, they bear nearly the same proportion to the obligations of women as the obligations of the law of nations do to those of the law of nature. 'Tis contrary to the interest of civil society that men should have an entire liberty of indulging their appetites in venereal enjoyment. But as this interest is weaker than in the case of the female sex, the moral obligation arising from it must be proportionably weaker. And to prove this we need only appeal to the practice and sentiments of all nations and ages.

NOTES

1. [Ed.] *chimerical*: fanciful.
2. [Ed.] *ductile*: pliant.

'OF LOVE AND MARRIAGE'*

I know not whence it proceeds that women are so apt to take amiss everything which is said in disparagement of the married state, and always consider a satire upon matrimony as a satire upon themselves. Do they mean by this, they are the parties principally concerned, and that, if a backwardness to enter the state should prevail in the world, they would be the greatest sufferers? Or, are they sensible that misfortunes and miscarriages of the married state are owing more to their sex than to ours? I hope they do not intend to confess either of these two particulars, or to give such an advantage to their adversaries, the men, as even to allow them to suspect it.

I have often had thoughts of complying with this humour of the fair sex, and of writing a panegyric[1] upon marriage: But in looking around for materials, they seemed to be of so mixed a nature that at the conclusion of my reflections, I found that I was as much disposed to write a satire which might be placed on the opposite pages of the panegyric: and I am afraid, that as satire is, on most occasions, thought to have more truth in it than panegyric, I should have done their cause more harm than good by

* From *Essays, Moral and Political* (Edinburgh, 1741), edited by Robert Lindsey.

this expedient. To misrepresent facts is what, I know, they will not require of me. I must be more a friend to truth than even to them, where their interests are opposite.

I shall tell the women what it is our sex complains of most in the married state; and if they be disposed to satisfy us in this particular, all the other differences will easily be accommodated. If I be not mistaken, 'tis their love of dominion which is the ground of the quarrel; though 'tis very likely that they will think it an unreasonable love of it in us, which makes us insist so much upon that point. However this may be, no passion seems to have more influence on female minds than this for power; and there is a remarkable instance in history of its prevailing above another passion, which is the only one that can be supposed a proper counterpoise for it. We are told, that all the women in Scythia[2] once conspired against the men, and kept the secret so well, that they executed their design before they were suspected. They surprised the men in drink, or asleep, bound them all fast in chains, and having called a solemn council of the whole sex, it was debated what expedient should be used to improve the present advantage, and prevent their falling again into slavery. To kill all the men did not seem to be the relish of any part of the assembly, notwithstanding the injuries formerly received; and they were afterwards pleased to make a great merit of this lenity of theirs. It was, therefore, agreed to put out the eyes of the whole male sex, and thereby resign for ever after all the vanity which they could draw from their beauty in order to secure their authority. 'We must no longer pretend to dress and show,' said they, 'but then we shall be free from slavery. We shall hear no more tender sighs, but in return we shall hear no more imperious commands. Love must for ever leave us; but he will carry subjection along with him.'

'Tis regarded by some as an unlucky circumstance, since the women were resolved to maim the men and deprive them of some of their senses in order to render them humble and dependent, that the sense of hearing could not serve their purpose, since 'tis probable the females would rather have attacked that than the sight: and I think it is agreed among the learned that in a married state 'tis not near so great an inconvenience to lose the former senses as the latter. However this may be, we are told by modern anecdotes that some of the Scythian women did secretly spare their husbands' eyes, presuming, I suppose, that they could govern them as well by means of that sense as without it. But so incorrigible and intractable were these men, that their wives were all obliged in a few years, as their youth and beauty decayed, to imitate the example of their sisters; which it was no difficult matter to do in a state where the female sex had once got the superiority.

I know not if our Scottish ladies derive anything of this humour from their Scythian ancestors; but I must confess that I have often been surprised to see a woman very well pleased to take a fool for her mate, that she might govern with the less control; and could not but think her sentiments, in this respect, still more barbarous than those of the Scythian women above mentioned, as much, as the eyes of the understanding are more valuable than those of the body.

But to be just, and to lay the blame more equally, I am afraid it is the fault of our sex if the women be so fond of rule, and that if we did not abuse our authority, they would never think it worth while to dispute it. Tyrants, we know, produce rebels, and all history informs us that rebels, when they prevail, are apt to become tyrants in their turn. For this reason, I could wish there were no pretensions to authority on either side; but that everything was carried on with perfect equality as betwixt two equal members of the same body. And to induce both parties to embrace those amicable sentiments, I shall deliver to them Plato's account of the origin of love and marriage.[3]

Mankind, according to that fanciful philosopher, were not, in their original, divided into male and female, as at present; but each individual was a compound of both sexes, and was in himself both husband and wife, melted down into one living creature. This union, no doubt, was very entire and the parts very well adjusted together, since there resulted a perfect harmony betwixt the male and female, although they were obliged to be inseparable companions. And so great were the harmony and happiness flowing from it, that the Androgynes,[4] (for so Plato calls them) or men–women, became insolent upon their prosperity, and rebelled against the gods. To punish them for this temerity, Jupiter[5] could contrive no better expedient than to divorce the male-part from the female, and make two imperfect beings of the compound which was before so perfect. Hence the origin of men and women as distinct creatures. But notwithstanding this division, so lively is our remembrance of the happiness we enjoyed in our primæval state, that we are never at rest in this situation; but each of these halves is continually searching through the whole species to find the other half which was broken from it; and when they meet, they join again with the greatest fondness and sympathy. But it often happens that they are mistaken in this particular that they take for their half what no way corresponds to them, and that the parts do not meet nor join in with each other as is usual in fractures. In this case the union is soon dissolved and each part is set loose again to hunt for its lost half, joining itself to every one it meets, by way of trial, and enjoying no rest till its perfect sympathy with its partner shows that it has at last been successful in its endeavours.

Were I disposed to carry on this fiction of Plato, which accounts for the mutual love betwixt the sexes in so agreeable a manner, I would do it by the following allegory:

When Jupiter had separated the male from the female, and had quelled their pride and ambition by so severe an operation, he could not but repent him of the cruelty of his vengeance and take compassion on poor mortals, who were now become incapable of any repose or tranquillity. Such cravings, such anxieties, such necessities arose, as made them curse their creation and think existence itself a punishment. In vain had they recourse to every other occupation and amusement. In vain did they seek after every pleasure of sense, and every refinement of reason. Nothing could fill that void which they felt in their hearts, or supply the loss of their partner who was so fatally separated from them. To remedy this disorder and to bestow some comfort, at least, on the human race in their forlorn situation, Jupiter sent down Love and Hymen,[6] to collect the broken halves of human kind, and piece them together in the best manner possible. These two deities found such a prompt disposition in mankind to unite again in their primitive state, that they proceeded on their work with wonderful success for some time, till, at last, from many unlucky accidents, dissension arose betwixt them. The chief counsellor and favourite of Hymen was Care, who was continually filling his patron's head with prospects of futurity; a settlement, family, children, servants; so that little else was regarded in all the matches they made. On the other hand, Love had chosen Pleasure for his favourite, who was as pernicious a counsellor as the other, and would never allow Love to look beyond the present momentary gratification, or the satisfying of the prevailing inclination. These two favourites became, in a little time, irreconcilable enemies, and made it their chief business to undermine each other in all their undertakings. No sooner had Love fixed upon two halves, which he was cementing together, and forming to a close union, but Care insinuates himself, and bringing Hymen along with him, dissolves the union produced by

Love, and joins each half to some other half which he had provided for it. To be revenged of this, Pleasure creeps in upon a pair already joined by Hymen, and calling Love to his assistance, they under-hand contrive to join each half by secret links to halves which Hymen was wholly unacquainted with. It was not long before this quarrel was felt in its pernicious consequences; and such complaints arose before the throne of Jupiter, that he was obliged to summon the offending parties to appear before him, in order to give an account of their proceedings. After hearing the pleadings on both sides, he ordered an immediate reconcilement betwixt Love and Hymen, as the only expedient for giving happiness to mankind: And that he might be sure this reconcilement should be durable, he laid his strict injunctions on them never to join any halves without consulting their favourites Care and Pleasure, and obtaining the consent of both to the conjunction. Where this order is strictly observed, the Androgyne is perfectly restored and the human race enjoy the same happiness as in their primæval state. The seam is scarce perceived that joins the two beings together; but both of them combine to form one perfect and happy creature.

NOTES

1. [Ed.] *panegyric*: public speech or writing in praise of a person, thing, or achievement.
2. [Ed.] *the women in Scythia*: source unknown. For a fuller discussion of this obscure allusion, see E. F. Miller's edition of Hume's *Essays Moral, Political and Literary* (Indianapolis: Liberty Fund, 1985). For a classical history of Scythia, see Herodotus, *Histories*, Book IV.
3. [Ed.] Cf. *Symposium* 190b–2e. Plato attributes this tale to Aristophanes.
4. [Ed.] *Androgynes*: hermaphrodites.
5. [Ed.] *Jupiter*: supreme Roman god.
6. [Ed.] *Hymen*: Greek god of marriage.

STUDY QUESTIONS

1. Hume's main contribution to western philosophy is his insistence that experience should be acknowledged as the basis for human knowledge. How might women's experience be used to challenge his account of the nature of woman?
2. 'Tyrants, we know, produce rebels.' What response might be made to Hume's account of male responsibility for female 'desire for power'?

SELECT BIBLIOGRAPHY

Also of interest by Hume on this subject, 'Of Polygamy and Divorces', from *Essays, Moral and Political* (1741/42); and *Enquiry Concerning the Principles of Morals*, section IV, 166–8; section VI, 165, which suggests a similar understanding of women to that offered in 'Of Chastity and Modesty'.

A. J. Ayer, *Hume* (Oxford: Oxford University Press, 1980).

S. Priest, *The British Empiricists* (Harmondsworth: Penguin, 1990).

E. C. Mossner, *The Life of David Hume* (Oxford: Oxford University Press, 1970).

B. Stroud, *Hume* (London: Routledge, 1977).

For feminist analysis

C. Battersby, 'An Enquiry Concerning the Humean Woman', *Philosophy*, vol. 56 (1981), pp. 303–12.

S. A. Macleod Burns, 'The Humean Female', in L. M. G. Clark and L. Lange (eds), *The Sexism of Social and Political Theory* (Toronto: University of Toronto Press, 1979).

L. Marcil-Lacoste, 'Hume's Method in Moral Reasoning', in L. M. G. Clark and L. Lange (eds), *The Sexism of Social and Political Theory* (Toronto: University of Toronto Press, 1979).

11 Immanuel Kant 1724–1804

Introduction and Background

Immanuel Kant's life was perhaps the least remarkable of all the philosophers. Totally committed to scholarship, he lived his life according to a strictly regimented regime. Legend has it that the people of Königsberg set their watches by the timing of his daily walk, a good indication of the disciplined life he led.

Kant's contribution to the discussion of gender and philosophy arises during his reflections on morality and aesthetics. According to Kant, the action which is truly moral is that which conforms to the dictates of duty. The task of reason is to decide where that duty lies. Moral action is determined by duty. As such, Kant denies that a truly moral action could arise if one were to act purely from personal inclination. In this sense, the 'cheery philanthropist' (in Kant's words, 'the friend of mankind') acts less morally than the person who acts from duty.

The connection between this 'duty-based' theory of morality and an account of the nature of woman is not readily apparent. However, examination of two passages from Kant's writings suggests a close connection between this understanding of morality and his account of the virtues pertaining to the masculine and the feminine. In the third section of his work *Of the Beautiful and Sublime* (1764), Kant offers his account of the difference between the sexes. He denies that men and women share a common nature; rather, male and female characteristics are understood to complement each other. Men have the potential to embody masculine qualities, women to embody feminine qualities. Included in the masculine qualities are nobility, depth, reflectiveness, learning, profundity, and the ability to be principled. The feminine qualities to which women can aspire include beauty, delicacy, modesty, compassion, sympathy and feeling.

His attitude to the status of these qualities is somewhat ambiguous. He seems to argue that these qualities are equally important, that they complement each other, and that in marriage the conjunction of these qualities contributes to the complete human life. Yet the claim that Kant advances an account of the sexes based upon complementarity not inequality is significantly undermined if a passage from the *Grounding for the Metaphysics of Morals* (1785) is considered. In this passage, Kant equates masculine values with the qualities necessary for genuine moral action; genuine moral action conforms to the dictates of duty, not the emotions. The qualities of sympathy and compassion, which he equates with the feminine in *Of the Beautiful and Sublime*, are given a low status in comparison with the virtues necessary for the moral life.[1] These virtues can be paralleled with Kant's description of masculine values. It is difficult to escape the conclusion that under Kant's schema women are incapable of acting morally; their 'morality' arises not from principle but from emotive responses to situations. If women are incapable of the highest form of virtue, it seems that Kant's thought leads to a hierarchical account of the relationship between men and women. Moreover, the age-old identification of woman with nature is built upon and developed anew. 'Inclination belongs to our determined physical and psychological nature'[2] and is to be conquered by obeying the dictates of duty. Once again, nature is to be subdued by reason, with the male corresponding most closely to the rational principle.

*OBSERVATIONS ON THE FEELING OF THE BEAUTIFUL AND SUBLIME**

Section Three: 'Of the Distinction of the Beautiful and Sublime in the Interrelations of the Two Sexes'

He who first conceived of woman under the name of the *fair sex* probably wanted to say something flattering, but he has hit upon it better than even he himself might have believed. For without taking into consideration that her figure in general is finer, her features more delicate and gentler, and her mien more engaging and more expressive of friendliness, pleasantry, and kindness than in the male sex, and not forgetting what one must reckon as

*Reprinted from Immanuel Kant, *Observations on the Feeling of the Beautiful and Sublime*, translated and edited by J. T. Goldthwait (University of California Press, 1960);

a secret magic with which she makes our passion inclined to judgments favourable to her – even so, certain specific traits lie especially in the personality of this sex which distinguish it clearly from ours and chiefly result in making her known by the mark of the beautiful. On the other side, we could make a claim on the title of the *noble sex*, if it were not required of a noble disposition to decline honorific titles and rather to bestow than to receive them. It is not to be understood by this that woman lacks noble qualities, or that the male sex must do without beauty completely. On the contrary, one expects that a person of either sex brings both together, in such a way that all the other merits of a woman should unite solely to enhance the character of the beautiful, which is the proper reference point; and on the other hand, among the masculine qualities the sublime clearly stands out as the criterion of his kind. All judgments of the two sexes must refer to these criteria, those that praise as well as those that blame; all education and instruction must have these before its eyes, and all efforts to advance the moral perfection of the one or the other – unless one wants to disguise the charming distinction that nature has chosen to make between the two sorts of human being. For here it is not enough to keep in mind that we are dealing with human beings; we must also remember that they are not all alike.

Women have a strong inborn feeling for all that is beautiful, elegant, and decorated. Even in childhood they like to be dressed up, and take pleasure when they are adorned. They are cleanly and very delicate in respect to all that provokes disgust. They love pleasantry and can be entertained by trivialities if only these are merry and laughing. Very early they have a modest manner about themselves, know how to give themselves a fine demeanour and be self-possessed – and this is at an age when our well-bred male youth is still unruly, clumsy, and confused. They have many sympathetic sensations, goodheartedness and compassion, prefer the beautiful to the useful, and gladly turn abundance of circumstance into parsimony, in order to support expenditure on adornment and glitter. They have very delicate feelings in regard to the least offence, and are exceedingly precise to notice the most trifling lack of attention and respect toward them. In short, they contain the chief cause in human nature for the contrast of the beautiful qualities with the noble, and they refine even the masculine sex.

I hope the reader will spare me the reckoning of the manly qualities, so far as they are parallel to the feminine, and be content only to consider both in comparison with each other. The fair sex has just as much understanding as the male, but it is a beautiful understanding, whereas ours should be a deep understanding, an expression that signifies identity with the sublime.

To the beauty of all actions belongs above all the mark that they display facility, and appear to be accomplished without painful toil. On the other hand, strivings and surmounted difficulties arouse admiration and belong to the sublime. Deep meditation, and a long-sustained reflection are noble but difficult, and do not well befit a person in whom unconstrained charms should show nothing else than a beautiful nature. Laborious learning or painful pondering, even if a woman should greatly succeed in it, destroy the merits that are proper to her sex, and because of their rarity they can make of her an object of cold admiration; but at the same time they will weaken the charms with which she exercises her great power over the other sex. A woman who has a head full of Greek, like Mme Dacier,[1] or carries on fundamental controversies about mechanics, like the Marquise de Châtelet,[2] might as well even have a beard; for perhaps that would express more obviously the mien of profundity for which she strives. The beautiful understanding selects for its objects everything closely related to the finer feeling, and relinquishes to the diligent, fundamental, and deep understanding abstract speculations or branches of knowledge useful but dry. A woman therefore will learn no geometry; of the principle of sufficient reason or monads she will know only so much as is needed to perceive the salt in a satire which the insipid grubs of our sex have censured. The fair can leave Descartes his vortices to whirl forever without troubling themselves about them, even though the suave Fontenelle[3] wished to afford them company among the planets; and the attraction of their charms loses none of its strength even if they know nothing of what Algarotti[4] has taken the trouble to sketch out for their benefit about the gravitational attraction of matter according to Newton. In history they will not fill their heads with battles, nor in geography with fortresses, for it becomes them just as little to reek of gunpowder as it does the males to reek of musk.

It appears to be a malicious stratagem of men that they have wanted to influence the fair sex to this perverted taste. For, well aware of their weakness before her natural charms and of the fact that a single sly glance sets them more in confusion than the most difficult problem of science, so soon as woman enters upon this taste they see themselves in a decided superiority and are at an advantage that otherwise they hardly would have, being able to succour their vanity in its weakness by a generous indulgence toward her. The content of woman's great science, rather, is humankind, and among humanity, men. Her philosophy is not to reason, but to sense. In the opportunity that one wants to give to women to cultivate their beautiful nature, one must always keep this relation before his eyes. One will seek to broaden their total moral feeling and not their memory, and that of course not by universal rules but by some judgment upon the conduct that they see about them. The examples one borrows from other times in order to examine the influence the fair sex has had in culture, the various relations to the masculine in which it has stood in other ages or in foreign lands, the character of both so far as it can be illustrated by these, and the changing taste in amusements – these comprise her whole history and geography. For the ladies, it is well to make it a pleasant diversion to see a map setting forth the entire globe or the principal parts of the world. This is brought about by showing it only with the intention of portraying the different characters of peoples that dwell there, and the differences of their taste and moral feeling, especially in respect to the effect these have upon the relations of sexes – together with a few easy illustrations taken from the differences of their climates, or their freedom or slavery. It is of little consequence whether or not the women know the particular subdivisions of these lands, their industry, power, and sovereigns. Similarly, they will need to know nothing more of the cosmos than is necessary to make the appearance of the heavens on a beautiful evening a stimulating sight to them, if they can conceive to some extent that yet more worlds, and in them yet more beautiful creatures, are to be found. Feeling for expressive painting and for music, not so far as it manifests artistry but sensitivity – all this refines or elevates the taste of this sex, and always has some connection with moral impulses. Never a cold and speculative instruction but always feelings, and those indeed which remain as close as possible to the situation of her sex. Such instruction is very rare because it demands talents, experience, and a heart full of feeling; and a woman can do very well without any other, as in fact without this she usually develops very well by her own efforts.

The virtue of a woman is a beautiful virtue.[5] That of the male sex should be a *noble virtue*. Women will avoid the wicked not because it is unright, but because it is ugly; and virtuous actions mean to them such as are morally beautiful. Nothing of duty, nothing of compulsion, nothing of obligation! Woman is intolerant of all commands and all morose constraint. They do something only because it pleases them, and the art consists in making only that please them which is good. I hardly believe that the fair sex is capable of principles, and I hope by that not to offend, for these are also extremely rare in the male. But in place of it Providence has put in their breast kind and benevolent sensations, a fine feeling for propriety, and a complaisant soul. One should not at all demand sacrifices and generous self-restraint. A man must never tell his wife if he risks a part of his fortune on behalf of a friend. Why should he fetter her merry talkativeness by burdening her mind with a weighty secret whose keeping lies solely upon him? Even many of her weaknesses are, so to speak, beautiful faults. Offence or misfortune moves her tender soul to sadness. A man must never weep other than magnanimous tears. Those he sheds in pain or over circumstances of fortune make him contemptible. Vanity, for which one reproaches the fair sex so frequently, so far as it is a fault in that sex, yet is only a beautiful fault. For – not to mention that the men who so gladly flatter a woman would be left in a strait if she were not inclined to take it well – by that they actually enliven their charms. This inclination is an impulsion to exhibit pleasantness and good demeanour, to let her merry wit play, to radiate through the changing devices of dress, and to heighten her beauty. Now in this there is not at all any offensiveness toward others, but rather so much courtesy, if it is done with good taste, that to scold against it with peevish rebukes is very ill-bred. A woman who is too inconstant and deceitful is called a coquette; which expression yet has not so harsh a meaning as what, with a changed syllable, is applied to man, so that if we understand each other, it can sometimes indicate a familiar flattery. If vanity is a fault that in a woman much merits excuse, a haughty bearing is not only as reproachable in her as in people in general, but completely disfigures the character of her sex. For this quality is exceedingly stupid and ugly, and is set completely in opposition to her captivating, modest charms. Then such a person is in a slippery position. She will suffer herself to be judged sharply and without any pity; for whoever presumes an esteem invites all around him to rebuke. Each disclosure of even the least fault gives everyone a true joy, and the word coquette here loses its mitigated meaning. One must always distinguish between vanity and conceit. The first seeks approbation and to some extent honours those on whose account it gives itself the trouble. The second believes itself already in full possession of approbation, and because it never strives to gain any, it wins none.

If a few ingredients of vanity do not deform a woman in the eyes of the male sex, still, the more apparent they are, the more they serve to divide the fair sex among themselves. Then they judge one another severely, because the one seems to obscure the charms of the other, and in fact, those who make strong presumptions of conquest actually are seldom friends of one another in a true sense.

Nothing is so much set against the beautiful as disgust, just as nothing sinks deeper beneath the sublime than the ridiculous. On this account no insult can be more painful to a man than being called a fool, and to a woman, than being called disgusting. The English *Spectator* maintains that no more insulting reproach could be made to a man than if he is considered a liar, and to a woman none more bitter than if she is held unchaste. I will leave this for what it is worth so far as it is judged according to strictness in morals. But here the question is not what of itself deserves the greatest rebuke, but what is actually felt as the harshest of all. And to that point I ask every reader whether, when he sets himself to thinking upon this matter, he must not assent to my opinion. The maid Ninon Lenclos[6] made not the least claims upon the honour of chastity, and yet she would have been implacably offended if one of her lovers should have gone so far in his pronouncements; and one knows the gruesome fate of Monaldeschi,[7] on account of an insulting expression of that sort, at the hands of a princess who had wanted to be thought no Lucretia.[8] It is intolerable that one should never once be capable of doing something wicked if one actually wanted to, because then even the omission of it remains only a very ambiguous virtue.

In order to remove ourselves as far as possible from these disgusting things, neatness, which of course well becomes any person, in the fair sex belongs among the virtues of first rank and can hardly be pushed too high among them, although in a man it sometimes rises to excess and then becomes trifling.

Sensitivity to shame is a secrecy of nature addressed to setting bounds to a very intractable inclination, and since it has the voice of nature on its side, seems always to agree with good moral qualities even if it yields to excess. Hence it is most needed, as a supplement to principles, for there is no instance in which inclination is so ready to turn Sophist, subtly to devise complaisant principles, as in this. But at the same time it serves to draw a curtain of mystery before even the most appropriate and necessary purposes of nature, so that a too familiar acquaintance with them might not occasion disgust, or indifference at least, in respect to the final purpose of an impulse onto which the finest and liveliest inclinations of human nature are grafted. This quality is especially peculiar to the fair sex and very becoming to it. There is also a coarse and contemptible rudeness in putting delicate modesty to embarrassment or annoyance by the sort of vulgar jests called obscenities. However, although one may go as far around the secret as one ever will, the sexual inclination still ultimately underlies all her remaining charms, and a woman, ever as a woman, is the pleasant object of a well-mannered conversation; and this might perhaps explain why otherwise polite men occasionally take the liberty to let certain fine allusions show through, by a little mischief in their jests, which make us call them loose or waggish. Because they neither affront by searching glances nor intend to injure anyone's esteem, they believe it justified to call the person who receives it with an indignant or brittle mien a prude. I mention this practice only because it is generally considered as a somewhat bold trait in polite conversation, and also because in point of fact much wit has been squandered upon it; however, judgment according to moral strictness does not belong here, because what I have to observe and explain in the sensing of the beautiful is only the appearances.

The noble qualities of this sex, which still, as we have already noted, must never disguise the feeling of the beautiful, proclaim themselves by nothing more clearly and surely than by modesty, a sort of noble simplicity and innocence in great excellences. Out of it shines a quiet benevolence and respect toward others, linked at the same time with a certain noble trust in oneself, and a reasonable self-esteem that is always to be found in a sublime disposition. Since this fine mixture at once captivates by charms and moves by respect, it puts all the remaining shining qualities in security against the mischief of censure and mockery. Persons of this temperament also have a heart for friendship, which in a woman can never be valued highly enough, because it is so rare and moreover must be so exceedingly charming.

As it is our purpose to judge concerning feelings, it cannot be unpleasant to bring under concepts, if possible, the difference of the impression that the form and features of the fair sex make on the masculine. This complete fascination is really overlaid upon the sex instinct. Nature pursues its great purpose, and all refinements that join together, though they may appear to stand as far from that as they will, are only trimmings and borrow their charm ultimately from that very source. A healthy and coarse taste, which always stays very close to this impulse, is little tempted by the charms of demeanour, of facial features, of eyes, and so on, in a woman, and because it really pertains only to sex, it oftentimes sees the delicacy of others as empty flirting.

If this taste is not fine, nevertheless it is not on that account to be disdained. For the largest part of mankind complies by means of it with the great order of nature, in a very simple and sure way.[9] Through it the greatest number of marriages are brought about, and indeed by the most diligent part of the human race; and because the man does not have his head full of fascinating expressions, languishing eyes, noble demeanour, and so forth, and understands nothing of all this, he becomes that much the more attentive to householders' virtues, thrift and such, and to the dowry. As for what relates to the somewhat finer taste, on whose account it might be necessary to make a distinction among the exterior charms of women, this is fixed either upon what in the form and the expression of the face is moral, or upon what is non-moral. In respect to the last-named sort of pleasantness, a lady is called pretty. A well-proportioned figure, regular features, colours of eyes and face which contrast prettily, beauties pure and simple which are also pleasing in a bouquet and gain a cool approbation. The face itself says nothing, although it is pretty, and speaks not to the heart. What is moral in the expression of the features, the eyes, and mien pertains to the feeling either of the sublime or of the beautiful. A woman in whom the agreeableness beseeming her sex particularly makes manifest the moral expression of the sublime is called beautiful in the proper sense; so far as the moral composition makes itself discernible in the mien or facial features, she whose features show qualities of beauty is agreeable, and if she is that to a high degree, charming. The first, under a mien of composure and a noble demeanour, lets the glimmer of a beautiful understanding play forth through discreet glances, and as in her face she portrays a tender feeling and a benevolent heart, she seizes possession of the affection as well as the esteem of a masculine heart. The second exhibits merriment and wit in laughing eyes, something of a fine mischief, the playfulness of just and sly coyness. She charms, while the first moves; and the feeling of love of which she is capable and which she stimulates in others is fickle but beautiful, whereas the feeling of the first is tender, combined with respect, and constant. I do not want to engage in too detailed an analysis of this sort, for in doing so the author always appears to depict his own inclination. I shall still mention, however, that the liking many women have for a healthy but pale colour can be explained here. For this generally accompanies a disposition of more inward feeling and delicate sensation, which belongs to the quality of the sublime; whereas the rosy and blooming complexion proclaims less of the first, but more of the joyful and merry disposition – but it is more suitable to vanity to move and to arrest, than to charm and to attract. On the other hand there can be very pretty persons completely without moral feeling and without any expression that indicates feeling; but they will neither move nor charm, unless it might be the coarse taste of which we have made mention, which sometimes grows somewhat more refined and then also selects after its fashion. It is too bad that this sort of beautiful creatures easily fall into the fault of conceit, through the consciousness of the beautiful figure their mirror shows them, and from a lack of finer sensations, for then they make all indifferent to them except the flatterer, who has ulterior motives and contrives intrigues.

Perhaps by following these concepts one can understand something of the different effect the figure of the same woman has upon the tastes of men. I do not concern myself with what in this impression relates too closely to the sex impulse and may be of a piece with the particular sensual illusion with which the feeling of everyone clothes itself, because it lies outside the compass of finer taste. Perhaps what M. Buffon supposes may be true: that the figure that makes the first impression, at the time when this impulse is still new and is beginning to develop, remains the pattern all feminine figures in the futures must more or less follow so as to be able to stir the fanciful ardour, whereby a rather coarse inclination is compelled to choose among the different objects of a sex. Regarding the somewhat finer taste, I affirm that the sort of beauty we have called the pretty figure is judged by all men very much alike, and that opinions about it are not so different as one generally maintains. The Circassian and Georgian maidens have always been considered extremely pretty by all Europeans who travel through their lands. The Turks, the Arabs, the Persians are apparently of one mind in this taste, because they are very eager to beautify their races through such fine blood, and one also notes that the Persian race has actually succeeded in this. The merchants of Hindustan likewise do not fail to draw great profit from a wicked commerce in such beautiful creatures, for they supply them to the self-indulgent rich men of their land. And it appears that, as greatly as the caprice of taste in these different quarters of the world may diverge, still, whatever is once known in any of these as especially pretty will also be considered the same in all the others. But whenever what is moral in the features mingles in the judgment upon the fine figure, the taste of different men is always very different, both because their moral feeling itself is dissimilar, and also on account of the different meaning that the expression of the face may have in every fancy. One finds that those formations that at first glance do not have any particular effect, because they are not pretty in any decided way, generally appear far more to captivate and to grow constantly more beautiful as soon as they begin to please upon nearer acquaintance. On the other hand, the pretty appearance that proclaims itself at once is later received with greater indifference. This probably is because moral charms, when they are evident, are all the more arresting because they are set in operation only on the occasion of moral sensations, and let themselves be discovered in this way, each disclosure of a new charm causing one to suspect still more of these; whereas all the agreeable features that do not at all conceal themselves, after exercising their entire effect at the beginning, can subsequently do nothing more than to cool off the enamoured curiosity and bring it gradually to indifference.

Along with these observations, the following comment naturally presents itself. The quite simple and coarse feeling in the sexual inclination leads directly to the great purpose of nature, and as it fulfils her claims it is fitted to make the person himself happy without digression; but because of its great universality it degenerates easily into excess and dissoluteness. On the other hand, a very refined taste serves to take away the wildness of an impetuous inclination, and although it limits this to few objects, to make it modest and decorous, such an inclination usually misses the great goal of nature. As it demands or expects more than nature usually offers, it seldom takes care to make the person of such delicate feeling happy. The first disposition becomes uncouth, because it is attracted to all the members of a sex; the second becomes oversubtle, because actually it is attracted to none. It is occupied only with an object that the enamoured inclination creates in thought, and ornaments with all the noble and beautiful qualities that nature seldom unites in one human being and still more seldom brings to him who can value them and perhaps would be worthy of such a possession.

Thence arises the postponement and finally the full abandonment of the marital bond; or what is perhaps just as bad, a peevish regret after making a choice that does not fulfil the great expectations one had made oneself – for not seldom the Aesopian cock[10] finds a pearl when a common barleycorn would have been better suited to him.

From this we can perceive in general that as charming as the impressions of the delicate feeling may be, one still might have cause to be on guard in its refinement, lest by excessive sensibility we subtly fabricate only much discontent and a source of evil. To noble souls I might well propose to refine as much as they can the feeling with respect to qualities that become them, or with respect to actions that they themselves perform, but to maintain this taste in its simplicity respecting what they enjoy or expect from others – if only I saw how this were possible to achieve. But if it were approached, they would make others happy and also be happy themselves. It is never to be lost sight of that in whatever way it might be, one must make no very high claims upon the raptures of life and the perfection of men; for he who always expects only something ordinary has the advantage that the result seldom refutes his hope, but sometimes he is surprised by quite unexpected perfections.

Finally age, the great destroyer of beauty, threatens all these charms; and if it proceeds according to the natural order of things, gradually the sublime and noble qualities must take the place of the beautiful, in order to make a person always worthy of a greater respect as she ceases to be attractive. In my opinion, the whole perfection of the fair sex in the bloom of years should consist in the beautiful simplicity that has been brought to its height by a refined feeling toward all that is charming and noble. Gradually, as the claims upon charms diminish, the reading of books and the broadening of insight could refill unnoticed the vacant place of the Graces with the Muses,[11] and the husband should be the first instructor. Nevertheless, when the epoch of growing old, so terrible to every woman, actually approaches, she still belongs to the fair sex, and that sex disfigures itself if in a kind of despair of holding this character longer, it gives way to a surly and irritable mood.

An aged person who attends a gathering with a modest and friendly manner, is sociable in a merry and sensible way, favours with a pleasant demeanour the pleasures of youth in which she herself no longer participates, and, as she looks after everything, manifests contentment and benevolence toward the joys that are going on around her, is yet a finer person than a man of like age, and perhaps even more attractive than a girl, although in another sense. Indeed the platonic love might well be somewhat too mystical, which an ancient philosopher asserted when he said of the object of his inclination, 'The Graces reside in her wrinkles, and my soul seems to hover upon my lips when I kiss her withered mouth'; but such claims must be relinquished. An old man who acts infatuated is a fool, and the like presumptions of the other sex at that age are disgusting. It never is due to nature when we do not appear with a good demeanour, but rather to the fact that we turn her upside down.

In order to keep close to my text, I want to undertake a few reflections on the influence one sex can have upon the other, to beautify or ennoble its feeling. Woman has a superior feeling for the beautiful, so far as it pertains to herself; but for the noble, so far as it is encountered in the male sex. Man on the other hand has a decided feeling for the noble, which belongs to his qualities, but for the beautiful, so far as it is to be found in woman. From this it must follow that the purposes of nature are directed still more to ennoble man, by the sexual inclination, and likewise still more to beautify woman. A woman is embarrassed little that she does not possess certain high insights, that she is timid, and not fit for serious employments, and so forth; she is beautiful and captivates, and that is enough. On the other hand, she demands all these qualities in a man, and the sublimity of her soul shows itself only in that she knows to treasure these noble qualities so far as they are found in him. How else indeed would it be possible that so many grotesque male faces, whatever merits they may possess, could gain such well-bred and fine wives! Man on the other hand is much more delicate in respect to the beautiful charms of woman. By their fine figure, merry naïveté, and charming friendliness he is sufficiently repaid for the lack of book learning and for other deficiencies that he must supply by his own talents. Vanity and fashion can give these natural drives a false direction and make out of many a male a sweet gentleman, but out of a woman either a prude or an Amazon; but still nature always seeks to reassert her own order. One can thereby judge what powerful influences the sexual inclination could have especially upon the male sex, to ennoble it, if instead of many dry instructions the moral feeling of woman were seasonably developed to sense properly what belongs to the dignity and the sublime qualities of the other sex, and were thus prepared to look upon the trifling fops with disdain and to yield to no other qualities than the merits. It is also certain that the power of her charms on the whole would gain through that; for it is apparent that their fascination for the most part works only upon nobler souls; the others are not fine enough to sense them. Just as the poet Simonides[12] said, when someone advised him to let the Thessalians hear his beautiful songs: 'These fellows are too stupid to be beguiled by such a man as I am.' It has been regarded moreover as an effect of association with the fair sex that men's customs have become gentler, their conduct more polite and refined, and their bearing more elegant; but the advantage of this is only incidental.[13] The principal object is that the man should become more perfect as a man, and the woman as a wife; that is, that the motives of the sexual inclination work according to the hint of nature, still more to ennoble the one and to beautify the qualities of the other. If all comes to the extreme, the man, confident in his merits, will be able to say: 'Even if you do not love me, I will constrain you to esteem me,' and the woman, secure in the might of her charms, will answer: 'Even if you do not inwardly admire me, I will still constrain you to love me.' In default of such principles one sees men take on femininity in order to please, and woman occasionally (although much more seldom) affect a masculine demeanour in order to stimulate esteem; but whatever one does contrary to nature's will, one always does very poorly.

In matrimonial life the united pair should, as it were, constitute a single moral person, which is animated and governed by the understanding of the man and the taste of the wife. For not only can one credit more insight founded on experience to the former, and more freedom and accuracy in sensation to the latter; but also, the more sublime a disposition is, the more inclined it is to place the greatest purpose of its exertions in the contentment of a beloved object, and likewise the more beautiful it is, the more it seeks to require these exertions by complaisance. In such a relation, then, a dispute over precedence is trifling and, where it occurs, is the surest sign of a coarse or dissimilarly matched taste. If it comes to such a state that the question is of the right of the superior to command, then the case is already utterly corrupted; for where the whole union is in reality erected solely upon inclination, it is already half destroyed as soon as the 'duty' begins to make itself heard. The presumption of the woman in this harsh tone is extremely ugly, and of the man is base and contemptible in the highest degree. However, the wise order of things so brings it about that all these niceties and delicacies of feeling have their whole strength only in the beginning, but subsequently gradually become duller through association and domestic concerns, and then degenerate into familiar love. Finally, the great skill consists in still preserving sufficient remainders of those feelings so that indifference and satiety do not put an end to the whole value of the enjoyment on whose account it has solely and alone been worth the trouble to enter such a union.

NOTES

1. [Ed.] Anne *Dacier*: (1654–1720) translator of the Latin classics into French.
2. [Ed.] *Marquise de Châtelet*: prize-winning scholar for her work on fire (1738).
3. [Ed.] *Fontenelle*: Fontenelle's work *Entretiens sur la Pluralité des Mondes*, is said to have arisen from women's conversations concerning astronomy.
4. [Ed.] *Algarotti*: (1702–64) commentator on Newton's ideas for women.
5. [Ed.] Kant notes: '[In Section II, "Of the Attributes of the Beautiful and Sublime in Man in General"] in a strict judgment this was called adoptive virtue; here, where on account of the character of the sex it deserves a favourable justification, it is generally called a beautiful virtue' [J. T. Goldthwait's translation].
6. [Ed.] *Ninon Lenclos*: (1616–1705) society hostess of dubious reputation.
7. [Ed.] Marchese Giovanni *Monaldeschi*: (d. 1657) equerry for Queen Christina of Sweden. Christina allegedly ordered him assassinated whilst at the French court.
8. [Ed.] *Lucretia*: Rape victim of Roman legend, she committed suicide after revealing her ordeal to her husband.
9. [Ed.] Kant notes: 'As all things in the world have their bad side, regarding this taste it is only to be regretted that easier than another it degenerates into dissoluteness. For as any other can extinguish the fire one person has lighted, there are not enough obstables that can confine an intractable inclination' [J. T. Goldthwait's translation].
10. [Ed.] *the Aesopian cock*: character from the fables of Aesop (*c.*6 BCE). The cock finds a pearl, but, as he is too ignorant to know its value, would prefer a barleycorn!
11. [Ed.] *the Graces with the Muses*: the Graces – goddesses which personify grace and beauty; the Muses – goddesses of poetry, music and dancing, activities which are often seen as the fruits of the Graces.
12. [Ed.] *Simonides*: (556–468 BCE) Greek poet and writer of epigrams. Wrote a satire on 'the different temper and character of women'.

13. [Ed.] Kant notes: 'This advantage itself is really much reduced by the observation that one will have made, that men who are too early and too frequently introduced into company where woman sets the tone generally become somewhat trifling, and in male society they are boring or even contemptible because they have lost the taste for conversation, which must be merry, to be sure, but still of actual content – witty, to be sure, but also useful through its earnest discourse' [J. T. Goldthwait's translation].

*GROUNDING FOR THE METAPHYSICS OF MORALS**

To be beneficent where one can is a duty; and besides this, there are many persons who are so sympathetically constituted that, without any further motive of vanity or self-interest, they find an inner pleasure in spreading joy around them and can rejoice in the satisfaction of others as their own work. But I maintain that in such a case an action of this kind, however dutiful and amiable it may be, has nevertheless no true moral worth. It is on a level with such actions as arise from other inclinations, e.g., the inclination for honour, which if fortunately directed to what is in fact beneficial and accords with duty and is thus honourable, deserves praise and encouragement, but not esteem; for its maxim lacks the moral content of an action done not from inclination but from duty. Suppose then the mind of this friend of mankind to be clouded over with his own sorrow so that all sympathy with the lot of others is extinguished, and suppose him still to have the power to benefit others in distress, even though he is not touched by their trouble because he is sufficiently absorbed with his own; and now suppose that, even though no inclination moves him any longer, he nevertheless tears himself from his deadly insensibility and performs the action without any inclination at all, but solely from duty – then for the first time his action has genuine moral worth. Further still, if nature has put little sympathy in this or that man's heart, if (while being an honest man in other respects) he is by temperament cold and indifferent to the sufferings of others, perhaps because as regards his own sufferings he is endowed with the special gift of patience and fortitude and expects or even requires that others should have the same; if such a man (who would truly not be nature's worst

*From the translation of Karl Vorländer's German text (Leipzig, 1906) by J. W. Ellington (Indianapolis: Hackett, 1981), pp. 11–12.

product) had not been exactly fashioned by her to be a philanthropist, would he not yet find in himself a source from which he might give himself a worth far higher than any that a good-natured temperament might have? By all means, because just here does the worth of the character come out; this worth is moral and incomparably the highest of all, viz., that he is beneficent, not from inclination, but from duty.

STUDY QUESTIONS

1. List the qualities from *Of the Beautiful and Sublime* which Kant describes as 'masculine' and the qualities he describes as 'feminine'.
2. Could a woman, according to Kant, be a philosopher?
3. How do the qualities necessary for attaining the higher moral virtues which Kant outlines in the passage from *Grounding for the Metaphysics of Morals* relate to the masculine and feminine qualities described in *Of the Beautiful and Sublime*? What implication does this connection have for Kant's theory of the complementarity of the sexes?

SELECT BIBLIOGRAPHY

General

R. Scruton, *Kant* (Oxford: Oxford University Press, 1982).
A. W. Wood, *Kant's Moral Religion* (Ithaca, NY: Cornell University Press, 1970).

For feminist analysis

E. Frazer, J. Hornsby and S. Lovibond, *Ethics: A Feminist Reader* (Oxford: Blackwell, 1992), Section II.
C. Gilligan, *In a Different Voice* (Cambridge, Mass.: Harvard, 1993).
J. Grimshaw, *Feminist Philosophers* (Brighton: Harvester Wheatsheaf, 1986).
G. Lloyd, *The Man of Reason* (London: Methuen, 1984), ch. 4.

12 Jean-Jacques Rousseau 1712–1778

Introduction and Background

As Joel Schwartz points out in his study of Rousseau's sexual politics, Rousseau's work is used in contradictory ways by feminists.[1] Some, like Susan Okin, see him as the arch-defender of the patriarchal family; a philosopher intent on maintaining the submissive position of women in relation to men. Others, such as Brigitte Berger, see him as the radical philosopher, rejecting the family as the structure which impedes human freedom.[2] Schwartz suggests that both interpretations are valid, for they echo the contradictory nature of Rousseau's ideas on women.

Rousseau's ambivalent attitude towards women is illustrated in two unpublished essays. The first, 'Sur les femmes', suggests an early 'pro-feminist' Rousseau who 'stresses the injustices done to women, the legal restrictions limiting their freedom',[3] and who goes on to argue for full equality between men and women. The second essay, 'Les Événements importants dont les femmes ont été la cause secrète', reveals a more critical Rousseau who seeks to expose the way in which women have exercised their power in secret. Schwartz suggests that Rousseau rejects his earlier feminist ideas 'not because he believes in the inequality of the sexes, but because he believes in the social utility of differentiating between the ways of life of the two equal sexes'.[4]

This issue forms the basis for Rousseau's arguments concerning the education of the sexes in what he considered to be the most important of his writings, *Émile* (1762). In this work he offers a method for educating the child which respects the dictates of nature, but which ultimately shapes the child to the demands of citizenship. Nature and society are seen to act in harmony; it is not a question of juxtaposing nature with society. Understanding nature and society as complementary ultimately influences the way in which Rousseau considers the roles of men and women, an understanding which dominates his educational theory. Rousseau advocates a 'needs-based' approach to education. Just as nature and society complement each other, so do the respective nature of men and women. As such, education must cater for the differing needs of males and females.

The vast majority of Rousseau's outworking of his theory on education concerns the way in which the boy – Émile – is to be educated. In chapter V – 'Sophy, or Woman' – Rousseau offers what he perceives as an appropriate education for women. Sophy is Rousseau's idealized woman. She is portrayed as warmhearted and attractive. She dresses well, but is not vain. She is a proficient singer, and is well-skilled in the womanly graces of needlework and managing the home. Sophy is portrayed as the ideal helpmeet for man. Woman is understood solely in relation to male needs; thus Rousseau offers her an education comprised chiefly of domestic crafts. This male-centred definition of woman has been challenged by feminist writers. Rousseau's earliest feminist critic was Catharine Sawbridge Macaulay-Graham (1731–91), who argued that 'it is not reason, it is not wit; it is pride and sensuality that speak in Rousseau'.[5] More famously, Mary Wollstonecraft in her *Vindication of the Rights of Woman* (1792) challenged

Rousseau's division of human virtues into masculine and feminine qualities. In rejecting his divisive and ultimately hierarchical account of the sexes, she argued for an account of the human virtues which is *independent* of male/female biological differences.[6]

In marked contrast to Wollstonecraft's comprehensive critique, Rousseau's commentators often deny the anti-feminist tone of his work. On occasion, the desire to remove the taint of misogyny from Rousseau's works betrays the sexism of the commentator's own position. A notable example of this is J. H. Broome. Broome denies that Rousseau preaches the inferiority of woman; rather, Rousseau is proclaiming the essential but complementary differences between men and women. Broome writes:

> A woman, in short, should *be* a woman, and not a man in skirts; just as a child has the right to *be* a child, and not treated merely as a miniature adult.[7]

The comparison drawn between woman and child is significant. The child, Broome writes, should be treated as a child, not 'a miniature adult'. If the child should not to be equated with a miniature adult, the woman should not to be equated with a *miniature* male. In comparing the child with the woman, a rather negative account of the latter emerges. Woman is paralleled with that which is not fully man. Just as a child should not be compared with an adult, so the woman should not be compared with the man. If she was, her true status would be revealed as something which could only be found wanting when compared with manhood.

Ultimately, an essentialist idea of what constitutes 'womanhood' pervades Broome's commentary:

> It seems hard when the same critics praise [Rousseau] for wanting children to be children, and condemn him for wanting women to be women.[8]

It is worth noting that Broome's definition of woman is taken from his reading of Rousseau. Individuality is denied to women; all women can be defined in the same way and allotted the same tasks. It seems that a philosophy which takes its lead from Rousseau must equate 'woman' with 'domestic helpmate'. As such, Rousseau's view of reality, like that offered by Kant, assumes an implicit hierarchy of male over female, despite the claims for *complementary* masculine and feminine qualities.

*ÉMILE**

It is not good that man should be alone. Émile is now a man, and we must give him his promised helpmeet. That helpmeet is Sophy. Where is her dwelling-place, where shall she be found? We must know beforehand what she is, and then we can decide where to look for her. . . .

* From the translation by Barbara Foxley (Dent & Sons, 1911; Everyman's Library, David Campbell).

Sophy, or Woman

Sophy should be as truly a woman as Émile is a man, i.e., she must possess all those characters of her sex which are required to enable her to play her part in the physical and moral order. Let us inquire to begin with in what respects her sex differs from our own.

But for her sex, a woman is a man; she has the same organs, the same needs, the same faculties. The machine is the same in its construction; its parts, its working, and its appearance are similar. Regard it as you will the difference is only in degree.

Yet where sex is concerned man and woman are unlike; each is the complement of the other; the difficulty in comparing them lies in our inability to decide, in either case, what is a matter of sex, and what is not. General differences present themselves to the comparative anatomist and even to the superficial observer; they seem not to be a matter of sex; yet they are really sex differences, though the connection eludes our observation. How far such differences may extend we cannot tell; all we know for certain is that where man and woman are alike we have to do with the characteristics of the species; where they are unlike, we have to do with the characteristics of sex. Considered from these two standpoints, we find so many instances of likeness and unlikeness that it is perhaps one of the greatest of marvels how nature has contrived to make two beings so like and yet so different.

These resemblances and differences must have an influence on the moral nature; this inference is obvious, and it is confirmed by experience; it shows the vanity of the disputes as to the superiority or equality of the sexes; as if each sex, pursuing the path marked out for it by nature, were not more perfect in that very divergence than if it more closely resembled the other. A perfect man and a perfect woman should no more be alike in mind than in face, and perfection admits of neither less nor more.

In the union of the sexes each alike contributes to the common end, but in different ways. From this diversity springs the first difference which may be observed between man and woman in their moral relations. The man should be strong and active; the woman should be weak and passive; the one must have both the power and the will; it is enough that the other should offer little resistance.

When this principle is admitted, it follows that woman is specially made for man's delight. If man in his turn ought to be pleasing in her eyes, the necessity is less urgent, his virtue is in his strength, he pleases because he is strong. I grant you this is not the law of love, but it is the law of nature, which is older than love itself.

If woman is made to please and to be in subjection to man, she ought to make herself pleasing in his eyes and not provoke him to anger; her strength is in her charms, by their means she should compel him to discover and use his strength. The surest way of arousing this strength is to make it necessary by resistance. Thus pride comes to the help of desire and each exults in the other's victory. This is the origin of attack and defence, of the boldness of one sex and the timidity of the other, and even of the shame and modesty with which nature has armed the weak for the conquest of the strong.

Who can possibly suppose that nature has prescribed the same advances to the one sex as to the other, or that the first to feel desire should be the first to show it? What strange depravity of judgment! The consequences of the act being so different for the two sexes, is it natural that they should enter upon it with equal boldness? How can any one fail to see that when the share of each is so unequal, if the one were not controlled by modesty as the other is controlled by nature, the result would be the destruction of both, and the human race would perish through the very means ordained for its continuance?

Women so easily stir a man's senses and fan the ashes of a dying passion, that if philosophy ever succeeded in introducing this custom into any unlucky country, especially if it were a warm country where more women are born than men, the men, tyrannized over by the women, would at last become their victims, and would be dragged to their death without the least chance of escape.

Female animals are without this sense of shame, but what of that? Are their desires as boundless as those of women, which are curbed by this shame? The desires of the animals are the result of necessity, and when the need is satisfied, the desire ceases; they no longer make a feint of repulsing the male, they do it in earnest. Their seasons of complaisance are short and soon over. Impulse and restraint are alike the work of nature. But what would take the place of this negative instinct in women if you rob them of their modesty?

The Most High has deigned to do honour to mankind; he has endowed man with boundless passions, together with a law to guide them, so that man may be alike free and self-controlled; though swayed by these passions man is endowed with reason by which to control them. Woman is also endowed with boundless passions; God has given her modesty to restrain them. Moreover, he has given to both a present reward for the right use of their powers, in the delight which springs from that right use of them, i.e., the taste for right conduct established as the law of our behaviour. To my mind this is far higher than the instinct of the beasts.

Whether the woman shares the man's passion or not, whether she is willing or unwilling to satisfy it, she always repulses him and defends herself, though not always with the same vigour, and therefore not always with the same success. If the siege is to be successful, the besieged must permit or direct the attack. How skilfully can she stimulate the efforts of the aggressor. The freest and most delightful of activities does not permit of any real violence; reason and nature are alike against it; nature, in that she has given the weaker party strength enough to resist if she chooses; reason, in that actual violence is not only most brutal in itself, but it defeats its own ends, not only because the man thus declares war against his companion and thus gives her a right to defend her person and her liberty even at the cost of the enemy's life, but also because the woman alone is the judge of her condition, and a child would have no father if any man might usurp a father's rights.

Thus the different constitution of the two sexes leads us to a third conclusion, that the stronger party seems to be master, but is as a matter of fact dependent on the weaker, and that, not by any foolish custom of gallantry, nor yet by the magnanimity of the protector, but by an inexorable law of nature. For nature has endowed woman with a power of stimulating man's passions in excess of man's power of satisfying those passions, and has thus made him dependent on her goodwill, and compelled him in his turn to endeavour to please her, so that she may be willing to yield to his superior strength. Is it weakness which yields to force, or is it voluntary self-surrender? This uncertainty constitutes the chief charm of the man's victory, and the woman is usually cunning enough to leave him in doubt. In this respect the woman's mind exactly resembles her body; far from being ashamed of her weakness, she is proud of it; her soft muscles offer no resistance, she professes that she cannot lift the lightest weight; she would be ashamed to be strong. And why? Not only to gain an appearance of refinement; she is too clever for that; she is providing herself beforehand with excuses, with the right to be weak if she chooses.

The experience we have gained through our vices has considerably modified the views held in older times; we rarely hear of violence for which there is so little occasion that it would hardly be credited. Yet such stories are common enough among the Jews and ancient Greeks; for such views belong to the simplicity of nature, and have only been uprooted by our profligacy. If fewer deeds of violence are quoted in our days, it is not that men are more temperate, but because they are less credulous, and a complaint which would have been believed among a simple people would only excite laughter among ourselves; therefore silence is the better course. There is a law in Deuteronomy, under which the outraged maiden was punished, along with her assailant, if the crime were committed in a town; but if in the country or in a lonely place, the latter alone was punished. 'For', says the law, 'the maiden cried for help and there was none to hear.' From this merciful interpretation of the law, girls learnt not to let themselves be surprised in lonely places.

This change in public opinion has had a perceptible effect on our morals. It has produced our modern gallantry. Men have found that their pleasures depend, more than they expected, on the goodwill of the fair sex, and have secured this goodwill by attentions which have had their reward.

See how we find ourselves led unconsciously from the physical to the moral constitution, how from the grosser union of the sexes spring the sweet laws of love. Woman reigns, not by the will of man, but by the decrees of nature herself; she had the power long before she showed it. That same Hercules who proposed to violate all the fifty daughters of Thespis was compelled to spin at the feet of Omphale,[1] and Samson, the strong man, was less strong than Delilah.[2] This power cannot be taken from woman; it is hers by right; she would have lost it long ago, were it possible.

The consequences of sex are wholly unlike for man and woman. The male is only a male now and again, the female is always a female, or at least all her youth; everything reminds her of her sex; the performance of her functions requires a special constitution. She needs care during pregnancy and freedom from work when her child is born; she must have a quiet, easy life while she nurses her children; their education calls for patience and gentleness, for a zeal and love which nothing can dismay; she forms a bond between father and child, she alone can win the father's love for his children and convince him that they are indeed his own. What loving care is required to preserve a united family! And there should be no question of virtue in all this, it must be a labour of love, without which the human race would be doomed to extinction.

The mutual duties of the two sexes are not, and cannot be, equally binding on both. Women do wrong to complain of the inequality of man-made laws; this inequality is not of man's making, or at any rate it is not the result of mere prejudice, but of reason. She to whom nature has entrusted the care of the children must hold herself responsible for them to their father. No doubt every breach of faith is wrong, and every faithless husband, who robs his wife of the sole reward of the stern duties of her sex, is cruel and unjust; but the faithless wife is worse; she destroys the family and breaks the bonds of nature; when she gives her husband children who are not his own, she is false both to him and them, her crime is not infidelity but treason. To my mind, it is the source of dissension and of crime of every kind. Can any position be more wretched than that of the unhappy father who, when he clasps his child to his breast, is haunted by the suspicion that this is the child of another, the badge of his own dishonour, a thief who is robbing his own children of their inheritance. Under such circumstances the family is little more than a group of secret enemies, armed against each other by a guilty woman, who compels them to pretend to love one another.

Thus it is not enough that a wife should be faithful; her husband, along with his friends and neighbours, must believe in her fidelity; she must be modest, devoted, retiring; she should have the witness not only of a good conscience, but of a good reputation. In a word, if a father must love his children, he must be able to respect their mother. For these reasons it is not enough that the woman should be chaste, she must preserve her reputation and her good name. From these principles there arises not only a moral difference between the sexes, but also a fresh motive for duty and propriety, which prescribes to women in particular the most scrupulous attention to their conduct, their manners, their behaviour. Vague assertions as to the equality of the sexes and the similarity of their duties are only empty words; they are no answer to my argument.

It is a poor sort of logic to quote isolated exceptions against laws so firmly established. Women, you say, are not always bearing children. Granted; yet that is their proper business. Because there are a hundred or so of large towns in the world where women live licentiously and have few children, will you maintain that it is their business to have few children? And what would become of your towns if the remote country districts, with their simpler and purer women, did not make up for the barrenness of your fine ladies? There are plenty of country places where women with only four or five children are reckoned unfruitful. In conclusion, although here and there a woman may have few children, what difference does it make? Is it any the less a woman's business to be a mother? And do not the general laws of nature and morality make provision for this state of things?

Even if there were these long intervals, which you assume, between the periods of pregnancy, can a woman suddenly change her way of life without danger? Can she be a nursing mother today and a soldier tomorrow? Will she change her tastes and her feelings as a chameleon changes his colour? Will she pass at once from the privacy of household duties and indoor occupations to the buffeting of the winds, the toils, the labours, the perils of war? Will she be now timid, now brave, now fragile, now robust? If the young men of Paris find a soldier's life too hard for them, how would a woman put up with it, a woman who has hardly ventured out of doors without a parasol and who has scarcely put a foot to the ground? Will she make a good soldier at an age when even men are retiring from this arduous business?

There are countries, I grant you, where women bear and rear children with little or no difficulty, but in those lands the men go half-naked in all weathers, they strike down the wild beasts, they carry a canoe as easily as a knapsack, they pursue the chase for 700 or 800 leagues, they sleep in the open on the bare ground, they bear incredible fatigues and go many days without food. When women become strong, men become still stronger; when men become soft, women become softer; change both the terms and the ratio remains unaltered.

I am quite aware that Plato, in the *Republic*, assigns the same gymnastics to women and men. Having got rid of the family there is no place for women in his system of government, so he is forced to turn them into men. That great genius has worked out his plans in detail and has provided for every contingency; he has even provided against a difficulty which in all likelihood no one would ever have raised; but he has not succeeded in meeting the real difficulty. I am not speaking of the alleged community of wives which has often been laid to his charge; this assertion only shows that his detractors have never read his works. I refer to that political promiscuity under which the same occupations are assigned to both sexes alike, a scheme which could only lead to intolerable evils; I refer to that subversion of all the tenderest of our natural feelings, which he sacrificed to an artificial sentiment which can only exist by their aid. Will the bonds of convention hold firm without some foundation in nature? Can devotion to the state exist apart from the love of those near and dear to us? Can patriotism thrive except in the soil of that miniature fatherland, the home? Is it not the good son, the good husband, the good father, who makes the good citizen?

When once it is proved that men and women are and ought to be unlike in constitution and in temperament, it follows that their education must be different. Nature teaches us that they should work together, but that each has its own share of the work; the end is the same, but the means are different, as are also the feelings which direct them. We have attempted to paint a natural man, let us try to paint a helpmeet for him.

You must follow nature's guidance if you would walk aright. The native characters of sex should be respected as nature's handiwork. You are always saying, 'Women have such and such faults, from which we are free.' You are misled by your vanity; what would be faults in you are virtues in them; and things would go worse if they were without these so-called faults. Take care that they do not degenerate into evil, but beware of destroying them.

On the other hand, women are always exclaiming that we educate them for nothing but vanity and coquetry, that we keep them amused with trifles that we may be their masters; we are responsible, so they say, for the faults we attribute to them. How silly! What have men to do with the education of girls? What is there to hinder their mothers educating them as they please? There are no colleges for girls; so much the better for them! Would God there were none for the boys, their education would be more sensible and more wholesome. Who is it that compels a girl to waste her time on foolish trifles? Are they forced, against their will, to spend half their time over their toilet, following the example set them by you? Who prevents you teaching them, or having them taught, whatever seems good in your eyes? Is it our fault that we are charmed by their beauty and delighted by their airs and graces, if we are attracted and flattered by the arts they learn from you, if we love to see them prettily dressed, if we let them display at leisure the weapons by which we are subjugated? Well then, educate them like men. The more women are like men, the less influence they will have over men, and then men will be masters indeed.

All the faculties common to both sexes are not equally shared between them, but taken as a whole they are fairly divided. Woman is worth more as a woman and less as a man; when she makes a good use of her own rights, she has the best of it; when she tries to usurp our rights, she is our inferior. It is impossible to controvert this, except by quoting exceptions after the usual fashion of the partisans of the fair sex.

To cultivate the masculine virtues in women and to neglect their own is evidently to do them an injury. Women are too clear-sighted to be thus deceived; when they try to usurp our privileges they do not abandon their own; with this result: they are unable to make use of two incompatible things, so they fall below their own level as women, instead of rising to the level of men. If you are a sensible mother you will take my advice. Do not try to make your daughter a good man in defiance of nature. Make her a good woman, and be sure it will be better both for her and us.

Does this mean that she must be brought up in ignorance and kept to housework only? Is she to be man's handmaid or his helpmeet? Will he dispense with her greatest charm, her companionship? To keep her a slave will he prevent her knowing and feeling? Will he make an automaton of her? No, indeed, that is not the teaching of nature, who has given women such a pleasant easy wit. On the contrary, nature means them to think, to will, to love, to cultivate their minds as well as their persons; she puts these weapons in their hands to make up for their lack of strength and to enable them to direct the strength of men. They should learn many things, but only such things as are suitable.

When I consider the special purpose of woman, when I observe her inclinations or reckon up her duties, everything combines to indicate the mode of education she requires. Men and women are made for each other, but their mutual dependence differs in degree; man is dependent on woman through his desires; woman is dependent on man through her desires and also through her needs; he could do without her better than she can do without him. She cannot fulfil her purpose in life without his aid, without his goodwill, without his respect; she is dependent on our feelings, on the price we put upon her virtue, and the opinion we have of her charms and her deserts. Nature herself has decreed that woman, both for herself and her children, should be at the mercy of man's judgment.

Worth alone will not suffice, a woman must be thought worthy; nor beauty, she must be admired; nor virtue, she must be respected. A woman's honour does not depend on her conduct alone, but on her reputation, and no woman who permits herself to be considered vile is really virtuous. A man has no one but himself to consider, and so long as he does right he may defy public opinion; but when a woman does right her task is only half finished, and what people think of her matters as much as what she really is. Hence her education must, in this respect, be different from man's education. 'What will people think?' is the grave of a man's virtue and the throne of a woman's.

The children's health depends in the first place on the mother's, and the early education of man is also in a woman's hands; his morals, his passions, his tastes, his pleasures, his happiness itself, depend on her. A woman's education must therefore be planned in relation to man. To be pleasing in his sight, to win his respect and love, to train him in childhood, to tend him in manhood, to counsel and console, to make his life pleasant and happy, these are the duties of woman for all time, and this is what she should be taught while she is young. The further we depart from this principle, the further we shall be from our goal, and all our precepts will fail to secure her happiness or our own.

Every woman desires to be pleasing in men's eyes, and this is right; but there is a great difference between wishing to please a man of worth, a really lovable man, and seeking to please those foppish manikins who are a disgrace to their own sex and to the sex which they imitate. Neither nature nor reason can induce a woman to love an effeminate person, nor will she win love by imitating such a person.

If a woman discards the quiet modest bearing of her sex, and adopts the airs of such foolish creatures, she is not following her vocation, she is forsaking it; she is robbing herself of the rights to which she lays claim. 'If we were different,' she says, 'the men would not like us.' She is mistaken. Only a fool likes folly; to wish to attract such men only shows her own foolishness. If there were no frivolous men, women would soon make them, and women are more responsible for men's follies than men are for theirs. The woman who loves true manhood and seeks to find favour in its sight will adopt means adapted to her ends. Woman is a coquette by profession, but her coquetry varies with her aims; let these aims be in accordance with those of nature, and a woman will receive a fitting education.

Even the tiniest little girls love finery; they are not content to be pretty, they must be admired; their little airs and graces show that their heads are full of this idea, and as soon as they can understand they are controlled by 'What will people think of you?' If you are foolish enough to try this way with little boys, it will not have the same effect; give them their freedom and their sports, and they care very little what people think; it is a work of time to bring them under the control of this law.

However acquired, this early education of little girls is an excellent thing in itself. As the birth of the body must precede the birth of the mind, so the training of the body must precede the cultivation of the mind. This is true of both sexes; but the aim of physical training for boys and girls is not the same; in the one case it is the development of strength, in the other of grace; not that these qualities should be peculiar to either sex, but that their relative values should be different. Women should be strong enough to do anything gracefully; men should be skilful enough to do anything easily.

The exaggeration of feminine delicacy leads to effeminacy in men. Women should not be strong like men but for them, so that their sons may be strong. Convents and boarding-schools, with their plain food and ample opportunities for amusements, races, and games in the open air and in the garden, are better in this respect than the home, where the little girl is fed on delicacies, continually encouraged or reproved, where she is kept sitting in a stuffy room, always under her mother's eye, afraid to stand or walk or speak or breathe, without a moment's freedom to play or jump or run or shout, or to be her natural, lively, little self; there is either harmful indulgence or misguided severity, and no trace of reason. In this fashion heart and body are alike destroyed.

As I have already said, the duties of their sex are more easily recognized than performed. They must learn in the first place to love those duties by considering the advantages to be derived from them – that is the only way to make duty easy. Every age and condition has its own duties. We are quick to see our duty if we love it. Honour your position as a woman, and in whatever station of life to which it shall please heaven to call you, you will be well off. The essential thing is to be what nature has made you; women are only too ready to be what men would have them.

The search for abstract and speculative truths, for principles and axioms in science, for all that tends to wide generalization, is beyond a woman's grasp; their studies should be thoroughly practical. It is their business to apply the principles discovered by men, it is their place to make the observations which lead men to discover those principles. A woman's thoughts, beyond the range of her immediate duties, should be directed to the study of men, or the acquirement of that agreeable learning whose sole end is the formation of taste; for the works of genius are beyond her reach, and she has neither the accuracy nor the attention for success in the exact sciences; as for the physical sciences, to decide the relations between living creatures and the laws of nature is the task of that sex which is more active and enterprising, which sees more things, that sex which is possessed of greater strength and is more accustomed to the exercise of that strength. Woman, weak as she is and limited in her range of observation, perceives and judges the forces at her disposal to supplement her weakness, and those forces are the passions of man. Her own mechanism is more powerful than ours; she has many levers which may set the human heart in motion. She must find a way to make us desire what she cannot achieve unaided and what she considers necessary or pleasing; therefore she must have a thorough knowledge of man's mind; not an abstract knowledge of the mind of man in general, but the mind of those who are about her, the mind of those men who have authority over her, either by law or custom. She must learn to divine their feelings from speech and action, look and gesture. By her own speech and action, look and gesture, she must be able to inspire them with the feelings she desires, without seeming to have any such purpose. The men will have a better philosophy of the human heart, but she will read more accurately in the heart of men. Woman should discover, so to speak, an experimental morality, man should reduce it to a system. Woman has more wit, man more genius; woman observes, man reasons; together they provide the clearest light and the profoundest knowledge which is possible to the unaided human mind; in a word, the surest knowledge of self and of others of which the human race is capable. In this way art may constantly tend to the perfection of the instrument which nature has given us.

NOTES

1. [Ed.] *Hercules . . . Omphale*: Hercules, a mythical Greek hero, celebrated for his courage, but also a figure with lustful appetites. Omphale, Queen of Lydia, to whom Hercules was sold as punishment for murdering Iphitus.

2. [Ed.] *Samson . . . Delilah*: Samson, judge of Israel, who, through his infatuation with Delilah, violated his commitment to God. She ultimately betrayed him to his Philistine enemies (see Judges 13–16).

STUDY QUESTIONS

1. 'But for her sex, a woman is a man.' What implications does this remark have for Rousseau's account of the nature of woman?
2. Rousseau appears to be arguing for the complementarity of the sexes. What parts of this passage suggest a hierarchy of male over female rather than an equality of these masculine/feminine qualities?
3. 'The male is only a male now and again, the female is always a female.' How does this idea relate to Rousseau's account of the way in which women should be treated by society?
4. '"What will people think?" is the grave of a man's virtue and the throne of a woman's.' What does Rousseau mean by this, and why might this lead to the conclusion that Rousseau is 'anti-feminist'?

SELECT BIBLIOGRAPHY

General

J. H. Broome, *Rousseau* (London: Edward Arnold, 1963).

R. Grimsley, *The Philosophy of Rousseau* (Oxford: Oxford University Press, 1973).

J. Schwartz, *The Sexual Politics of Jean-Jacques Rousseau* (Chicago: University of Chicago Press, 1984).

For feminist analysis

C. Battersby, *Gender and Genius: Towards a Feminist Aesthetics* (London: The Women's Press, 1989).

K. Green, *The Woman of Reason* (Cambridge: Polity Press, 1995).

J. Grimshaw, *Feminist Philosophers* (Brighton: Harvester Wheatsheaf, 1986).

M. Le Doeuff, *The Philosophical Imaginary* (London: Athlone Press, 1989).
M. J. Falco (ed.), *Feminist Interpretations of Mary Wollstonecraft* (Pennsylvania: Pennsylvania State University Press, 1996).
G. Lloyd, *The Man of Reason* (London: Methuen, 1984).
S. Okin, *Women in Western Political Thought* (London: Virago, 1980).
C. Sawbridge Macaulay-Graham, *Letters on Education* (London: C. Dilly, 1790).
M. E. Waithe, 'Women Philosophers of the Seventeenth, Eighteenth and Nineteenth Centuries', in M. E. Waithe (ed.), *A History of Women Philosophers*, vol. 3 (Dordrecht: Kluwer Academic Press, 1991), pp. 217–22.
M. Wollstonecraft, *A Vindication of the Rights of Woman* (Harmondsworth: Pelican, 1975).

13 G. W. F. Hegel 1770–1831

Introduction and Background

Hegel's philosophy is notoriously difficult, principally because of his complex and distinctive terminology. Yet, as Peter Singer comments in his highly accessible introduction to Hegel's ideas, his philosophy has had the most profound influence.

Hegel's main claim is that the change encountered in human life is not without meaning; change is symptomatic of the progress of history. According to Hegel, 'the history of the world is none other than the progress of the consciousness of freedom'.[1] For Hegel, 'freedom' should not be defined as freedom from constraint; rather conformity to reason is the basis of true freedom. In this sense, Hegel's thought builds on that of Kant. Consequently, Hegel's ideal of freedom lies not with the principle of universal suffrage. On the contrary, he rejects the concept of democracy, feeling that people do not vote according to the dictates of reason; rather, personal likes and dislikes too often dominate the ideas of the masses. His ideal form of government is constitutional monarchy. This political structure coheres with Hegel's account of 'the organic community'. In this structure, all work towards the good of society. All have their place in a society which conforms to the strict hierarchy defining a society which conforms to the supremacy of reason.

Hegel's understanding of the subordinate place of women within such a society is hardly surprising given the hierarchical structure he proposes. Man is defined as 'the one', woman as 'the other'. Man is 'powerful and active', woman 'passive and subjective'. Moreover, reason is equated with the male, who is said to embody the ideal, whilst woman is equated with nature, notably with feeling and intuitive responses. This distinction affects his notion of who should practise philosophy, and Hegel adopts Kant's belief that only men can be philosophers. This claim is grounded in his understanding of male and female. Women cannot be effective philosophers because, unlike men, they do not concern themselves with universal principles. According to Hegel, women make decisions on the basis of what he terms 'contingent inclination': in other words, their judgements are based on feelings and emotions.

The theories of two of the most influential thinkers of the nineteenth century are indebted to Hegel. Karl Marx was to adapt Hegel's view of history to show the inexorable march of the proletariat. Ludwig Feuerbach developed the connection Hegel made between the idea of God and the ideals of humanity. 'God', according to Feuerbach, is the repository for human values.[2] This idea has been developed in the last part of the twentieth century by 'non-realists' such as Don Cupitt, and by feminists engaged in the task of exposing the way in which the concept of God has deified key masculinist values.[3] Hegel's ideas thus remain influential. Is this influence problematic if one considers the understanding of woman which arises from his key concepts?

ELEMENTS OF THE PHILOSOPHY OF RIGHT (1821)*

The one [sex] is therefore spirituality which divides itself up into personal sufficiency with being *for itself* and the knowledge and volition of *free universality*, i.e. into the self-consciousness of conceptual thought and the volition of the objective and ultimate end. And the *other* is spirituality which maintains itself in unity as knowledge and volition of the substantial in the form of concrete *individuality* and *feeling*. In its external relations, the former is powerful and active, the latter passive and subjective. Man therefore has his actual substantial life in the state, in learning, etc., and otherwise in work and struggle with the external world and with himself, so that it is only through his division that he fights his way to self-sufficient unity with himself. In the family, he has a peaceful intuition of this unity, and an emotive and subjective ethical life. Woman, however, has her substantial vocation in the family, and her ethical disposition consists in this [family] *piety*.

> In one of the most sublime presentations of piety – the *Antigone* of Sophocles[1] – this quality is therefore declared to be primarily the law of woman, and it is presented as the law of emotive and subjective substantiality, of inwardness which has not yet been fully actualized, as the law of ancient gods and of the chthonic real [*des Unterirdischen*] as an eternal law of which no one knows whence it came, and in opposition to the public law, the law of the state – an opposition of the highest order in ethics and therefore in tragedy, and one which is individualized in femininity and masculinity in the same play.

*From the translation by H. B. Nisbet, edited by Allen W. Wood (Cambridge: Cambridge University Press, 1991).

Addition

Women may be well educated, but they are not made for the higher sciences, for philosophy and certain artistic productions which require a universal element. Women may have insights, taste, and delicacy, but they do not possess the ideal. The difference between man and woman is the difference between animal and plant; the animal is closer in character to man, the plant to woman, for the latter is a more peaceful [process of] unfolding whose principle is the more indeterminate unity of feeling. When women are in charge of government, the state is in danger, for their actions are based not on the demands of universality but on contingent inclination and opinion. The education of women takes place imperceptibly, as if through the atmosphere of representational thought, more through living than through the acquisition of knowledge, whereas man attains his position only through the attainment of thought and numerous technical exertions.

NOTE

1. [Ed.] *Antigone*: heroine of Sophocles' play, Antigone is the daughter of Oedipus. Her brothers, Polynices and Eteocles, die fighting each other for control of Thebes. Creon, King of Thebes, refuses to bury Polynices who died attacking Thebes. Antigone refuses to accept this decree, loyalty to her family being more important to her than loyalty to the state. For this, Creon condemns her to death.

STUDY QUESTIONS

1. To what extent does this passage offer examples of the reason/nature dichotomy common in western philosophical thinking?
2. 'The difference between man and woman is the difference between animal and plant.' What elements of woman's 'nature' lead Hegel to this conclusion?

SELECT BIBLIOGRAPHY

General

P. Singer, *Hegel* (Oxford: Oxford University Press, 1983).
C. Taylor, *Hegel and Modern Society* (Cambridge: Cambridge University Press, 1979).

For feminist analysis

M. Le Doeuff, *The Philosophical Imaginary*, translated by C. Gordon (London: Athlone Press, 1989).

J. Hodge, 'Women and the Hegelian State', in E. Kennedy and S. Mendus (eds), *Women in Western Political Philosophy* (Brighton: Wheatsheaf, 1987).

P. Jagentowicz Mills (ed.), *Feminist Interpretations of Hegel* (Pennsylvania: Pennsylvania State University Press, 1996).

L. Irigaray, 'The Eternal Irony of Community', in *Speculum of the Other Woman*, translated by G. Gill (Ithaca, NY: Cornell, 1985).

G. Lloyd, *The Man of Reason* (London: Methuen, 1984).

PART V

MISOGYNY IN THE MODERN AGE

14 ARTHUR SCHOPENHAUER 1788–1860

Introduction and Background

With the possible exception of Tertullian and the *Malleus Maleficarum*, it is difficult to find a more vitriolic attack on women than that offered by Schopenhauer in his essay 'On Women'. It is tempting to dismiss Schopenhauer's writings on the nature of woman as hyperbole isolated from the broad mass of philosophical writings. Indeed his complex relationship with his mother Johanna, a successful society hostess and popular novelist, may go some way to explaining his misogynistic views. However, his views cannot be understood in isolation from the main body of philosophical material within the western tradition. Like Kant, Schopenhauer argues that women's inferior powers of reason have an impact upon their ability to be moral. Like Rousseau, he advocates an education for woman commensurate with her status and function in life. Presaging Freud, his views suggest a belief that 'biology is destiny', woman's body bearing testimony to her inherent inferiority to man. Schopenhauer's thought is not, then, an aberration in the western tradition, for he explicitly builds upon and develops attitudes towards women implicit in the arguments of his fellow philosophers.

The timing of Schopenhauer's onslaught is interesting, and it could be argued that it arises at precisely the time when 'the Rights of Woman' was starting to become a real issue. Mary Wollstonecraft wrote her *Vindication of the Rights of Woman* in 1792. Nine years after Schopenhauer's death John Stuart Mill's treatise for female equality, *On the Subjection of Women*, was published, a work which owed much to the ideas of Mill's wife, Harriet Taylor. The 'spirit of the age' seemed to be moving in the direction of women's rights. In such a setting a passionate backlash was likely, and Schopenhauer appears to have provided it.

*ON WOMEN**

Schiller's[1] poem in honour of women, *Würde der Frauen*, is the result of much careful thought, and it appeals to the reader by its antithetic style and its use of contrast; but as an expression of the true praise which should be accorded to them, it is, I think, inferior to these few words of Jouy's:[2] 'Without women the beginning of our life would be helpless; the middle, devoid of pleasure; and the end, of consolation.' The same thing is more feelingly expressed by Byron in *Sardanapalus*:

* From *Schopenhauer Selections*, edited by D. H. Parker, translated by T. D. Saunders (New York: Charles Scribner, 1928).

> The very first
> Of human life must spring from women's breast,
> Your first small words are taught you from her lips,
> Your first tears quench'd by her, and your last sighs
> Too often breathed out in a woman's hearing,
> When men have shrunk from the ignoble care
> Of watching the last hour of him who led them.
> (Act I, Scene 2)

These two passages indicate the right standpoint for appreciation of women.

You need only look at the way in which she is formed to see that woman is not meant to undergo great labour, whether of the mind or of the body. She pays the debt of life not by what she does but by what she suffers; by the pains of childbearing and care for the child, and by submission to her husband, to whom she should be a patient and cheering companion. The keenest sorrows and joys are not for her, nor is she called upon to display a great deal of strength. The current of her life should be more gentle, peaceful and trivial than man's, without being essentially happier or unhappier.

Women are directly fitted for acting as the nurses and teachers of our early childhood by the fact that they are themselves childish, frivolous and short-sighted; in a word, they are big children all their life long – a kind of intermediate stage between the child and the full grown man, who is 'man' in the strict sense of the word. See how a girl will fondle a child for days together, dance with it and sing to it; and then think what a man, with the best will in the world, could do if he were put in her place.

With young girls Nature seems to have had in view what, in the language of the drama, is called a *coup de théâtre*.[3] For a few years she dowers them with a wealth of beauty and is lavish in her gift of charm, at the expense of the rest of their life, in order that during those years they may capture the fantasy of some man to such a degree that he is hurried into undertaking the honourable care of them, in some form or other, as long as they live – a step for which there would not appear to be any sufficient warranty if reason only directed his thoughts. Accordingly Nature has equipped woman, as she does all her creatures, with the weapons and implements requisite for the safeguarding of her existence, and for just as long as it is necessary for her to have them. Here, as elsewhere, Nature proceeds with her usual economy; for just as the female ant, after fecundation, loses her wings, which are then superfluous, nay, actually a danger to the business of breeding; so, after giving birth to one or two children, a woman generally loses her beauty; probably, indeed, for similar reasons.

And so we find that young girls, in their hearts, look upon domestic affairs or work of any kind as of secondary importance, if not actually as a mere jest. The only business that really claims their earnest attention is love, making conquests, and everything connected with this – dress, dancing, and so on.

The nobler and more perfect a thing is, the later and slower it is in arriving at maturity. A man reaches the maturity of his reasoning powers and mental faculties hardly before the age of twenty-eight; a woman, at eighteen. And then, too, in the case of woman, it is only reason of a sort – very niggard in its dimensions. This is why women remain children their whole life long; never seeing anything but what is quite close to them, cleaving to the present moment, taking appearance for reality, and preferring trifles to matters of the first importance. For it is by virtue of his reasoning faculty that man does not live in the present only, like the brute, but looks about him and considers the past and the future; and this is the origin of prudence, as well as of that care and anxiety which many people exhibit. Both the advantages and the disadvantages which this involves, are shared in by the woman to a smaller extent because of her weaker power of reasoning. She may, in fact, be described as intellectually short-sighted, because, while she has an intuitive understanding of what lies quite close to her, her field of vision is narrow and does not reach to what is remote: so that things which are absent or past or to come have much less effect upon women than upon men. This is the reason why women are more often inclined to be extravagant, and sometimes carry their inclination to a length that borders upon madness. In their hearts women think that it is men's business to earn money and theirs to spend it – if possible during their husband's life, but, at any rate, after his death. The very fact that their husband hands them over his earnings for purposes of housekeeping strengthens them in this belief.

However many disadvantages all this may involve, there is at least this to be said in its favour: that the woman lives more in the present than the man, and that, if the present is at all tolerable, she enjoys it more eagerly. This is the source of that cheerfulness which is peculiar to woman, fitting her to amuse man in his hours of recreation, and, in case of need, to console him when he is borne down by the weight of his cares.

It is by no means a bad plan to consult women in matters of difficulty, as the Germans used to do in ancient times; for their way of looking at things is quite different from ours, chiefly in the fact that they like to take the shortest way to their goal, and, in general, manage to fix their eyes upon what lies before them; while we, as a rule, see far beyond it, just because it is in front of our noses. In cases like this, we need to be brought back to the right standpoint, so as to recover the near and simple view.

Then, again, women are decidedly more sober in their judgment than we are, so that they do not see more in things than is really there; whilst, if our passions are aroused, we are apt to see things in an exaggerated way, or imagine what does not exist.

The weakness of their reasoning faculty also explains why it is that women show more sympathy for the unfortunate than men do, and so treat them with more kindness and interest; and why it is that, on the contrary, they are inferior to men in point of justice, and less honourable and conscientious. For it is just because their reasoning power is weak that present circumstances have such a hold over them, and those concrete things which lie directly before their eyes exercise a power which is seldom counteracted to any extent by abstract principles of thought, by fixed rules of conduct, firm resolutions, or, in general, by consideration for the past and the future, or regard for what is absent and remote. Accordingly, they possess the first and main elements that go to make a virtuous character, but they are deficient in those secondary qualities which are often a necessary instrument in the formation of it.

Hence it will be found that the fundamental fault of the female character is that it has *no sense of justice*. This is mainly due to the fact, already mentioned, that women are defective in the powers of reasoning and deliberation; but it is also traceable to the position which Nature has assigned to them as the weaker sex. They are dependent, not upon strength, but upon craft; and hence their instinctive capacity for cunning, and their ineradicable tendency to say what is not true. For as lions are provided with claws and teeth, and elephants and boars with tusks, bulls with horns, and the cuttle fish with its cloud of inky fluid, so Nature has equipped woman, for her defence and protection, with the arts of dissimulation; and all the power which Nature has conferred upon man in the shape of physical strength and reason has been bestowed upon women in this form. Hence dissimulation is innate in woman, and almost as must a quality of the stupid as of the clever. It is as natural for them to make use of it on every occasion as it is for those animals to employ their means of defence when they are attacked; they have a feeling that in doing so they are only within their rights. Therefore a woman who is perfectly truthful and not given to dissimulation is perhaps an impossibility, and for this very reason they are so quick at seeing through dissimulation in others that it is not a wise thing to attempt it with them. But this fundamental defect which I have stated, with all that it entails, gives rise to falsity, faithlessness, treachery, ingratitude, and so on. Perjury in a court of justice is more often committed by women than by men. It may, indeed, be generally questioned whether women ought to be sworn at all. From time to time one finds repeated cases everywhere of ladies, who want for nothing, taking things from shop-counters when no one is looking and making off with them.

Nature has appointed that the propagation of the species shall be the business of men who are young, strong and handsome; so that the race may not degenerate. This is the firm will and purpose of Nature in regard to the species, and it finds its expression in the passions of women. There is no law that is older or more powerful than this. Woe, then, to the man who sets up claims and interests that will conflict with it; whatever he may say and do, they will be unmercifully crushed at the first serious encounter. For the innate rule that governs women's conduct, though it is secret and unformulated, nay, unconscious in its working, is this: *We are justified in deceiving those who think they have acquired rights over the species by paying little attention to the individual, that is, to us. The constitution and, therefore, the welfare of the species have been placed in our hands and committed to our care, through the control we obtain over the next generation, which proceeds from us; let us discharge our duties conscientiously*. But women have no abstract knowledge of this leading principle; they are conscious of it only as a concrete fact; and they have no other method of giving expression to it than the way in which they act when the opportunity arrives. And then their conscience does not trouble them so much as we fancy; for in the darkest recesses of their heart they are aware that, in committing a breach of their duty towards the individual, they have all the better fulfilled their duty towards the species, which is infinitely greater.

And since women exist in the main solely for the propagation of the species, and are not destined for anything else, they live, as a rule, more for the species than for the individual, and in their hearts take the affairs of the species more seriously than those of the individual. This gives their whole life and being a certain levity; the general bent of their character is in a direction fundamentally different from that of man; and it is this which produces that discord in married life which is so frequent, and almost the normal state.

The natural feeling between men is mere indifference, but between women it is actual enmity. The reason of this is that trade-jealousy which, in the case of men, does not go beyond the confines of their own particular pursuit but with women embraces the whole sex; since they have only one kind of business. Even when they meet in the street women look at one another like Guelphs and Ghibellines.[4] And it is a patent fact that when two women make first acquaintance with each other they behave with more constraint and dissimulation than two men would show in a like case; and hence it is that an exchange of compliments between two women is a much more ridiculous proceeding than between two men. Further, whilst a man will, as a general rule, always preserve a certain amount of consideration and humanity in speaking to others, even to those who are in a very inferior position, it is intolerable to see how proudly and disdainfully a fine lady will generally behave towards one who is in a lower social rank (I do not mean a woman who is in her service), whenever she speaks to her. The reason of this may be that, with women, differences of rank are much more precarious than with us; because, while a hundred considerations carry weight in our case, in theirs there is only one, namely, with which man they have found favour; as also that they stand in much nearer relations with one another than men do, in consequence of the one-sided nature of their calling. This makes them endeavour to lay stress upon differences of rank.

It is only the man whose intellect is clouded by his sexual impulses that could give the name of *the fair sex* to that undersized, narrow-shouldered, broad-hipped, and short-legged race: for the whole beauty of the sex is bound up with this impulse. Instead of calling them beautiful, there would be more warrant for describing women as the unaesthetic sex. Neither for music, nor for poetry, nor for fine art, have they really and truly any sense or susceptibility; it is a mere mockery if they make a pretence of it in order to assist their endeavour to please. Hence, as a result of this, they are incapable of taking a *purely objective interest* in anything; and the reason of it seems to me to be as follows. A man tries to acquire *direct* mastery over things, either by understanding them or by forcing them to do his will. But a woman is always and everywhere reduced to obtaining this mastery *indirectly*, namely through a man; and whatever direct mastery she may have is entirely confined to him. And so it lies in woman's nature to look upon everything only as a means for conquering man; and if she takes an interest in anything else it is simulated – a mere roundabout way of gaining her ends by coquetry and feigning what she does not feel. Hence even Rousseau declared: 'Women have, in general, no love of any art; they have no proper knowledge of any; and they have no genius' [*Lettre à d'Alembert*].

No one who sees at all below the surface can have failed to remark the same thing. You need only observe the kind of attention women bestow upon a concert, an opera, or a play – the childish simplicity, for example, with which they keep on chattering during the finest passages in the greatest masterpieces. If it is true that the Greeks excluded women from their theatres, they were quite right in what they did; at any rate you would have been able to hear what was said upon the stage. In our day, besides, or in lieu of saying, 'Let a woman keep silence in the church,' it would be much to the point to say, 'Let a woman keep silence in the theatre.' This might, perhaps, be put up in big letters on the curtain.

And you cannot expect anything else of women if you consider that the most distinguished intellects among the whole sex have never managed to produce a single achievement in the fine arts that is really great, genuine, and original; or given to the world any work of permanent value in any sphere. This is most strikingly shown in regard to painting, where mastery of technique is at least as much within their power as within ours – and hence they are diligent in cultivating it; but still, they have not a single great painting to boast of, just because they are deficient in that objectivity of mind which is so directly indispensable in painting. They never get beyond a subjective point of view. It is quite in keeping with this that ordinary women have no real susceptibility for art at all; for Nature proceeds in strict sequence – *non facit saltum*. The case is not altered by particular and partial exceptions; taken as a whole, women are, and remain, thorough-going philistines, and quite incurable. Hence, with that absurd arrangement which allows them to share the rank and title of their husbands, they are a constant stimulus to his ignoble ambitions. And, further, it is just because they are philistines that modern society, where they take the lead and set the tone, is in such a bad way. Napoleon's saying – that *women have no rank* – should be adopted as the right standpoint in determining their position in society; and as regards their other qualities Chamfort makes the very true remark: 'They are made to trade with our own weaknesses and our follies, but not with our reason. The sympathies that exist between them and men are skin-deep only, and do not touch the mind or the feelings or the character.' They form the *sexus sequior* – the second sex, inferior in every respect to the first; their infirmities should be treated with consideration; but to show them great reverence is extremely ridiculous, and lowers us in their eyes. When Nature made two divisions of the human race, she did not draw the line exactly through the middle. These divisions are polar and opposed to each other, it is true; but the difference between them is not qualitative merely, it is also quantitative.

This is just the view which the ancients took of woman, and the view which people in the East take now; and their judgment as to her proper position is much more correct than ours, with our old French notions of gallantry and our preposterous system of reverence – that highest product of Teutonico-Christian stupidity. These notions have served only to make women more arrogant and overbearing; so that one is occasionally reminded of the holy apes in Benares, who in the consciousness of their sanctity and inviolable position think they can do exactly as they please.

But in the West the woman, and especially the *lady*, finds herself in a false position; for woman, rightly called by the ancients *sexus sequior*, is by no means fit to be the object of our honour and veneration, or to hold her head higher than man and be on equal terms with him. The consequences of this false position are sufficiently obvious. Accordingly it would be a very desirable thing if this Number Two of the human race were in Europe also relegated to her natural place, and an end put to that lady-nuisance, which not only moves all Asia to laughter but would have been ridiculed by Greece and Rome as well. It is impossible to calculate the good effects which such a change would bring about in our social, civil and political arrangements. There would be no necessity for the Salic law:[5] it would be a superfluous truism. In Europe the *lady*, strictly so called, is a being who should not exist at all; she should be either a housewife or a girl who hopes to become one; and she should be brought up, not to be arrogant, but to be thrifty and submissive.

It is just because there are such people as *ladies* in Europe that the women of the lower classes, that is to say, the great majority of the sex, are much more unhappy than they are in the East. And even Lord Byron says: 'Thought of the state of women under the ancient Greeks – convenient enough. Present state, a remnant of the barbarism of the chivalric and the feudal ages – artificial and unnatural. They ought to mind home – and be well fed and clothed – but not minded in society. Well educated, too, in religion – but to read neither poetry nor politics – nothing but books of piety and cookery. Music – drawing – dancing – also a little gardening and ploughing now and then. I have seen them mending the roads in Epirus with good success. Why not, as well as haymaking and milking?'

The laws of marriage prevailing in Europe consider the woman as the equivalent of the man – start, that is to say, from a wrong position. In our part of the world where monogamy is the rule, to marry means to halve one's rights and double one's duties. Now when the laws gave women equal rights with man, they ought to have also endowed her with a masculine intellect. But the fact is that, just in proportion as the honours and privileges which the laws accord to women exceed the amount which Nature gives, there is a diminution in the number of women who really participate in these privileges; and all the remainder are deprived of their natural rights by just so much as is given to the other over and above their share. For the institution of monogamy, and the laws of marriage which it entails, bestow upon the woman an unnatural position of privilege, by considering her throughout as the full equivalent of the man, which is by no means the case; and seeing this men who are shrewd and prudent very often scruple to make so great a sacrifice and to acquiesce in so unfair an arrangement.

Moreover, the bestowal of unnatural rights upon women has imposed upon them unnatural duties, and nevertheless a breach of these duties makes them unhappy. Let me explain. A man may often think that his social or financial position will suffer if he marries, unless he makes some brilliant alliance. His desire will then be to win a woman of his own choice under conditions other than those of marriage, such as will secure her position and that of the children. However fair, reasonable, fit and proper these conditions may be, if the woman consents by forgoing that undue amount of privilege which marriage alone can bestow, she to some extent loses her honour, because marriage is the basis of civic society; and she will lead an unhappy life, since human nature is so constituted that we pay an attention to the opinion of other people which is out of all proportion to its value. On the other hand, if she does not consent, she runs the risk either of having to be given in marriage to a man whom she does not like, or of being landed high and dry as an old maid; for the period during which she has a chance of being settled for life is very short. And in view of this aspect of the institution of monogamy, Thomasius' profoundly learned treatise *On Concubinage* is well worth reading; for it shows that, amongst all nations and in all ages, down to the Lutheran Reformation, concubinage was permitted; nay, that it was an institution which was to a certain extent actually recognized by law, and attended with no dishonour. It was only the Lutheran Reformation that degraded it from this position. It was seen to be a further justification for the marriage of the clergy; and then, after that, the Catholic Church did not dare to remain behindhand in the matter.

The first love of a mother for her child is, with the lower animals as with men, of a purely *instinctive* character, and so it ceases when the child is no longer in a physically helpless condition. After that, the first love should give way to one that is based on habit and reason; but this often fails to make its appearance, especially where the mother did not love the father. The love of a father for his child is of a different order, and more likely to last; because it has its foundation in the fact that in the child he recognizes his own inner self; that is to say, his love for it is metaphysical in its origin.

In almost all nations, whether of the ancient or the modern world, even amongst the Hottentots, property is inherited by the male descendants alone; it is only in Europe that a departure has taken place; but not amongst the nobility, however. That the property which has cost men long years of toil and effort, and been won with so much difficulty, should afterwards come into the hands of women, who then, in their lack of reason, squander it in a short time, or otherwise fool it away, is a grievance and a wrong, as serious as it is common, which should be prevented by limiting the right of women to inherit. In my opinion the best arrangement would be that by which women, whether widows or daughters, should never receive anything beyond the interest for life on property secured by mortgage, and in no case the property itself, or the capital, except where all male descendants fail. The people who make money are men, not women; and it follows from this that women are neither justified in having unconditional possession of it, nor fit persons to be entrusted with its administration. When wealth, in any true sense of the word, that is to say, funds, houses or land, is to go to them as an inheritance, they should never be allowed the free disposition of it. In their case a guardian should always be appointed; and hence they should never be given the free control of their own children, wherever it can be avoided. The vanity of women, even though it should not prove to be greater than that of men, has this much danger in it that it takes an entirely material direction. They are vain, I mean, of their personal beauty, and then of finery, show and magnificence. That is just why they are so much in their element in society. It is this, too, which makes them so inclined to be extravagant, all the more as their reasoning power is low. But with men vanity often takes the direction of non-material advantages, such as intellect, learning, courage.

That woman is by nature meant to obey may be seen by the fact that every woman who is placed in the unnatural position of complete independence, immediately attaches herself to some man, by whom she allows herself to be guided and ruled. It is because she needs a lord and master. If she is young, it will be a lover; if she is old, a priest.

NOTES

1. [Ed.] Johann Christoph Friedrich von *Schiller*: (1759–1805) poet; philosophically important for his work on aesthetics. Schopenhauer is referring to his poem on 'the Dignity of Women'.
2. [Ed.] Victor *Jouy*: (1764–1846) dramatist.
3. [Ed.] *coup de théâtre*: stage effect.
4. [Ed.] *Guelphs and Ghibellines*: two opposing parties in Renaissance Italian politics. 'Guelphs' was the name given to the Pope's faction, 'Ghibellines' to the Emperor's faction.
5. [Ed.] *Salic law*: French law by which females were excluded from succession to the crown.

STUDY QUESTIONS

1. Schopenhauer describes woman as an intermediate stage between child and man, arguing that it is 'the full-grown man who is "man" in the strict sense of the word'. What implications might this statement have for claims that the generic 'man' includes 'woman'?
2. Which parts of this essay might be used to support the claim that Schopenhauer is building upon Kant's work?
3. Schopenhauer argues that women have 'failed' to produce great art or 'any work of permanent value'. What factors are lacking in his

analysis? (You might like to consider Karen Petersen and J. J. Wilson, *Women Artists* (Harper & Row, 1976), who show that throughout history there have been well-known women artists.)

SELECT BIBLIOGRAPHY

General

P. Gardiner, *Schopenhauer* (Harmondsworth: Penguin, 1963).
B. Magee, *The Philosophy of Schopenhauer* (Oxford: Oxford University Press, 1983), which includes useful appendices documenting Schopenhauer's influence on other writers.

For feminist analysis

C. Battersby, *Gender and Genius: Towards a Feminist Aesthetics* (London: The Women's Press, 1989).

15 Friedrich Nietzsche 1844–1900

Introduction and Background

Nietzsche's influence on twentieth-century thinking has been considerable. His proclamation of the death of God, in particular, has caught the imagination of philosophers and theologians concerned with the phenomenon of 'post-modernity'.[1] Nietzsche uses this dramatic image of a dead God to describe the declining power of notions of transcendent truth. If there is no transcendent repository of value, human beings are to be responsible for creating their own notions of good and evil. While this notion reverberates throughout the concepts of postmodernity, his call for creative approaches to morality has found unlikely support in the work of radical feminists like Mary Daly, who have built upon his idea of the autonomous individual who actively affirms all aspects life.[2]

Nietzsche's own life was far removed from his idyll of the *Übermensch* (in the translation that follows, the 'Overman', but more usually translated as the 'Superman'). Nietzsche lived a painfully ascetic life, consistently troubled by ill-health. He lived alone. His relationships with women were few and short-lived. He suffered a long, debilitating death, possibly caused by syphilis contracted whilst a student.

Nietzsche's unfortunate experience of women may go some way to explaining his highly negative attitude towards them. In the following passage from *Thus Spake Zarathustra*, written in the aftermath of Lou Salome's rejection of his proposal of marriage, woman is identified with evil; his ideas on women appear to reflect the pain of that rejection, rather than the conclusions of rational enquiry.

This fascinating woman, whose motto was 'dare everything, need nothing', was one of the first women to practise psychotherapy, and was a confidante of Sigmund Freud. Nietzsche ignores the possibility of woman's intellectual capabilities in direct contrast to his experience of Salome's talents. Like his mentor Schopenhauer, particular concrete experience lies at the centre of his apparently universal generalizations of women.

'OLD AND YOUNG GIRLS'*

'Why dost thou steal along so timidly in the twilight, Zarathustra? And what dost thou hide so carefully under thy mantle?

'Is it a treasure which has been given thee? or a child which has been born to thee? Or dost thou now go on a thief's errand, thou friend of the wicked?'

'Verily, my brother,' said Zarathustra, 'it is a treasure which has been given me: it is a little truth which I carry.

'But it is naughty, like a baby; and when I do not hold its mouth it cries too loud.

'Today, as I went on my way alone, at the time the sun goes down, an old girl met me, and spake thus to my soul:

'"Much has Zarathustra spoken to us women, but never has he spoken to us about women."

'And I answered her: "One should only speak to men about women."

'"Speak also to me of woman," said she; "I am old enough to forget it again immediately."

'And I complied with the old girl's request, and spake thus to her:

'"Everything in woman is a riddle, and everything in woman has one solution – namely, pregnancy.

'"Man is for woman a means; the purpose is always the child. But what is woman for man?

'"The true man wants two different things: danger and diversion. He therefore wants woman, as the most dangerous plaything.

'"Man must be trained for war, and woman for the relaxation of the warrior; all else is folly.

'"Too sweet fruits – these the warrior does not like. He therefore likes woman – even the sweetest woman is bitter.

* From *Thus Spake Zarathustra*, translated by T. Common (London: William Reeves, 1902).

'"Woman understands children better than man does, but man is more childish than woman.

'"In the true man there is a child hidden; it wants to play. Up then, ye women, discover, I pray you, the child in man!

'"Let woman be a pastime-object, divine and fine like the precious stone, illumined with the virtues of a world not yet dawned.

'"May the beam of a star shine in your love! Let your hope be – 'may I bear the overman!'

'"May there be valour in your love. Ye must attack with your love him who inspires you with fear!

'"Let your honour be in your love! Woman understands little about honour otherwise. But let this be your honour: always to love more than ye are loved, and never be the second.

'"Let man be afraid of woman when she loves: she then makes every sacrifice, and regards everything else as worthless.

'"Let man be afraid of woman when she hates; for man is merely evil in his innermost soul: woman, however, is bad there.

'"Whom does woman hate most? Thus spake the iron to the magnet: 'I hate thee most, because thou attractest, but art not strong enough to pull to thee.'

'"The happiness of man is: 'I will.' The happiness of woman is: 'He will.'

'"'Lo, the world has now become perfect!' – thus thinks every woman when she obeys with all her love.

'"And woman must obey and find a depth for her surface. Woman's nature is surface, an unstable, stormy film on a shallow water.

'"Man's nature, however, is deep, its current gushes in subterranean caverns; woman conjectures its power, but does not comprehend it."

'Here the old girl replied to me: "Many pretty things has Zarathustra said, especially for those who are young enough for them.

'"It is strange! Zarathustra knows little about women, and yet he is right with regard to them. Does that happen because nothing is impossible with women?

'"And now accept a little truth by way of thanks! I am surely old enough for it!

'"Swaddle it up and hold its mouth, otherwise it will cry too loud, the little truth."

'"Give me thy little truth," said I. And thus spake the old girl:

'"Thou goest to women? Do not forget thy whip!"'
Thus spake Zarathustra.

STUDY QUESTIONS

1. 'One should only speak to men about women.' What might this suggest about the way in which philosophers, including Nietzsche, have formulated their views on women?
2. According to Nietzsche, 'Woman's nature is surface. . . . Man's nature . . . is deep.' How might this idea relate to Kant's ideas on the nature of the sexes?

SELECT BIBLIOGRAPHY

General

W. Kaufmann, *Nietzsche* (Princeton: Princeton University Press, 1974).
J. P. Stern, *Nietzsche* (London: Fontana, 1978).
W. D. Williams, 'Nietzsche's Masks', in *Nietzsche: Imagery and Thought*, ed. M. Parsley (London: Methuen, 1978).

For feminist analysis

M. Daly, *Pure Lust* (London: Women's Press, 1984).
J. Grimshaw, *Feminist Philosophers* (Brighton: Harvester Wheatsheaf, 1986).
E. Kennedy, 'Nietzsche: Women as *Untermensch*', in E. Kennedy and S. Mendus, *Women in Western Political Philosophy* (Brighton: Wheatsheaf, 1987).

16 Sigmund Freud 1856–1939

Introduction and Background

While some would not characterize Freud's work as 'philosophical', this would seem to take too narrow an account of his work. In defining the parameters of psychoanalytic discourse, Freud employs philosophical ideas. If philosophy is understood as a method employed to expose lazy or uncritical thinking, then Freud's work is profoundly philosophical. Moreover, his impact upon many aspects of contemporary western thought remains.[1]

As Rosalind Miles documents, the end of the nineteenth century and the beginning of the twentieth century saw increased activity on the part of women not only to achieve the vote, but to take charge of their own bodies.[2] The demand for universal suffrage was paralleled with an increased demand for women to take control of their sexuality, and primarily the reproductive process. From 1840 onwards came the development of better and more effective contraception; 1882 saw the world's first birth control clinic.[3] The quality of women's lives seemed to be improving. An end to the all-too-frequent deaths on the 'birthing' bed was in view. With this assurance came the possibility that control over their own fertility would enable women to compete on equal terms with men in the male world.

Analysis of Freud's ideas is profitable on two fronts. On the one hand, his ideas of female sexuality are grounded in ideas of the nature of woman consistent in the western philosophical canon. In particular, Freud re-states male sexual experience as the 'norm'. Male experience is taken as normative, and woman is defined in relation to the male. Aristotle's claim that women are 'mutilated males', defined in relation to men and found wanting, resonates in Freud's writings on female sexual development. Like Augustine, Freud moves from writing of 'gender' (i.e. 'masculine' and 'feminine' traits and qualities) to associating these 'qualities' with the sexes. So, men are 'masculine', women are 'feminine'. The claims of Kant and Schopenhauer that a woman's sexuality hinders her ability to act in a truly moral way is reiterated in Freud's comments on 'feminine' morality.

At the same time, Freud's writings do more than reiterate notions of woman present in the western philosophical tradition. His ideas exemplify the connection between a writer's ideas and 'his' socio-historical context. Freud's account of human sexuality was formulated through his work with the bourgeoisie of nineteenth-century Vienna. Family life in this social group was governed by strict rules of conduct; in some cases this resulted in extreme repression of the emotions. The strongly patriarchal structure of the family resulted in distant, rather cold relationships between husband and wife, which in turn determined the way in which children developed emotionally. Is it possible – or indeed adequate – to move from conclusions grounded in this specific social setting to make universal claims about human relationships and development? While such a comment is not primarily concerned with issues of philosophical clarity, the connection between ideas and their context is important, for it suggests that all philosophers should be wary of making false generalizations.

*SOME PSYCHICAL CONSEQUENCES OF THE ANATOMICAL DISTINCTION BETWEEN THE SEXES**

In examining the earliest mental shapes assumed by the sexual life of children we have been in the habit of taking as the subject of our investigations the male child, the little boy. With little girls,

*From *The Standard Edition of the Complete Psychological Works of Sigmund Freud*, vol. 19 (1923–5), translated and edited by J. Strachy. Reprinted by permission of Sigmund Freud Copyrights, The Institute of Psycho-Analysis and The Hogarth Press.

so we have supposed, things must be similar, though in some way or other they must nevertheless be different. The point in development at which this difference lay could not be clearly determined.

In boys the situation of the Oedipus complex[1] is the first stage that can be recognized with certainty. It is easy to understand, because at that stage a child retains the same object which he previously cathected with his libido – not as yet a genital one – during the preceding period while he was being suckled and nursed. The fact, too, that in this situation he regards his father as a disturbing rival and would like to get rid of him and take his place is a straightforward consequence of the actual state of affairs. I have shown elsewhere how the Oedipus attitude in little boys belongs to the phallic phase, and how its destruction is brought about by the fear of castration – that is, by narcissistic interest in their genitals. The matter is made more difficult to grasp by the complicating circumstance that even in boys the Oedipus complex has a double orientation, active and passive, in accordance with their bisexual constitution; a boy also wants to take his *mother's* place as the love-object of his *father* – a fact which we describe as the feminine attitude.

As regards the prehistory of the Oedipus complex in boys we are far from complete clarity. We know that that period includes an identification of an affectionate sort with the boy's father, an identification which is still free from any sense of rivalry in regard to his mother. Another element of that stage is invariably, I believe, a masturbatory activity in connection with the genitals, the masturbation of early childhood, the more or less violent suppression of which by those in charge of the child sets the castration complex in action. It is to be assumed that this masturbation is attached to the Oedipus complex and serves as a discharge for the sexual excitation belonging to it. It is, however, uncertain whether the masturbation has this character from the first, or whether on the contrary it makes its first appearance spontaneously as an activity of a bodily organ and is only brought into relation with the Oedipus complex at some later date; this second possibility is by far the more probable. Another doubtful question is the part played by bed-wetting and by the breaking of that habit through the intervention of training measures. We are inclined to make the simple connection that continued bed-wetting is a result of masturbation and that its suppression is regarded by boys as an inhibition of their genital activity – that is, as having the meaning of a threat of castration; but whether we are always right in supposing this remains to be seen. Finally, analysis shows us in a shadowy way how the fact of a child at a very early age listening to his parents copulating may set up his first sexual excitation, and how that event may, owing to its after-effects, act as a starting-point for the child's whole sexual development. Masturbation, as well as the two attitudes in the Oedipus complex, later on become attached to this early experience, the child having subsequently interpreted its meaning. It is impossible, however, to suppose that these observations of coitus are of universal occurrence, so that at this point we are faced with the problem of 'primal phantasies'. Thus the prehistory of the Oedipus complex, even in boys, raises all of these questions for sifting and explanation; and there is the further problem of whether we are to suppose that the process invariably follows the same course, or whether a great variety of different preliminary stages may not converge upon the same terminal situation.

In little girls the Oedipus complex raises one problem more than in boys. In both cases the mother is the original object; and there is no cause for surprise that boys retain that object in the Oedipus complex. But how does it happen that girls abandon it and instead take their father as an object? In pursuing this question I have been able to reach some conclusions which may throw light precisely on the prehistory of the Oedipus relation in girls.

Every analyst has come across certain women who cling with especial intensity and tenacity to the attachment to their father and to the wish in which it culminates of having a child by him. We have good reason to suppose that the same wishful phantasy was also the motive force of their infantile masturbation, and it is easy to form an impression that at this point we have been brought up against an elementary and unanalysable fact of infantile sexual life. But a thorough analysis of these very cases brings something different to light – namely, that here the Oedipus complex has a long prehistory and is in some respects a secondary formation.

The old paediatrician Lindner[2] once remarked that a child discovers the genital zones (the penis or the clitoris) as a source of pleasure while indulging in sensual sucking (thumb-sucking). I shall leave it an open question whether it is really true that the child takes the newly found source of pleasure in exchange for the recent loss of the mother's nipple – a possibility to which later phantasies (fellatio) seem to point. Be that as it may, the genital zone is discovered at some time or other, and there seems no justification for attributing any psychical content to the first activities in connection with it. But the first step in the phallic phase which begins in this way is not the linking-up of the masturbation with the object-cathexes of the Oedipus complex, but a momentous discovery which little girls are destined to make. They notice the penis of a brother or playmate, strikingly visible and of large proportions, at once recognize it as the superior counterpart of their own small and inconspicuous organ, and from that time forward fall a victim to envy for the penis.

There is an interesting contrast between the behaviour of the two sexes. In the analogous situation, when a little boy first catches sight of a girl's genital region, he begins by showing irresolution and lack of interest; he sees nothing or disavows what he has seen, he softens it down or looks about for expedients for bringing it into line with his expectations. It is not until later, when some threat of castration has obtained a hold upon him, that the observation becomes important to him: if he then recollects or repeats it, it arouses a terrible storm of emotion in him and forces him to believe in the reality of the threat which he has hitherto laughed at. This combination of circumstances leads to two reactions, which may become fixed and will in that case, whether separately or together or in conjunction with other factors, permanently determine the boy's relations to women: horror of the mutilated creature or triumphant contempt for her. These developments, however, belong to the future, though not to a very remote one.

A little girl behaves differently. She makes her judgment and her decision in a flash. She has seen it and knows that she is without it and wants to have it.

Here what has been named the masculinity complex of women branches off. It may put great difficulties in the way of their regular development towards femininity, if it cannot be got over soon enough. The hope of some day obtaining a penis in spite of everything and so of becoming like a man may persist to an incredibly late age and may become a motive for strange and otherwise unaccountable actions. Or again, a process may set in which I should like to call a 'disavowal', a process which in the mental life of children seems neither uncommon nor very dangerous but which in an adult would mean the beginning of a psychosis. Thus a girl may refuse to accept the fact of being castrated, may harden herself in the conviction that she *does* possess a penis, and may subsequently be compelled to behave as though she were a man.

The psychical consequences of envy for the penis, in so far as it does not become absorbed in the reaction-formation of the masculinity complex, are various and far-reaching. After a woman has become aware of the wound to her narcissism she develops, like a scar, a sense of inferiority. When she has passed beyond her first attempt at explaining her lack of a penis as being a punishment personal to herself and has realized that that sexual character is a universal one, she begins to share the contempt felt by men for a sex which is the lesser in so important a respect, and, at least in holding that opinion, insists on being like a man.

Even after penis-envy has abandoned its true object, it continues to exist: by an easy displacement it persists in the character-trait of *jealousy*. Of course, jealousy is not limited to one sex and has a wider foundation than this, but I am of opinion that it plays a far larger part in the mental life of women than of men and that is because it is enormously reinforced from the direction of displaced penis-envy. While I was still unaware of this source of jealousy and was considering the phantasy 'a child is being beaten', which occurs so commonly in girls, I constructed a first phase for it in which its meaning was that another child, a rival of whom the subject was jealous, was to be beaten. This phantasy seems to be a relic of the phallic period in girls. The peculiar rigidity which struck me so much in the monotonous formula 'a child is being beaten' can probably be interpreted in a special way. The child which is being beaten (or caressed) may ultimately be nothing more nor less than the clitoris itself, so that at its very lowest level the statement will contain a confession of masturbation, which has remained attached to the content of the formula from its beginning in the phallic phase till later life.

A third consequence of penis-envy seems to be a loosening of the girl's affectionate relation with her maternal object. The situation as a whole is not very clear, but it can be seen that in the end the girl's mother, who sent her into the world so insufficiently equipped, is almost always held responsible for her lack of a penis. The way in which this comes about historically is often that soon after the girl has discovered that her genitals are unsatisfactory she begins to show jealousy of another child on the ground that her mother is fonder of it than of her, which serves as a reason for her giving up her attachment to her mother. It will fit in with this if the child which has been preferred by her mother is made into the first object of the beating-phantasy which ends in masturbation.

There is yet another surprising effect of penis-envy, or of the discovery of the inferiority of the clitoris, which is undoubtedly the most important of all. In the past I had often formed an impression that in general women tolerate masturbation worse than men, that they more frequently fight against it and that they are unable to make use of it in circumstances in which a man would seize upon it as a way of escape without any hesitation. Experience would no doubt elicit innumerable exceptions to this statement, if we attempted to turn it into a rule. The reactions of human individuals of both sexes are of course made up of masculine and feminine traits. But it appeared to me nevertheless as though masturbation were further removed from the nature of women than of men, and the solution of the problem could be assisted by the reflection that masturbation, at all events of the clitoris, is a masculine activity and that the elimination of clitoridal sexuality is a necessary precondition for the development of femininity. Analyses of the remote phallic period have now taught me that in girls, soon after the first signs of penis-envy, an intense current of feeling against masturbation makes its appearance, which cannot be attributed exclusively to the educational influence of those in charge of the child. This impulse is clearly a forerunner of the wave of repression which at puberty will do away with a large amount of the girl's masculine sexuality in order to make room for the development of her femininity. It may happen that this first opposition to auto-erotic activity fails to attain its end. And this was in fact the case in the instances which I analysed. The conflict continued, and both then and later the girl did everything she could to free herself from the compulsion to masturbate. Many of the later manifestations of sexual life in women remain unintelligible unless this powerful motive is recognized.

I cannot explain the opposition which is raised in this way by little girls to phallic masturbation except by supposing that there is some concurrent factor which turns her violently against that pleasurable activity. Such a factor lies close at hand. It cannot be anything else than her narcissistic sense of humiliation which is bound up with penis-envy, the reminder that after all this is a point on which she cannot compete with boys and that it would therefore be best for her to give up the idea of doing so. Thus the little girl's recognition of the anatomical distinction between the sexes forces her away from masculinity and masculine masturbation on to new lines which lead to the development of femininity.

So far there has been no question on the Oedipus complex, nor has it up to this point played any part. But now the girl's libido slips into a new position along the line – there is no other way of putting it – of the equation 'penis–child'. She gives up her wish for a penis and puts in place of it a wish for a child: and *with that purpose in view* she takes her father as a love-object. Her mother becomes the object of her jealousy. The girl has turned into a little woman. If I am to credit a single analytic instance, this new situation can give rise to physical sensations which would have to be regarded as a premature awakening of the female genital apparatus. When the girl's attachment to her father comes to grief later on and has to be abandoned, it may give place to an identification with him and the girl may thus return to her masculinity complex and perhaps remain fixated in it.

I have now said the essence of what I had to say: I will stop, therefore, and cast an eye over our findings. We have gained some insight into the prehistory of the Oedipus complex in girls. The corresponding period in boys is more or less unknown. In girls the Oedipus complex is a secondary formation. The operations of the castration complex precede it and prepare for it. As regards the relation between the Oedipus and castration complexes there is a fundamental contrast between the two sexes. *Whereas in boys the Oedipus complex is destroyed by the castration complex, in girls it is made possible and led up to by the castration complex.* This contradiction is cleared up if we reflect that the castration complex always operates in the sense implied in its subject-matter: it inhibits and limits masculinity and encourages femininity. The difference between the sexual development of males and females at the stage we have been considering is an intelligible consequence of the anatomical distinction between their genitals and of the psychical situation involved in it; it corresponds to the difference between a castration that has been carried out and one that has merely been threatened. In their essentials, therefore, our findings are self-evident and it should have been possible to foresee them.

The Oedipus complex, however, is such an important thing that the manner in which one enters and leaves it cannot be without its effects. In boys (as I have shown at length in the paper to which I have just referred[3] and to which all of my present remarks are closely related) the complex is not simply repressed, it is literally smashed to pieces by the shock of threatened castration. Its libidinal[4] cathexes are abandoned, desexualized and in part sublimated; its objects are incorporated into the ego,[5] where they form the nucleus of the super-ego[6] and give that new structure its characteristic qualities. In normal, or, it is better to say, in ideal cases, the Oedipus complex exists no longer, even in the unconscious: the super-ego has become its heir. Since the penis owes its extraordinarily high narcissistic cathexis to its organic significance for the propagation of the species, the catastrophe to the Oedipus complex (the abandonment of incest and the institution of conscience and morality) may be regarded as a victory of the race over the individual. This is an interesting point of view when one considers that neurosis is based upon a struggle of the ego against the demands of the sexual function. But to leave the standpoint of individual psychology is not of any immediate help in clarifying this complicated situation.

In girls the motive for the demolition of the Oedipus complex is lacking. Castration has already had its effect, which was to force the child into the situation of the Oedipus complex. Thus the Oedipus complex escapes the fate which it meets with in boys: it may be slowly abandoned or dealt with by repression, or its effects may persist far into women's normal mental life. I cannot evade the notion (though I hesitate to give it expression) that for women the level of what is ethically normal is different from what it is in men. Their super-ego is never so inexorable, so impersonal, so independent of its emotional origins as we require it to be in men. Character-traits which critics of every epoch have brought up against women – that they show less sense of justice than men, that they are less ready to submit to the great exigencies of life, that they are more often influenced in their judgements by feelings of affection or hostility – all these would be amply accounted for by the modification in the formation of their super-ego which we have inferred above. We must not allow ourselves to be deflected from such conclusions by the denials of the feminists, who are anxious to force us to regard the two sexes as completely equal in position and worth; but we shall, of course, willingly agree that the majority of men are also far behind the masculine ideal and that all human individuals, as a result of their bisexual disposition and of cross-inheritance, combine in themselves both masculine and feminine characteristics, so that pure masculinity and femininity remain theoretical constructions of uncertain content.

I am inclined to set some value on the considerations I have brought forward upon the psychical consequences of the anatomical distinction between the sexes. I am aware, however, that this opinion can only be maintained if my findings, which are based on a handful of cases, turn out to have general validity and to be typical. If not, they would remain no more than a contribution to our knowledge of the different paths along which sexual life develops.

NOTES

1. [Ed.] *Oedipus complex*: Freud's term for what he viewed as the key stage of child sexual development. The developing child/boy views the father as a rival for his mother's love, and wishes him dead. 'Oedipus' is taken from the name of the King in Greek mythology who kills his father and marries his mother.
2. [Ed.] *S. Lindner*: Freud is citing his work 'Das Saugen an den Fingern, Lippen, etc., bei den Kindern (Ludeln)', published in 1879.
3. [Ed.] Freud is referring to 'The Dissolution of the Oedipus Complex' (1924), which can be found in the *Standard Edition* of his works, vol. 19, published by the Hogarth Press.
4. [Ed.] *libidinal*: related to 'libido'; lustfulness, sex drive.
5. [Ed.] *ego*: the 'I'; the conscious, thinking subject.
6. [Ed.] *super-ego*: the internalized external authority, related to the capacity to make moral decisions; the ability of the ego to comment on its own actions.

STUDY QUESTIONS

1. 'They notice the penis of a brother or playmate, strikingly visible and of large proportions, at once recognize it as the superior counterpart of their own small and inconspicuous organ, and from that time forward fall victim to envy for the penis.'

   Compare Freud's account of 'penis-envy' with that given by Shulamith Firestone: 'It is safer to view this as a metaphor. Even when an actual preoccupation with genitals does occur it is that anything that physically distinguishes the envied male will be envied . . .' (S. Firestone, *The Dialectic of Sex* (London: Women's Press, 1979), p. 57).

   In a male-dominated society, why might women 'envy' the possession of a penis?
2. To what extent can Freud's account of the psychological development of women be related to the philosophical texts considered so far in this reader?

SELECT BIBLIOGRAPHY

General

R. W. Clark, *Freud: The Man and the Cause* (London: Paladin, 1982).
M. Jahoda, *Freud and the Dilemmas of Psychology* (London: Hogarth Press, 1977).

For feminist analysis

T. Brennan (ed.), *Between Feminism and Psychoanalysis* (London: Routledge, 1989).
N. J. Chodorow, *Feminism and Psychoanalytic Theory* (Cambridge: Polity Press, 1989).
S. Firestone, *The Dialectic of Sex* (London: Women's Press, 1979).
R. Morgan and G. Steinem, 'The International Crime of Genital Mutilation', in G. Steinem (ed.), *Outrageous Acts and Everyday Rebellions* (London: Signet, 1983).
N. Tuana, *The Less Noble Sex* (Indianapolis: Indiana University Press, 1993), Section II.4.

17 Otto Weininger 1880–1903

Introduction and Background

One of the forgotten philosophers of the late nineteenth/early twentieth century, Otto Weininger's ideas had a considerable impact on the work of others – most notably on the work of Ludwig Wittgenstein. Born in 1880, Weininger was more celebrated in his death than in his work. On 4 October 1903 he committed suicide. His death prompted a romantic attitude to suicide in the young Viennese men of his generation. His work *Sex and Character* had been published that year, and, unlike his death, it had not been well-received. Claiming that contemporary society was in a state of decay, his argument revolved around the polarization of masculine and feminine qualities. All positive achievements were associated with the masculine, all destructive ideas with the feminine. The Aryan race were equated with the masculine, and thus with the positive aspects of contemporary society; the Jewish race was characterized by the feminine, and thus associated with the negative. His death came to be seen as the logical outcome of these ideas, for he was both a Jew and a homosexual (the latter being equatable in Weininger's terms with a 'feminized man').

Drawing specifically upon the ideas of Plato, Kant and Schopenhauer, Weininger develops their ideas in relation to woman with remorseless logic. Platonic and Aristotelian distinctions between form and matter are explicitly applied to male and female. The male is the active agent, the female the passive partner who finds her meaning in the male. Kant's account of the masculine qualities, equated with the higher forms of morality, is drawn out and developed by Weininger. Kant's claim that the 'feminine virtues' are of little worth when it comes to living the moral life is pursued by Weininger to its logical conclusion. Even the worst kind of man has a spark of morality; in contrast, no woman can be said to be truly moral. Thus man is defined by individuality (he is 'the monad'), whilst woman is subsumed by Nature, which is closely identified with sexuality. Like Schopenhauer, Weininger sees woman as the plaything of men and children.

The misogyny of Weininger's work is thus clearly identifiable. Yet what is interesting is the extent to which Weininger's ideas are echoed by some feminist writers. In many ways this is the importance of his work, for it warns against adopting an easy essentialism concerning 'the nature of woman'. Feminists such as Susan Griffin have argued for a close connection between woman and nature.[1] The sexuality of woman has been affirmed and accepted, in contrast to the postulations of some fathers of the tradition directed against the castrating womb.[2] To an extent, Weininger's ideas follow a similar path to these feminist arguments. Indeed, his claim that only men have immortal longings can be paralleled with strands of feminist thought which suggest that the belief in immortality arises from the masculinist desire to transcend the world.[3]

It would be tempting to consign Weininger's rather rambling writings on woman to obscurity were it not for this connection between his thought and contemporary feminist ideas. At the same time, his work demonstrates with remorseless logic the extent to which misogynistic ideas have framed the western philosophical canon. In grappling with his work we arrive at the supreme example of the misogyny underlying philosophical method. Feminists ignore his negative rendition of male/female distinctions at their peril. In reclaiming the earth, we must also be aware of the dangers of reinstituting old distinctions between male and female.

*THE NATURE OF WOMAN AND HER SIGNIFICANCE IN THE UNIVERSE**

The further we go in the analysis of woman's claim to esteem the more we must deny her of what is lofty and noble, great and beautiful. As this chapter is about to take the deciding and most extreme step in that direction, I should like to make a few remarks as to my position. The last thing I wish to advocate is the Asiatic standpoint with regard to the treatment of women. Those who have carefully followed my remarks as to the injustice that all forms of sexuality and erotics visit on woman will surely see that this work is not meant to plead for the harem. But it is quite possible to desire the legal equality of men and women without

*From Otto Weininger, *Sex and Character* (London: Heinemann, 1910).

believing in their moral and intellectual equality, just as in condemning to the utmost any harshness in the male treatment of the female sex, one does not overlook the tremendous, cosmic, contrast and organic differences between them. There are no men in whom there is no trace of the transcendent, who are altogether bad; and there is no woman of whom that could truly be said. However degraded a man may be, he is immeasurably above the most superior woman, so much so that comparison and classification of the two are impossible; but even so, no one has any right to denounce or defame woman, however inferior she must be considered. A true adjustment of the claims for legal equality can be undertaken on no other basis than the recognition of a complete, deep-seated polar opposition of the sexes. . . .

Woman is neither high-minded nor low-minded, strong-minded nor weak-minded. She is the opposite of all these. Mind cannot be predicated of her at all; she is mindless. That, however, does not imply weak-mindedness in the ordinary sense of the term, the absence of the capacity to 'get her bearings' in ordinary everyday life. Cunning, calculation, 'cleverness', are much more usual and constant in the woman than in the man, if there be a personal selfish end in view. A woman is never so stupid as a man can be.

But has woman no meaning at all? Has she no general purpose in the scheme of the world? Has she not a destiny; and, in spite of all her senselessness and emptiness, a significance in the universe?

Has she a mission, or is her existence an accident and an absurdity? . . .

[*At this point, Weininger suggests that the 'purpose' of a woman's life is to be found in 'matchmaking'.*]

. . . The idea of union is always eagerly grasped and never repelled whatever form it may take (even where animals are concerned). She experiences no disgust at the nauseating details of the subject, and makes no attempt to think of anything pleasanter. This accounts for a great deal of what is so apparently mysterious in the psychic life of woman. Her wish for the activity of her own sexual life is her strongest impulse, but it is only a special case of her deep, her only vital interest, the interest that sexual unions shall take place; the wish that as much of it as possible shall occur, in all cases, places, and times.

This universal desire may either be concentrated on the act itself or on the (possible) child; in the first case, the woman is of the prostitute type and participates merely for the sake of the act; in the second, she is of the mother type, but not merely with the idea of bearing children herself; she desires that every marriage she knows of or has helped to bring about should be fruitful, and the nearer she is to the absolute mother the more conspicuous is this idea; the real mother is also the real grandmother (even if she remains a virgin; Johann Tesman's marvellous portrayal of Tante Jule in Ibsen's *Hedda Gabler*[1] is an example of what I mean). Every real mother has the same purpose, that of helping on matrimony; she is the mother of all mankind; she welcomes every pregnancy.

It is convenient to recapitulate at this point what my investigation has shown as to the sexuality of women. I have shown that woman is engrossed exclusively by sexuality, not intermittently, but throughout her life; that her whole being, bodily and mental, is nothing but sexuality itself. I added, moreover, that she was so constituted that her whole body and being continually were in sexual relations with her environment, and that just as the sexual organs were the centre of woman physically, so the sexual idea was the centre of her mental nature. The idea of pairing is the only conception which has positive worth for women. The woman is the bearer of the thought of the continuity of the species. The high value which she attaches to the idea of pairing is not selfish and individual, it is super individual, and, if I may be forgiven the desecration of the phrase, it is the transcendental function of woman. And just as femaleness is no more than the embodiment of the idea of pairing, so is it sexuality in the abstract. Pairing is the supreme good for the woman; she seeks to effect it always and everywhere. Her personal sexuality is only a special case of this universal, generalized, impersonal instinct.

The effort of woman to realize this idea of pairing is so fundamentally opposed to that conception of innocence and purity, the higher virginity which man's erotic nature has demanded from women, that not all his erotic incense would have obscured her real nature but for one factor. I have now to explain this factor which has veiled from man the true nature of woman, and which in itself is one of the deepest problems of woman, I mean her absolute duplicity. Her pairing instinct and her duplicity, the latter so great as to conceal even from woman herself what is the real essence of her nature, must be explained together. . . .

In order to understand these fallacious contradictions one must first of all remember the tremendous 'accessibility', to use another word, the 'impressionability', of women. Their extraordinary aptitude for anything new, and their easy acceptance of other people's views have not yet been sufficiently emphasized in this book.

As a rule, the woman adapts herself to the man, his views become hers, his likes and dislikes are shared by her, every word he says is an incentive to her, and the stronger his sexual influence on her the more this is so. Woman does not perceive that this influence which man has on her causes her to deviate from the line of her own development; she does not look upon it as a sort of unwarrantable intrusion; she does not try to shake off what is really an invasion of her private life; she is not ashamed of being receptive; on the contrary, she is really pleased when she can be so, and prefers man to mould her mentally. She rejoices in being dependent, and her expectations from man resolve themselves into the moment when she may be perfectly passive.

But it is not only from her lover (although she would like that best), but also from her father and mother, uncles and aunts, brothers and sisters, near relations and distant acquaintances, that a woman takes what she thinks and believes, being only too glad to get her opinions 'ready made'.

It is not only inexperienced girls but even elderly and married women who copy each other in everything, from the nice new dress or pretty coiffure down to the places where they get their things, and the very recipes by which they cook.

And it never seems to occur to them that they are doing something derogatory on their part, as it ought to do if they possessed an individuality of their own and strove to work out their own salvation. A woman's thoughts and actions have no definite, independent relations to things in themselves; they are not the result of the reaction of her individuality to the world. They accept what is imposed on them gladly, and adhere to it with the greatest firmness. That is why woman is so intolerant when there has been a breach of conventional laws. . . .

The extraordinary way in which woman can be influenced by external agencies is similar in its nature to her suggestibility, which is far greater and more general than man's; they are both in accordance with woman's desire to play the passive and never the active part in the sexual act and all that leads to it.[2]

It is the universal passivity of woman's nature which makes her accept and assume man's valuations of things, although these are utterly at variance with her nature. The way in which woman can be impregnated with the masculine point of view, the saturation of her innermost thoughts with a foreign element, her false recognition of morality, which cannot be called hypocrisy because it does not conceal anything anti-moral, her assumption and practice of things which in themselves are not in her realm, are all very well if the woman does not try to use her own judgment, and they succeed in keeping up the fiction of her superior morality. Complications first arise when these acquired valuations come into collision with the only inborn, genuine, and universally feminine valuation, the supreme value she sets on pairing. . . .

Woman is not a free agent; she is altogether subject to her desire to be under man's influence, herself and all others: she is under the sway of the phallus, and irretrievably succumbs to her destiny, even if it leads to actively developed sexuality. At the most a woman can reach an indistinct feeling of her un-freedom, a cloudy idea of the possibility of controlling her destiny – manifestly only a flickering spark of the free, intelligible subject, the scanty remains of inherited maleness in her, which, by contrast, gives her even this slight comprehension. It is also impossible for a woman to have a clear idea of her destiny, or of the forces within her: it is only he who is free who can discern fate, because he is not chained by necessity; part of his personality, at least, places him in the position of spectator and a combatant outside his own fate and makes him so far superior to it. One of the most conclusive proofs of human freedom is contained in the fact that man has been able to create the idea of causality. Women consider themselves most free when they are most bound; and they are not troubled by the passions, because they are simply the embodiment of them. It is only a man who can talk of the *dira necessitas* within him; it is only he could have created the idea of destiny, because it is only he who, in addition to the empirical, conditioned existence, possesses a free, intelligible ego.

As I have shown, woman can reach no more than a vague half-consciousness of the fact that she is a conditioned being, and so she is unable to overcome the sexuality that binds her. Hysteria is the only attempt on her part to overcome it, and, as I have shown, it is not a genuine attempt. The hysteria itself is what the hysterical woman tries to resist, and the falsity of this effort against slavery is the measure of its hopelessness. The most notable examples of the sex . . . may feel that it is because they wish it that servitude is a necessity for them, but this realization does not give them power to resist it; at the last moment they will kiss the man who ravishes them, and succumb with pleasure to those whom they have been resisting violently. It is as if woman were under a curse. At times she feels the weight of it, but she never flees from it. Her shrieks and ravings are not really genuine, and she succumbs to her fate at the moment when it has seemed most repulsive to her.

After a long analysis, then, it has been found that there is no exception to the complete absence in women of any true, inalienable relation to worth. Even what is covered by such current terms as 'womanly love', 'womanly virtue', 'womanly devoutness', 'womanly modesty', has failed to invalidate my conclusions. I have maintained my ground in face of the strongest opposition, even including that which comes from woman's hysterical imitations of the male morality.

Woman, the normal receptive woman of whom I am speaking, is impregnated by the man not only physically (and I set down the astonishing mental alteration in women after marriage to a physical phenomenon akin to telegony), but at every age of her life, by man's consciousness and by man's social arrangements. Thus it comes about that although woman lacks all the characters of the male sex, she can assume them so cleverly and so slavishly that it is possible to make mistakes such as the idea of the higher morality of women.

But this astounding receptivity of woman is not isolated, and must be brought into practical and theoretical connection with the other positive and negative characteristics of woman. . . .

[*Weininger goes on to distinguish between two sets of characteristics.*]

I may group the two sets of factors as follows:

Common to men and animals, fundamentally organic.	*Limited to mankind, and in particular to the males of mankind.*
Individuation	Individuality
Recognition	Memory
Pleasure	Sense of worth or value
Sexual desire	Love
Limitation of the field of consciousness	Faculty of 'taking notice'
Impulse	Will

The series shows that man possesses not only each character which is found in all living things, but also an analogous and higher character peculiar to himself. The old tendency at once to identify the two series and to contrast them seems to show the existence of something binding together the two series, and at the same time separating them. One may recall in this connection the Buddhistic conception of there being in man a superstructure added to the characters of lower existences. It is as if man possessed all the properties of the beasts, with, in each case, some special quality added. What is this that has been added? How far does it resemble, and in what respects does it differ from, the more primitive set?

The terms in the left-hand row are fundamental characteristics of all animal and vegetable life. All such life is individual life, not the life of undivided masses; it manifests itself as the impulse to satisfy needs, as sexual impulse for the purpose of reproduction. Individuality, memory, will, love, are those qualities of a second life, which, although related to organic life to a certain extent, are *toto coelo* different from it.

This brings us face to face with the religious idea of the eternal, higher, *new* life, and especially with the Christian form of it.

. . . Just as all earthly life is sustained by earthly food, this other life requires spiritual sustenance (symbolized in the communion service). The birth and death of the former have their counterparts in the latter – the moral re-birth of man, the 'regeneration' – and the end: the final loss of the soul through error or crime. The one is determined from without by the bonds of natural causation; the other is ruled by the moral imperative from within. The one is limited and confined to a definite purpose; the other is unlimited, eternal and moral. The characters which are in the left row are common to all forms of lower life; those in the right-hand column are the corresponding presages of eternal life, manifestations of a higher existence in which man, and only man, has a share. The perpetual intermingling and the fresh complications which arise between the higher and lower natures are the making of all history of the human mind; this is the plot of the history of the universe.

It is possible that some may perceive in this second life something which in man might have been derived from the other lower characters; such a possibility dismiss at once.

A clearer grasp of this sensuous, impressionable lower life will make it clear that, as I have explained in earlier chapters, the case is reversed; the lower life is merely a projection of the higher on the world of the senses, a reflection of it in the sphere of necessity, as a degradation of it, or its Fall. And the great problem is how the eternal, lofty idea came to be bound with earth. This problem is the guilt of the world. My investigation is now on the threshold of what cannot be investigated; of a problem that so far no one has dared to answer, and that never will be answered by any human being. It is the riddle of the universe and of life; the binding of the unlimited in the bonds of space, of the eternal in time, of the spirit in matter. It is the relation of freedom to necessity, of something to nothing, of God to the devil. The dualism of the world is beyond comprehension; it is the plot of the story of man's Fall, the primitive riddle. It is the binding of eternal life in a perishable being, of the innocent in the guilty. . . .

As the absolute female has no trace of individuality and will, no sense of worth or of love, she can have no part in the higher, transcendental life. The intelligible, hyperempirical existence of the male transcends matter, space, and time. He is certainly mortal, but he is immortal as well. And so he has the power to choose between the two, between the life which is lost with death and the life to which death is only a stepping-stone. The deepest will of man is towards this perfect, timeless existence; he is compact of the desire for immortality. That the woman has no craving for perpetual life is too apparent; there is nothing in her of that eternal which man tries to interpose and must interpose between his real self and his projected, empirical self. Some sort of relation to the idea of supreme value, to the idea of the absolute, that perfect freedom which he has not yet attained, because he is bound by necessity, but which he can attain because mind is superior to matter; such a relation to the purpose of things generally, or to the divine, every man has. And although his life on earth is accompanied by separation and detachment from the absolute, his mind is always longing to be free from the taint of original sin.

Just as the love of his parents was not pure in purpose, but sought more or less a physical embodiment, the son, who is the outcome of that love, will possess his share of mortal life as well as of eternal: we are horrified at the thought of death, we fight against it, cling to this mortal life, and prove from that that we were anxious to be born as we were born, and that we still desire to be born of this world.

But since every male has a relation to the idea of the highest value, and would be incomplete without it, no male is really ever happy. It is only women who are happy. No man is happy, because he has a relation to freedom, and yet during his earthly life he is always bound in some way. None but a perfectly passive being, such as the absolute female, or a universally active being, like the divine, can be happy. Happiness is the sense of perfect consummation, and this feeling a man can never have; but there are women who fancy themselves perfect. The male always has problems behind him and efforts before him: all problems originate in the past; the future is the sphere for efforts. Time has no objective, no meaning, for woman; no woman questions herself as to the reason of her existence; and yet the sole purpose of time is to give expression to the fact that this life can and must mean something.

Happiness for the male! That would imply wholly independent activity, complete freedom; he is always bound, although not with the heaviest bonds, and his sense of guilt increases the further he is removed from the idea of freedom.

Mortal life is a calamity, and must remain so whilst mankind is a passive victim of sensation; so long as he remains not form, but merely the matter on which form is impressed. Every man, however, has some glimmer of higher things; the genius most certainly and most directly. This trace of light, however, does not come from his perceptions; so far as he is ruled by these, man is merely a passive victim of surrounding things. His spontaneity, his freedom, come from his power of judging as to values, and his highest approach to absolute spontaneity and freedom comes from love and from artistic or philosophical creation. Through these he obtains some faint sense of what happiness might be.

Woman can really never be quite unhappy, for happiness is an empty word for her, a word created by unhappy men. Women never mind letting others see their unhappiness, as it is not real; behind it there lies no consciousness of guilt, no sense of the sin of the world.

The last and absolute proof of the thoroughly negative character of woman's life, of her complete want of a higher existence, is derived from the way in which women commit suicide.

Such suicides are accompanied practically always by thoughts of other people, what they will think, how they will mourn over them, how grieved – or angry – they will be. Every woman is convinced that her unhappiness is undeserved at the time she kills herself; she pities herself exceedingly with the sort of self-compassion which is only a 'weeping with others when they weep'.

How is it possible for a woman to look upon her unhappiness as personal when she possesses no idea of a destiny? The most appallingly decisive proof of the emptiness and nullity of women is that they never once succeed in knowing the problem of their own lives, and death leaves them ignorant of it, because they are unable to realize the higher life of personality.

I am now ready to answer the question which I put forward as the chief object of this portion of my book, the question as to the significance of the male and female in the universe. Women have no existence and no essence; they are not, they are nothing. Mankind occurs as male or female, as something or nothing. Woman has no share in ontological reality, no relation to the thing-in-itself, which, in the deepest interpretation, is the absolute, is God. Man in his highest form, the genius, has such a relation, and for him the absolute is either the conception of the highest worth of existence, in which case he is a philosopher; or it is the wonderful fairyland of dreams, the kingdom of absolute beauty, and then he is an artist. But both views mean the same. Woman has no relation to the idea, she neither affirms nor denies it; she is neither moral nor anti-moral; mathematically speaking, she has no sign; she is purposeless, neither good nor bad, neither angel nor devil, never egoistical (and therefore has often been said to be altruistic); she is as non-moral as she is non-logical. But all existence is moral and logical existence. So woman has no existence.

Woman is untruthful. An animal has just as little metaphysical reality as the actual woman, but it cannot speak, and consequently it does not lie. In order to speak the truth one must *be* something; truth is dependent on an existence, and only that can have a relation to an existence which is in itself something. Man desires truth all the time; that is to say, he all along desires only to be something. The cognition-impulse is in the end identical with the desire for immortality. Any one who objects to a statement without ever having realized it; any one who gives outward acquiescence without the inner affirmation, such persons, like woman, have no real existence and must of necessity lie. So that woman always lies, even if, objectively, she speaks the truth.

Woman is the great emissary of pairing. The living units of the lower forms of life are individuals, organisms; the living units of the higher forms of life are individualities, souls, monads, 'meta-organisms'. . . .

Each monad, however, is differentiated from every other monad, and is as distinct from it as only two things can be. Monads have no windows, but instead, have the universe in themselves. Man as monad, as a potential or actual individuality, that is, as having genius, has in addition differentiation and distinction, individuation and discrimination; the simple undifferentiated unit is exclusively female. Each monad creates for itself a detached entity, a whole; but it looks upon every other ego as a perfect totality also, and never intrudes upon it. Man has limits, and accepts them and desires them; woman, who does not recognize her own entity, is not in a position to regard or perceive the privacy of those around her, and neither respects, nor honours, nor leaves it alone: as there is no such thing as one-ness for her there can be no plurality, only an indistinct state of fusion with others. Because there is no 'I' in woman she cannot grasp the 'thou'; according to her perception the I and thou are just a pair, an undifferentiated one; this makes it possible for woman to bring people together, to match-make. The object of her love is that of her sympathy – the community, the blending of everything.[3]

Woman has no limits to her ego which could be broken through, and which she would have to guard. . . .

At this stage it well may be asked if women are really to be considered human beings at all, or if my theory does not unite them with plants and animals? For, according to the theory, women, just as little as plants and animals, have any real existence, any relation to the intelligible whole. Man alone is a microcosm, a mirror of the universe.

In Ibsen's *Little Eyolf* there is a beautiful and apposite passage.

Rita 'After all, we are only human beings.'
Allmers 'But we have some kinship with the sky and the sea, Rita.'
Rita 'You, perhaps; not me.'

Woman, according to the poet, according to Buddha, and in my interpretation, has no relation to the all, to the world whole, to God. Is she then human, or an animal, or a plant?

Anatomists will find the question ridiculous, and will at once dismiss the philosophy which could lead up to such a possibility. For them woman is the female of *Homo sapiens*, differentiated from all other living beings, and occupying the same position with regard to the human male that the females of other species occupy with regard to their males. And he will not allow the philosopher to say, 'What has the anatomist to do with me? Let him mind his own business.'

As a matter of fact, women are sisters of the flowers, and are in close relationship with the animals. Many of their sexual perversities and affections for animals (Pasiphäe[4] myth and Leda[5] myth) indicate this. But they are human beings. Even the absolute woman, whom we think of as without any trace of intelligible ego, is still the complement of man. And there is no doubt that the fact of the special sexual and erotic completion of the human male by the human female, even if it is not the moral phenomenon which advocates of marriage would have us believe, is still of tremendous importance to the woman problem. Animals are mere individuals; women are persons, although they are not personalities.

An appearance of discriminative power, though not the reality, language, though not conversation, memory, though it has no continuity or unity of consciousness – must all be granted to them.

They possess counterfeits of everything masculine, and thus are subject to those transformations which the defenders of womanliness are so fond of quoting. The result of this is a sort of amphi-sexuality of many ideas (honour, shame, love, imagination, fear, sensibility, and so on), which have both a masculine and feminine significance. . . .

The contrast between the subject and the object in the theory of knowledge corresponds ontologically to the contrast between form and matter. It is no more than a translation of this distinction from the theory of experience to metaphysics. Matter, which in itself is absolutely unindividualized and so can assume any form, of itself has no definite and lasting qualities, and has as little essence as mere perception, the matter of experience, has in itself any existence. If the Platonic conception is followed out, it will be apparent that that great thinker asserted to be nothing what the ordinary Philistine regards as the highest form of reality. According to Plato, the negation of existence is no other than matter. Form is the only real existence. Aristotle carried the Platonic conception into the regions of biology. For Plato form is the parent and creator of all reality. For Aristotle, in the sexual process the male principle is the active, formative agent, the female principle the passive matter on which the form is impressed. In my view, the significance of woman in humanity is explained by the Platonic and Aristotelian conception. Woman is the material on which man acts. Man as the microcosm is compounded of the lower and higher life. Woman is matter, is nothing. This knowledge gives us the keystone to our structure, and it makes everything clear that was indistinct, it gives things a coherent form. Woman's sexual part depends on contact; it is the absorbing and not the liberating impulse. It coincides with this, that the keenest sense woman has, and the only one she has more highly developed than man, is the sense of touch. The eye and the ear lead to the unlimited and give glimpses of infinity; the sense of touch necessitates physical limitations to our own actions: one is affected by what one feels; it is the eminently sordid sense, and suited to the physical requirements of an earth-bound being.

Man is form, woman is matter: if that is so it must find expression in the relations between their respective psychic experiences.

The summing up of the connected nature of man's mental life, as opposed to the inarticulate and chaotic condition of woman's, illustrates the above antithesis of form and matter.

Matter needs to be formed: and thus woman demands that man should clear her confusion of thought, give meaning to her henid ideas. Women are matter, which can assume any shape. Those experiments which ascribe to girls a better memory for learning by rote than boys are explained in this way: they are due to the nullity and inanity of women, who can be saturated with anything and everything, whilst man only retains what has an interest for him, forgetting all else.

This accounts for what has been called woman's submissiveness, the way she is influenced by the opinions of others, her suggestibility, the way in which man moulds her formless nature. Woman is nothing; therefore, and only, therefore, she can become everything, whilst man can only remain what he is. A man can make what he likes of a woman: the most a woman can do is to help a man to achieve what he wants.

A man's real nature is never altered by education: woman, on the other hand, by external influences, can be taught to suppress her most characteristic self, the real value she sets on sexuality.

Woman can appear everything and deny everything, but in reality she is never anything.

Women have neither this nor that characteristic; their peculiarity consists in having no characteristics at all; the complexity and terrible mystery about women come to this; it is this which makes them above and beyond man's understanding – man, who always wants to get to the heart of things. . . .

Woman is first created by man's will – he dominates her and changes her whole being (hypnotism). Here is the explanation of the relation of the psychical to the physical in man and woman. Man assumes a reciprocal action of body and mind, in the sense rather that the dominant mind creates the body, than that the mind merely projects itself on phenomena, whilst the woman accepts both mental and psychical phenomena empirically. None the less, even in the woman there is some reciprocal action. However, whilst in the man, as Schopenhauer truly taught, the human being is his own creation, his own will makes and re-makes the body, the woman is bodily influenced and changed by an alien will (suggestion).

Man not only forms himself, but woman also – a far easier matter. The myths of the book of Genesis and other cosmogonies, which teach that woman was created out of man, are nearer the truth than the biological theories of descent, according to which males have been evolved from females.

We have now to come to the question left open in Chapter IX, as to how woman, who is herself without soul or will, is yet able to realize to what extent a man may be endowed with them; and we may now endeavour to answer it. Of this one must be certain, that what woman notices, that for which she has a sense, is not the special nature of man, but only the general fact and possibly the grade of his maleness. It is quite erroneous to suppose that woman has an innate capacity to understand the individuality of a man. The lover, who is so easily fooled by the unconscious simulation of a deeper comprehension on the part of his sweetheart, may believe that he understands himself through a girl; but those who are less easily satisfied cannot help seeing that women only possess a sense of the fact not of the individuality of the soul, only for the formal general fact, not for the differentiation of the personality. In order to perceive and apperceive the special form, matter must not itself be formless; woman's relation to man, however, is nothing but that of matter to form, and her comprehension of him nothing but willingness to be as much formed as possible by him; the instinct of those without existence for existence. Furthermore, this 'comprehension' is not theoretical, it is not sympathetic, it is only a desire to be sympathetic; it is importunate and egoistical. Woman has no relation to man and no sense of man, but only for maleness; and if she is to be considered as more sexual than man, this greater claim is nothing but the intense desire for the fullest and most definite formation, it is the demand for the greatest possible quantity of existence.

And, finally, match-making is nothing else than this. The sexuality of women is super-individual, because they are not limited, formed, individualized entities, in the higher sense of the word. . . .

It is thus that the duality of man and woman has gradually developed into complete dualism, to the dualism of the higher and lower lives, of subject and object, of form and matter, something and nothing. All metaphysical, all transcendental existence is logical and moral existence; woman is non-logical and non-moral. She has no dislike for what is logical and moral, she is not anti-logical, she is not anti-moral. She is not the negation, she is, rather, nothing. She is neither the affirmation nor the denial. A man has in himself the possibility of being the absolute something or the absolute nothing, and therefore his actions are directed towards the one or the other; woman does not sin, for she herself is the sin which is a possibility in man.

The abstract male is the image of God, the absolute something; the female, and the female element in the male, is the symbol of nothing; that is the significance of the woman in the universe, and in this way male and female complete and condition one another. Woman has a meaning and a function in the universe as the opposite of man; and as the human male surpasses the animal male, so the human female surpasses the female of zoology. It is not that limited existence and limited negation (as in the animal kingdom) are at war in humanity; what there stand in opposition are unlimited existence and unlimited negation. And so male and female make up humanity.

The meaning of woman is to be meaningless. She represents negation, the opposite pole from the Godhead, the other possibility of humanity. And so nothing is so despicable as a man become female, and such a person will be regarded as the supreme criminal even by himself. And so also is to be explained the deepest fear of man; the fear of the woman, which is the fear of unconsciousness, the alluring abyss of annihilation.

An old woman manifests once for all what woman really is. The beauty of woman, as may be experimentally proved, is only created by love of a man; a woman becomes more beautiful when a man loves her because she is passively responding to the will which is in her lover; however deep this may sound, it is only a matter of everyday experience.

All the qualities of woman depend on her non-existence, on her want of character; because she has no true, permanent, but only a mortal life, in her character as the advocate of pairing she furthers the sexual part of life, and is fundamentally transformed by and susceptible to the man who has a physical influence over her.

Thus the three fundamental characters of woman with which this chapter has dealt come together in the conception of her as the non-existent. Her instability and untruthfulness are only negative deductions from the premiss of her non-existence. Her only positive character, the conception of her as the pairing agent, comes from it by a simple process of analysis. The nature of woman is no more than pairing, no more than super-individual sexuality. . . .

Her existence is bound up with the Phallus, and so that is her supreme lord and welcome master.

Sex, in the form of man, is woman's fate; the Don Juan is the only type of man who has complete power over her.

The curse, which was said to be heavy on woman, is the evil will of man: nothing is only a tool in the hand of the will for nothing. The early Fathers expressed it pathetically when they called woman the handmaid of the devil. For matter in itself is nothing, it can only obtain existence through form. The fall of 'form' is the corruption that takes place when form endeavours to relapse into the formless. When man became sexual he formed woman. That woman is at all has happened simply because man has accepted his sexuality. Woman is merely the result of this affirmation; she is sexuality itself. Woman's existence is dependent on man; when man, as man, in contradistinction to woman, is sexual, he is giving woman form, calling her into existence. Therefore woman's one object must be to keep man sexual. She desires man as Phallus, and for this she is the advocate of pairing. She is incapable of making use of any creature except as a means to an end, the end being pairing; and she has but one purpose, that of continuing the guilt of man, for she would disappear the moment man had overcome his sexuality. . . .

. . . Woman is nothing but man's expression and projection of his own sexuality. Every man creates himself a woman, in which he embodies himself and his own guilt.

But woman is not herself guilty; she is made so by the guilt of others, and everything for which woman is blamed should be laid at man's door.

Love strives to cover guilt, instead of conquering it; it elevates woman instead of nullifying her. The 'something' folds the 'nothing' in its arms, and thinks thus to free the universe of negation and drown all objections; whereas the nothing would only disappear if the something put it away.

Since man's hatred for woman is not conscious hatred of his own sexuality, his love is his most intense effort to save woman as woman, instead of desiring to nullify her in himself. And the consciousness of guilt comes from the fact that the object of guilt is coveted instead of being annihilated. . . .

NOTES

1. [Ed.] *Tante Jule in Ibsen's 'Hedda Gabler'*: maiden aunt in Ibsen's drama, she appears to take a perverse interest in the possibility of Hedda being pregnant.
2. [Ed.] *Weininger notes*: 'The quiescent, inactive, large egg-cells are sought out by the mobile, active, and slender spermatozoa.'
3. [Ed.] *Weininger notes*: 'All individuality is an enemy of the community. This is seen most markedly in men of genius, but it is just the same with regard to the sexes.'
4. [Ed.] *Pasiphäe*: mythical wife of King Minos of Crete who fell in love with a bull. The offspring from this match was the Minotaur – half man, half bull.
5. [Ed.] *Leda*: loved by Zeus, he raped her in the form of a swan.

STUDY QUESTIONS

1. Weininger felt that his ideas were the logical outcome of those offered by Plato, Kant and Schopenhauer. What examples can you find in this piece which echo the ideas of other philosophers within the tradition?
2. Weininger writes that woman 'is nothing but sexuality itself'. How might this claim relate to previous ideas on this connection between woman and nature? What implications does that connection have for Weininger's subsequent discussion of 'rape'?
3. Weininger claims that only man has a sense of immortality as only man is truly an individual. Feminist writers might want to challenge the notion of immortality on the grounds that it supports the egocentric/anthropocentric claims of masculinist thinking. What common

ground might there be between Weininger and these feminists, and why might this be problematic?

FURTHER READING

Little has been written on Weininger's ideas in their own right. For Weininger's influence on Wittgenstein, see Ray Monk, *Ludwig Wittgenstein: The Duty of Genius* (London: Vintage, 1991). For feminist analysis, see Christine Battersby, *Gender and Genius: Towards a Feminist Aesthetics* (London: The Women's Press, 1989), pp. 163–9, and briefly, Nancy Tuana, *The Less Noble Sex* (Indianapolis: Indiana University Press, 1993), pp. 64–6, 87–8.

18 OSWALD SPENGLER 1880–1936

Introduction and Background

> Oswald Spengler, who died in 1936, performed one of the most curious feats in the history of modern thought: in a remarkably short time he has achieved a kind of highly topical oblivion.[1]

So writes Erich Heller of the little-known philosopher Oswald Spengler. Spengler's apocalyptic work *The Decline of the West* outlines the spiritual bankruptcy of the modern western world. This is hardly an uncommon theme, yet what interested Spengler's admirers – who included Wittgenstein – was the way in which Spengler argued his case.

According to Spengler, cultures are similar to human beings in that they have their own life-cycles, their own development, their own declines. 'Civilization' was the term Spengler gave to the last stage of a culture; this was the point at which stratification set in, followed by a period of decline. According to Spengler, twentieth-century western civilization is currently in this last stage. For Spengler, there is no such thing as progress, there are no absolutes to which we can adhere. The only absolute to which we can cling is the absolute spiritual bankruptcy which defines our age.

In accepting that there are no absolutes, Spengler offers a relativist approach to values. All values must be understood in relation to the culture in which they were developed. It might be assumed that these ideas augur well for his understanding of the role of women. Yet it is at this point that Spengler's argument becomes contradictory. Whilst denying all absolutes, he maintains an absolute distinction between male and female. In particular, Spengler focuses upon the distinction between Reason and Nature, and gives it its fullest expression. He equates this distinction with the distinction between male and female. The difference between male and female is evident when Spengler offers a sharply polarized view of human history. Man's history, the history of conquest and 'culture', is juxtaposed with women's history, a history of children, the home, and ultimately of nature. These two approaches to human life are in constant tension with one another. Needless to say, the higher form of history and culture is that which lies with the male.

*THE STATE**

A fathomless secret of the cosmic flowings that we call Life is their separation into two sexes. Already in the earth-bound existence-streams of the plant world they are trying to part from one another, as the symbol of the flower tells us – into a something that *is* this existence and a something that keeps it going. Animals are free, little worlds in a big world – the cosmic – closed off as microcosms and set up against the macrocosm. And, more and more decisively as the animal kingdom unfolds its history, the dual direction of dual being, of the masculine and the feminine, manifests itself.

The feminine stands closer to the Cosmic. It is rooted deeper in the earth and it is immediately involved in the grand cyclic rhythms of Nature. The masculine is freer, more animal, more mobile – as to sensation and understanding as well as otherwise – more awake and more tense.

The male livingly experiences Destiny, and he *comprehends* Causality, the causal logic of the Become. The female, on the contrary, *is herself* Destiny and Time and the organic logic of the Becoming, and for that very reason the principle of Causality is for ever alien to her. Whenever Man has tried to give Destiny any tangible form, he has felt it as of feminine form, and he has called it Moirai, Parcæ, Norns.[1] The supreme deity is never itself Destiny, but always either its representative or its master – just as man represents or controls woman. Primevally, too, woman is the seeress, and not because she knows the future, but because she *is* the future. The priest merely interprets the oracle; the woman is the oracle itself, and it is Time that speaks through her.

The man *makes* History, the woman *is* History. Here, strangely clear yet enigmatic still, we have a dual significance of all living

* From Oswald Spengler, *The Decline of the West*, vol. II, translated by C. F. Atkinson. Reprinted by permission of George, Allen & Unwin, an imprint of HarperCollins Publishers Ltd.

happenings – on the one hand we sense cosmic flow as such, and on the other hand the chain and train of successive individuals brings us back to the microcosms themselves as the recipients, containers, and preservers of the flowing. It is this 'second' history that is characteristically masculine – political, social, more conscious, freer, and more agitated than the other. It reaches back deep into the animal world, and receives highest symbolic and world-historical expression in the life-courses of the great Cultures. Feminine, on the contrary, is the primary, the eternal, the maternal, the plantlike (for the plant ever has something female in it), *the cultureless history of the generation-sequence*, which never alters, but uniformly and stilly passes through the being of all animal and human species, through all the short-lived individual Cultures. In retrospect, it is synonymous with Life itself. This history, too, is not without its battles and its tragedies. Woman in childbed wins through to her victory. The Aztecs – the Romans of the Mexican Culture – honoured the woman in labour as a battling warrior, and if she died, she was interred with the same formulæ as the fallen hero. Policy for Woman is eternally the conquest of the Man, through whom she can become mother of children, through whom she can become History and Destiny and Future. The target of her profound shyness, her tactical finesse, is ever the father of her son. The man, on the contrary, whose centre of gravity lies essentially in the other kind of History, wants that son as *his* son, as inheritor and carrier of his blood and historical tradition.

Here, in man and in woman, *the two kinds of History* are fighting for power. Woman is strong and wholly what she is, and she experiences the Man and the Sons only in relation to herself and her ordained rôle. In the masculine being, on the contrary, there is a certain contradiction; he is this man, and he is something else besides, which woman neither understands nor admits, which she feels as robbery and violence upon that which to her is holiest. This secret and fundamental war of the sexes has gone on ever since there were sexes, and will continue – silent, bitter, unforgiving, pitiless – while they continue. In it, too, there are policies, battles, alliances, treaties, treasons. Race-feeling of love and hate, which originate in depths of world-yearning and primary instincts of directedness, prevail between the sexes – and with a still more uncanny potency than in the other History that takes place between man and man. There are love-lyrics and war-lyrics, love-dances and weapon-dances, there are two kinds of tragedy – *Othello*[2] and *Macbeth*.[3] But nothing in the political world even begins to compare with the abysses of a Clytaemnestra's[4] or a Kriemhild's[5] vengeance.

And so woman despises that other History – man's politics – which she never comprehends, and of which all that she sees is that it takes her sons from her. What for her is a triumphant battle that annihilates the victories of a thousand childbeds? Man's history sacrifices woman's history to itself, and no doubt there is a female heroism too, that proudly brings the sons to the sacrifice . . . but nevertheless there was and is and ever will be a secret politic of the woman – of the female of the animal world even – that seeks to draw away her male from his kind of history and to weave him body and soul into her own plantlike history of generic succession – that is, into herself. And yet all that is accomplished in the man-history is accomplished under the battle-cries of hearth and home, wives and children, race and the like, and its very object is the covering and upholding of this history of birth and death. The conflict of man and man is ever on account of the blood, of woman. *Woman, as Time, is that for which there is history at all* . . .

Thus history has two meanings, neither to be blasphemed. It is cosmic or politic, it *is* being or it *preserves* being. There are two sorts of Destiny, two sorts of war, two sorts of tragedy – *public and private*. Nothing can eliminate this duality from the world. It is radical, founded in the essence of the animal that is both microcosm and participant in the cosmic. It appears at all significant conjunctures in the form of a conflict of duties, which exists only for the man, not for the woman, and in the course of a higher Culture it is never overcome, but only deepened. There are public life and private life, public law and private law, communal cults and domestic cults. As Estate, Being is 'in form' for the one history; as race, breed, it is in flow as *itself* the other history. This is the old German distinction between the 'sword side' and the 'spindle side' of blood-relationships. The double significance of directional Time finds its highest expression in the ideas of *the State* and *the Family*.

[*Spengler notes:* And not until women cease to have race enough to have or to want children, not until they cease to *be* history, does it become possible for them to make or to copy the history of men. Conversely, it is deeply significant that we are in the habit of calling thinkers, doctrinaires, and humanity-enthusiasts of anti-political tendency 'old women'. They wish to imitate the other history, the history of woman, although they – cannot.]

NOTES

1. [Ed.] *Moirai, Parcæ, Norns*: the Greek Fates (Spengler also names their Roman and Norse counterparts), represented as three old women spinning the destinies of human beings.
2. [Ed.] Spengler understands Shakespeare's play as a love-tragedy. Othello, out of a misplaced jealousy, kills his wife Desdemona.
3. [Ed.] *Macbeth*: Spengler apparently understands Shakespeare's play as a political, rather than a personal, tragedy.
4. [Ed.] *Clytaemnestra*: wife of the mythical Greek King Agamemnon. While Agamemnon was participating in the Trojan war, she took a lover, Aegisthus. Agamemnon returned to Mycenae with his lover Cassandra, and Clytaemnestra killed them both.
5. [Ed.] *Kriemhild*: (i) wife of Attila the Hun, she murdered him on her wedding day and bathed in his blood;
or (ii) wife of Siegfried in the *Nibelungenlied*, she plots revenge upon those who murdered her husband.

STUDY QUESTIONS

1. To what extent do Spengler's views on woman mirror Hegel's?
2. What other parallels might be made between Spengler's ideas and those offered by other philosophers?

SELECT BIBLIOGRAPHY

E. Heller, *The Disinherited Mind* (Harmondsworth: Penguin, 1961).

19 J. R. Lucas 1973

Introduction and Background

J. R. Lucas in his discussion of equality offers a more recent example of the philosophical preoccupation with the nature and role of woman. Writing at a time of increased activity by feminists challenging the extent to which society defined the role of women, he identifies the core of the debate to reside with the question of the extent to which women should be understood to be 'the same' as men. His discussion of this issue leads Rajlukshmee Debee Bhattacharya to comment that 'while Plato thought that women should be treated in the same way as men (although they are not quite so good), Mr Lucas seems to think that they should be treated differently (though they are almost as good)'.[1]

Central to Lucas's argument is his refusal to accept the claim that sex is only relevant to the sexual act. He argues that genetic theory suggests that sex determines our predisposition to certain activities; as an example, he cites statistics which suggest that men are decidedly better at maths than women. This claim is of dubious worth. Even if such statistics are accepted, it could be argued that this has more to do with socialization than with genetics. Yet Lucas uses such ideas to support his belief that sex determines ability. Indeed, he goes further in using this example to support his account of the nature of women. Women, he argues, are disadvantaged in a discipline as 'pure' as mathematics, for it is a discipline which relies totally upon logic and the mind. Women, he argues, are better represented in disciplines which use all of their faculties. Thus Lucas reiterates the philosophical identification of men with reason, women with nature.

Lucas's article contains comments which suggest an idiosyncratic understanding of gender issues. He argues that 'Many feminists are dualists'.[2] As much feminist scholarship has been concerned with the attempt to reject dualistic thinking, this seems an odd conclusion to draw. Likewise, Lucas rejects claims that women 'failed' to create great works of art because of social mores. Recent feminist attempts to reclaim women's voices suggest that women have consistently produced work of artistic or philosophical merit, but that this work has tended to be lost or forgotten.[3] At times, the consistency of his argument breaks down: whilst arguing against legislation which would deny someone the fruits of their education, he paradoxically argues that no matter how good a woman might be as a soldier, she should not be allowed to serve alongside men as her sex might lead to a breakdown in discipline.

Lucas's article is noteworthy for its use of humour. It could be argued that what he finds amusing draws attention to the ideas which inform his stance on the issue of equality. His examples tend to focus on women's sexuality (so, the disturbance 'Miss Amazon' might create in the barrackroom; the idea that nursery nurses must be feminine, etc.). This emphasis is not surprising, for it merely reiterates the identification of woman with nature and thus sexuality, which predominates in the western tradition.

'BECAUSE YOU'RE A WOMAN'*

Plato was the first feminist. In the *Republic* he puts forward the view that women are just the same as men, only not quite so good. It is a view which has often been expressed in recent years, and generates strong passions. Some of these have deep biological origins, which a philosopher can only hope to recognize and not to assuage. But much of the heat engendered is due to unnecessary friction between views which are certainly compatible and probably correct. And here a philosopher can help. If we

*From *Philosophy*, vol. 48 (1973), pp. 161–71. Reprinted by kind permission of the author and Cambridge University Press.

can divide the issues neatly, at the joints, then we need not quarrel with one another for saying something, probably true, because what is being maintained is misconstrued and taken to mean something else, probably false.

The feminist debate turns on the application of certain concepts of justice, equality and humanity. Should the fact – 'the mere fact' – of a person's being a woman disqualify her from being a member of the Stock Exchange, the Bench of Bishops or the House of Lords, or from obtaining a mortgage, owning property, having a vote or going to heaven? Is it not, say the feminists, just as irrational and inequitable as disqualifying a man on the grounds of the colour of his hair? Is it not, counter the anti-feminists, just as rational as drawing a distinction between men on the one hand and children, animals, lunatics, Martians and computers on the other? Whereupon we come to enunciate the formal platitude that women are the same as men in some respects, different from them in others, just as men are the same in some respects as children, animals, lunatics, Martians and computers, and different in others. And then we have to embark on more substantial questions of the respects in which men and women are the same, and those in which they are different; and of whether any such differences could be relevant to the activity or institution in question, or could be comparable to the differences, generally acknowledged to exist, between *homo sapiens* and the rest of creation. Even if women are different from men, a feminist might argue, why should this be enough to debar them from the floor of the Stock Exchange, when, apparently, there is no objection to the presence of computers?

We are faced with two questions. We need to know first what exactly are the ways in which women differ from men, and this in turn raises issues of the methods whereby such questions may be answered. Only when these methodological issues have been discussed can we turn to the more substantial ones of morals and politics concerned with whether it can ever be right to treat a woman differently from a man on account of her sex, or whether that is a factor which must always be regarded as in itself irrelevant.

I

The facts of femininity are much in dispute. The development of genetic theory is some help, but not a decisive one. We know that men differ from women in having one Y chromosome and only one X chromosome whereas women have two X chromosomes. Apart from the X and Y chromosomes, exactly the same sort of chromosomes turn up in men and women indifferently. The genetic make-up of each human being is constituted by his chromosomes, which occur in pairs, one of each pair coming from the father, the other from the mother. Men and Women share the same gene pool. So far as chromosomes, other than the X and Y ones, are concerned, men and women of the same breeding community are far more alike than members of different species, or even men of different races. This constitutes a powerful argument against the doctrine, attributed by some to the Mahometans, that women have no souls; contrary to the view of many young males, they are not just birds; or, in more modern parlance, it gives empirical support to arguments based on the principle of Universal Humanity. Women are worthy of respect, for the same reasons as men are. If it is wrong to hurt a man, to harm him, humiliate him or frustrate him, then it is wrong to hurt, harm, humiliate or frustrate a woman; for she is of the same stock as he, and they share the same inheritance and have almost all their chromosome-types in common.

Early genetic theory assumed a one–one correlation between pairs of hereditary genetic factors and their manifested effects in the individual. Whether I had brown eyes or blue eyes depended on whether I had the pair of factors BB, Bb or bB, in all of which cases I should have brown eyes, or whether I had bb, in which case I should have blue eyes. No other genetic factor was supposed to be relevant to the colour of my eyes, nor was the possession of a B or a b gene relevant to anything else about me. If this theory represented the whole truth, the feminist case would be simple. Sex is irrelevant to everything except sex. The fact of a man's being male or a woman's being female would be a 'mere fact' with no bearing on anything except sexual intercourse and the procreation of children. It would be rational to hold that only a male could be guilty of rape, and it might be permissible to have marriage laws which countenanced only heterosexual unions, and to look for proofs of paternity as well as of maternity. Perhaps we might go a very little further, and on the same grounds as we admit that negroes are not really eligible for the part of Iago, admit that males could not really expect to be employed as models for female fashions, and vice versa. Beyond these few and essentially unimportant exceptions, it would be as wrong for the law to discriminate between the sexes as it would be if it were to prefer blondes.

Simple genetic theory is, however, too simple. It needs to be complicated in two ways. First, although chromosomes occur in pairs, each single one being inherited more or less independently of every other one, each chromosome contains not just one, but many, many genetic factors, and these are not all independently inherited, and some, indeed, like the one responsible for haemophilia, are sex-linked. There are, so far as we know, relatively few effects – and those mostly bad – which are caused by factors contained in the Y chromosome, and there is a slight *a priori* argument against many features being thus transmitted (because the Y chromosome is much smaller than the others, and so, presumably, carries less genetic information): but there could well be more complicated effects due to a relatively rare recessive gene not being marked in the male as it probably would have been in the female. Mathematical talent might be like haemophilia or colour-blindness: it is consonant with what we know of genetic theory that only one in a thousand inherit the genetic factor, which if it is inherited by a boy then becomes manifest, but which if it is inherited by a girl, still in 999 cases out of a thousand is marked by a dominant unmathematicality. The second complication is more fundamental than the first. Genetic factors not only are not inherited independently of the others, but do not operate independently of the others. What is important is not simply whether I have BB, Bb, or bb, but whether I have one of these pairs in conjunction with some set of other pairs of factors. In particular, whether a person is male or female may affect whether or not some other hereditary factor manifests itself or not. Only men go bald. There are many physical features and physiological processes which are affected by whether a person is male or female. So far as our bodies are concerned, the fact of a person's being a man or a woman is not 'a mere fact' but a fundamental one. Although there are many similarities between men and women, the differences are pervasive, systematic and of great biological significance. Almost the first question a hospital needs to ask is 'M or F?'

Many feminists are dualists, and while conceding certain bodily differences between men and women, deny that there is any inheritance of intellectual ability or traits of character at all. Genetic theory, as far as it goes, is against them. There is reasonable evidence for the inheritance of skills and patterns of behaviour in other animals, and in particular of those patterns of behaviour we should normally ascribe to the maternal instinct. Human beings are far too complicated to manifest many abilities or traits of character that are simple enough to be susceptible of scientific test; and although we often detect family resemblances in ways of walking and talking, as well as in temperament and emotion, it is not clear how far these are due to inherited factors and how far they have been acquired by imitation or learning. It is, however, a common experience to note resemblances between different members of the same family who have never seen each other and have had no opportunity of imitating one another. Such instances, when cited, are often dismissed as mere anecdotes, belonging to mythology rather than science, and unworthy of the attention of modern-minded thinkers in this day and age. It is difficult to stand one's ground in the face of the charge of being unscientific, for the word 'scientific' has strong evaluative overtones, and to be 'unscientific' smacks of quackery and prejudice. But it remains the case that all discussions about political and social issues must be 'unscientific' in that they are not exclusively based on the measurable results of repeatable experiments. For what we are concerned with is what people feel, decide, and ought to do about these things, and people are different, and feel differently and decide to do different things. If we refuse to admit to the argument any evidence other than the measurable results of reputable experiments, we may still be able to discuss questions of public health, but cannot even entertain those of justice or the political good. And if the feminist rejects all anecdotal evidence on principle, then she is making good her dualism by stipulation, because she is not prepared to recognize intellectual abilities or traits of character in the way in which they normally are recognized. This, of course, is not to urge that every story a boozy buffer cares to tell should be accepted as true or relevant; but only that the word 'scientific' needs to be handled with caution, and not used to rule out of court whole ranges of evidence and whole realms of experience. The canons of scientific evidence are, very properly, strictly drawn; and scientists accept the corollary that the topics amenable to scientific research are correspondingly limited. There are many discussions which cannot be evaluated within the canon of scientific argument upon the basis of scientific observations alone, among them discussions about what is right and good for individuals and societies. But they need not be any the worse for that, although they will be if the participants do not show the same fairness and reasonableness in their discussions as scientists do in their researches.

Another methodological issue is raised by those who acknowledge that there have been and are differences in the intellectual achievements and the typical behaviour of women as compared with men, but attribute all of them exclusively to the social pressures brought to bear upon women which have prevented them from exercising their talents to the full or giving rein to their natural inclinations. When the advocate of male supremacy marshals his masses of major poets against a solitary Sappho,[1] the feminist explains that women have been so confined by domestic pressures and so inhibited by convention that those few with real poetic talent have never had opportunity to bring it to flower. Poets might be poor, but at least they could listen to the Muse undistracted by baby's cries: whereas potential poetesses, unless their lot were cast in Lesbos, were married off and made to think of clothes and nappies to the exclusion of all higher thoughts.

It is difficult to find hard evidence either for or against this thesis. In this it is like many rival explanations or interpretations in history or literature. What moves us to adopt one rather than another is that it seems to us more explanatory or more illuminating than the alternative; and what seems to us more explanatory or illuminating depends largely on our own experience and understanding – and our own prejudices. But although we are very liable to be swayed by prejudice, it does not follow that we inevitably are, and although we are often guided by subjective considerations in deciding between various hypotheses, it does not follow that there is nothing, really, to choose between them. We can envisage evidence, even if we cannot obtain it, which would decide between the two alternatives. The feminist claim would be established if totally unisex societies sprang up and flourished; or if there were as many societies in which the rôles of men and women were reversed as there were traditional ones. Indeed, the existence of any successful and stable society in which the rôles of the sexes are reversed is evidence in favour of the claim. Evidence against is more difficult to come by. Few people deny that social pressures have a very considerable bearing on our behaviour and capacities. Some people argue from the analogy with other animals, whose behaviour is indubitably determined genetically and differs according to their sex; or argue, as I have done, by extrapolation from purely physical features. Both arguments are respectable, neither conclusive. Man is an animal, but very unlike other animals, particularly in respect of the extreme plasticity of human behaviour, nearly all of which is learned. Very few of our responses are purely instinctive; and it is unsafe to claim confidently that maternal feelings must be. What would constitute evidence against the feminist claim would be some intellectual ability or character trait which seemed to be both relatively independent of social circumstance and distributed unevenly between the sexes. Mathematical talent might be a case in point. It seems to be much more randomly distributed in the population than other forms of intellectual ability. If Ramanujan[2] could triumph over his circumstances, then surely numerate sisters to Sappho should abound. But this is far from being a conclusive argument.

There are no conclusive arguments about feminine abilities and attitudes. But the discoveries of the scientists, so far as they go, lend some support to traditional views. It could well be the case that intellectual and psychological characteristics are, like physical ones, influenced by genetic factors. If this is so, the way in which a particular pair of genes in an individual genotype will be manifested in the phenotype will depend on the other genes in the genotype, and may depend greatly on whether there are two X chromosomes or one X and one Y. It could be that the masculine mind is typically more vigorous and combative, and the feminine mind typically more intuitive and responsive, with correspondingly different ranges of interests and inclinations. It would make evolutionary sense if it were, and would fit in with what else we know about the nature of man: but it is still possible to maintain the contrary view; and even if there are in fact differences between men and women, it does not follow that their treatment should be different too.

II

If it could be established that there were no innate intellectual or emotional differences between men and women, the feminists' case would be pretty well made; but it does not follow that to admit that there are differences carries with it an adequate justification for every sort of discrimination, and it is useful to consider what sort of bearing various types of difference might have. Suppose, for example, that mathematical ability were distributed unevenly and according to the same pattern as haemophilia, so that only one in n males have it and only one in n_2 females. This would be a highly relevant factor in framing our educational policy. It would justify the provision of far more opportunities for boys to study higher mathematics than for girls. But it would not justify the total exclusion of girls. Most girls prefer nursing to numeracy, but those few who would rather solve differential equations ought not to be prevented from doing so on the grounds that they are female. Two principles underlie this judgment. First that the connexion between sex and mathematical ability is purely contingent; and secondly that we are in a position in which considerations of the individual's interests and deserts are paramount. Even if there are very few female mathematicians, there is no reason why any particular woman should not be a mathematician. And if any particular woman is, then her being a woman is irrelevant to her actual performance in mathematics. Her being a woman created a presumption, a purely contingent although usually reliable presumption, that she was no good at mathematics. It is like presumptive evidence in a court of law, which could be rebutted, and in this case was, and having been rebutted is of no more relevance in this individual situation, which is all we are concerned with.

Female mathematicians are rare. Few disciplines are so pure as mathematics. In most human activities – even in most academic pursuits – the whole personality is much more involved, and the irrelevance of a person's sex far more dubious. Differences between the sexes are likely to come into play most in ordinary human relations where one person tells another what to do, or persuades, or cajoles or encourages or warns or threatens or acquiesces. In so far as most positions in society are concerned with social relations, it cannot be argued that the differences between the sexes are, of necessity, irrelevant. Although it might be the case that working men would as readily take orders from a fore-woman as a foreman, or that customers would be as pleased to find a handsome boy receptionist as a pretty girl, there is no reason to suppose that it must be so. Moreover, life is not normally either an examination or a trial. It is one of the disadvantages of our meritocratic age that we too readily assume that all social transactions are exclusively concerned with the individual, who needs to be given every opportunity and whose rights must be zealously safeguarded. But examinations and trials are artificial and cumbersome exceptions to the general rule, in which no one individual is the centre of concern. To deny people the fruits of their examination success or to deprive them of their liberty on any grounds irrelevant to their own desert is wrong: but it is not so evidently wrong to frustrate Miss Amazon's hopes of a military career in the Grenadier Guards on the grounds not that she would make a bad soldier but that she would be a disturbing influence in the mess room. Laws and institutions are characteristically two-faced. They set norms for the behaviour of different parties, and need to take into consideration the interests and claims of more than one person. They also need to apply generally, and cannot be tailor-made to each particular situation: they define rôles rather than fit actual personalities, and roles need to fit the typical rather than the special case. Even if Miss Amazon is sure not to attract sidelong glances from the licentious soldiery, her sisters may not be; and it may be easier to operate an absolute bar than leave it to the recruiting officer to decide whether a particular woman is sufficiently unattractive to be safe. This type of case tuns up in many other laws and public regulations. We lay down rigid speed limits because they are easier to apply. There are many towns in which to drive at 30 mph would be dangerous, and many suburbs in which to drive at 45 mph would sometimes be safe. Some boys of ten are better informed about public affairs than other voters of thirty. But the advantage of having a fixed speed limit or a fixed voting age outweighs its admitted unfairness.

We can now see what sort of facts would bring what sort of principles to bear upon our individual decisions and the general structure of our laws and institutions. We need to know not only whether there are differences, but whether these differences are integrally or only contingently connected with a person's sex, and whether they apply in all cases or only as a rule. The more integrally and the more invariably a difference is connected with a person's sex, the more we are entitled to insist that the mere fact of being male or female can constitute a conclusive reason against being allowed to do something. The less integral a difference is, the more the arguments from Formal Equality (or Universalizability) and from Justice will come into play, requiring us to base our decisions only on the features relevant to the case in hand. The less invariable a difference is, the more the arguments from Humanity and again from Justice will come into play, requiring us to pay respect to the interests and inclinations of each individual person, and to weigh her actual interests, as against those of the community at large, on the basis of her actual situation and actual and reasonable desires.

However much I, a male, want to be a mother, a wife or a girlfriend, I am disqualified from those roles on account of my sex, and I cannot reasonably complain. Not only can I not complain if individuals refuse to regard me as suitable in those rôles, but I have to acknowledge that it is reasonable for society generally to do so, and for the state to legislate accordingly. The state is justified in not countenancing homosexual 'marriages', because of our general understanding of what marriage really is, and the importance we attach to family life. For exactly the same reasons, women are debarred from being regarded in a fatherly or husbandly light; and hence also in those parts of the Christian Church that regard priests as being essentially fathers in God from being clergymen or bishops. How far rôles should be regarded as being integrally dependent on sex is a matter of dispute. In very intimate and personal relationships it is evident that the whole personality is involved, and that since a man – or at least many, non-Platonic men – responds to a woman in a different way from that in which he responds to a man, or a woman to a woman, it is natural that these rôles should be essentially dependent on sex. But as the rôles become more limited, so the dependence becomes less. I could hardly complain if I was not given the part of Desdemona or a job as an *au pair* boy on account of my sex: but if I had very feminine features and had grown my hair long and golden, or if I were particularly deft at changing nappies, I might feel a little aggrieved, and certainly I could call in question any law that forbade a man to play the part of a woman or be a nursemaid. Some substantial public good would need to be shown to justify a legal decision enforceable by penal sanctions being uniformly based not on my actual inability to fill the rôle required but only my supposed unsuitability on account of my sex. We demand a higher standard of cogency in arguments justifying what laws there should be than in those concerned only with individual decisions; and although this standard can be satisfied, often by admitting considerations of the public good, yet the arguments need to be adduced, because, in framing laws, we need to be sensitive to individual rights and careful about our criteria of relevance. Although it may be the case that a nurse is a better nurse for having the feminine touch, we hesitate to deem it absolutely essential; and although many more women than men have been good nurses, we do not believe that it must invariably be so. There are male nurses. We reckon it reasonable to prefer a woman in individual cases, but do not insist upon it in all cases by law. We are reluctant to impose severe legal disqualifications, but equally would hesitate to impose upon employers an obligation not to prefer women to play female parts or to be nurses or to join a family in an *au pair* capacity. For we recognize that a person's sex can reasonably be regarded as relevant to his or her suitability for particular posts, and that many institutions will operate on this basis, and are entitled to. I am justified in refusing to employ a male *au pair* girl or a female foreman, although if there are many males anxious to be looking after young children or many women anxious to supervise the work of others, it may be desirable on grounds of Humanity to establish special institutions in which they can fulfil their vocations. If we will not let Miss Amazon join the Grenadier Guards, let there be an ATS or WRAC for her to join instead.

Although we are rightly reluctant to impose legal disqualifications on individuals on grounds extraneous to their individual circumstances, it is inherent in all political thinking that we may find considerations of the general case over-riding those of the individual one; and often we frame our laws with an eye to what men and women are generally like rather than what they invariably are. A man may not adopt an infant girl unless she is more than twenty-five years younger than he; for some men might otherwise use adoption to acquire not so much a daughter as a wife. In many societies women have less freedom in disposing of their property than men; for else, things being as they are, some women would be prevailed upon to divest themselves of it to their long-term disadvantage. Ardent feminists have chafed at the shackles of marriage, and demand freedom from this degrading institution for their sisters as well as themselves. But if this freedom were established it would be the libertine males who would enjoy the benefits of liberation, being then free to leave the women to bear the burdens of parenthood all on their own. If most mothers care more for their children and their homes than most fathers do, then in the absence of institutions that recognize the fact they will in fact be disadvantaged. Some discrimination is needed to redress the balance. But discrimination, even positive discrimination, can work to the disadvantage of individuals, however much it may benefit most people on the whole.

The would-be female Stakhanovite[3] is penalized by the law forbidding firms to employ female labour for sixty hours a week, just as the youthful entrepreneur is handicapped by his legal incapacity, as a minor, to pledge his credit except for the necessities of life, and the skilled racing motorist by the law forbidding him to drive, however safely, at more than 70 miles per hour. In each case the justification is the same: the restriction imposed on the individual, although real and burdensome, is not so severe as to outweigh the benefits that are likely to accrue in the long run to women in general, or to minors, or to motorists. It is in the nature of political society that we forgo some freedoms in order that either we ourselves or other people can secure some good. All we can in general demand is that our sacrifices should not be fruitless, and that if we give up some liberty or immunity it is at least arguable that it will be on balance for the best.

Arguments in politics are nearly always mixed, and involve appeals to different principles, according to how the question is construed. We can elucidate some canons of relevance for some of the principles which may be invoked. Where the principle is that of Universal Humanity, the reason 'Because you are a woman' is always irrelevant to its general applicability, though it may affect the way it is specified: perhaps women feel more strongly about their homes than men do, so that although we ought not, on grounds of humanity, to hurt either men or women, deprivation of her home would constitute a greater hurt to a woman than to a man. The principle of Universal Humanity is pervasive in its applications, but is conclusive only over a much more limited range. It is always wrong to torture; but often we cannot help hurting people's feelings or harming their interests if other values – justice, liberty, the public good – are to be preserved. And therefore arguments based on the principle of universal humanity may be over-ridden by ones based on other principles, also valuable. When the principle invoked is that of Formal Equality (or Universalizability) the reason 'Because you are a woman' cannot be dismissed out of hand as necessarily irrelevant. A person's sex is not a 'mere fact', evidently and necessarily separate from all other facts, and such that it is immediately obvious that no serious argument can be founded upon it. Particularly with those rôles that involve relationships with other people, and especially where those relationships are fairly personal ones, it is likely to matter whether it is a man or a woman that is chosen. When some principle of Justice is at stake, the criteria of relevance become fairly stringent. We are concerned only with the individual's actions, attitudes and abilities, and the reason 'Because you are a woman' must either be integrally connected with matter in issue (as in 'Why cannot I marry the girl I love?') or be reliably, although only contingently, connected with it (as in 'Why cannot I get myself employed for

60 hours a week?'); and in the latter case we feel that Justice has been compromised, although perhaps acceptably so, if there is no way whereby an individual can prove she is an exception to the rule and be treated as such. As the interests of the individual become more peripheral, or can be satisfied in alternative ways that are available, the principle of justice recedes, and we are more ready to accept rules and institutions based on general principles of social utility or tradition, and designed only to fit the general case. It is legitimate to base public feeling on such differences as seem to be relevant, but the more a law or an institution is based on merely a contingent, and not an integral, concomitance, the more ready we should be to cater for exceptions.

With sufficient care we may be able to disentangle what is true in the feminists' contention from what is false. At least we should be able to avoid the dilemma, which seems to be taken for granted by most participants in the debate, that we must say that women either are in all respects exactly the same as men or else are in all respects different from, and inferior to, them, and not members of the same universe of discourse at all. I do not share Plato's feelings about sex. I think the sexes are different, and incomparable. No doubt, women are not quite as good as men, *in some respects*: but since men are not nearly as good as women in others, this carries with it no derogatory implication of uniform inferiority. Exactly what these differences are, and, indeed, what sort of differences they are, is a matter for further research; and exactly what bearing they should have in the application of the various principles we value in making up our mind about social matters is a matter for further philosophical thought. But without any further thought we can align our emotions with the proponents of Women's Lib on the most important issue of all. What angers them most is the depersonalization of women in the Admass society: and one cannot but sympathize with their protest against women being treated as mere objects of sexual gratification by men; but cannot avoid the conclusion that their arguments and activities in fact lead towards just that result which they deplore. If we are insensitive to the essential femininity of the female sex, we shall adopt an easy egalitarianism which, while denying that there are any genetic differences, allows us to conclude in most individual cases that women, judged by male standards of excellence, are less good than their male rivals. Egalitarianism ends by depersonalizing women and men alike.

NOTES

1. [Ed.] *Sappho*: *c*.7th century BCE. Poet from the island of Lesbos. The common understanding of 'Lesbian' appears to have come from comments of the poet Anacreon (*c*.6th century BCE) on the practice of female homosexuality on the island.

2. [Ed.] *Ramanujan*: (1889–1920) self-taught mathematical genius.

3. [Ed.] *Stakhanovite*: from Soviet miner Aleksei Grigorevich Stakhanov (1906–77), used as examplar to other workers for his prodigious output of coal. A 'Stakhanovite' worker secured greater privileges during the 1930–40 Soviet Industrial Revolution.

STUDY QUESTIONS

1. 'Many feminists are dualists . . .' What does Lucas mean by this? How might an awareness of the way in which women have been defined by philosophers challenge this assumption?
2. Why are women under-represented in subjects like mathematics? Give Lucas's ideas and your own.
3. Why might an analysis of Lucas's work benefit from an awareness of the tone of this piece? (For example, what do phrases like 'most girls prefer nursing to numeracy' and 'Miss Amazon' suggest about the seriousness with which Lucas approaches gender issues?)

SELECT BIBLIOGRAPHY

Response to Lucas

Rajlukshmee Debee Bhattacharya, 'Because He is a Man', *Philosophy*, vol. 49 (1974), p. 96.

NOTES

Introduction: A Fling with the Philosophers

1. M. Whitford, *Feminist Philosophers* (Brighton: Harvester Wheatsheaf, 1986), pp. 1–2.
2. As such, feminist philosophy can learn from the work of feminist theologians, such as Rosemary Radford Ruether, who have wished to use women's experience as the criterion for 'truth'.
3. See L. Irigaray, *This Sex Which Is Not One*, translated by C. Porter (Ithaca, NY: Cornell University Press, 1985), p. 162.
4. Ibid., p. 150.
5. Cf. J. Plant, *Healing the Wounds: The Promise of Ecofeminism* (Philadelphia: New Society Publishers, 1989).
6. Cf. Hume's essay 'On Chastity and Modesty' from *Treatise of Human Nature*, in Part IV of this volume.
7. R. Swinburne, *The Christian God* (Oxford: Oxford University Press, 1994), pp. 125–6.
8. R. Swinburne, 'The Problem of Evil', in *Reason and Religion*, edited by S. C. Brown (Ithaca, NY: Cornell University Press, 1977), p. 88 – my emphasis.
9. For example, ibid., p. 89: 'But surely a father ought to interfere if his younger son is really getting badly hurt . . .'.
10. Irigaray, *This Sex Which Is Not One*, p. 151.
11. A. Plantinga, 'A Modal Version of the Ontological Argument', in *Readings in the Philosophy of Religion*, edited by W. L. Rowe and W. J. Wainwright (Orlando: Harcourt Brace Jovanovich, 1989), p. 117.
12. K. Power, *Veiled Desire: Augustine's Writing on Women* (London: Darton, Longman & Todd, 1995).
13. Hume and Freud are notable examples.
14. M. Warnock (ed.), *Women Philosophers* (London: Dent & Son, 1996).
15. Ibid., p. xxix.
16. Ibid., p. xxxiii.
17. See M. Daly, *Beyond God the Father* (London: Women's Press, 1986), ch. 4. For discussion of Daly's use of Nietzsche, see J Grimshaw, *Feminist Philosophers* (Brighton: Harvester Wheatsheaf, 1986), pp. 153ff.
18. Irigaray, *This Sex Which Is Not One*, p. 76.
19. Ibid., p. 76.
20. Ibid., p. 78.
21. L. Irigaray, *An Ethics of Sexual Difference*, translated by C. Burke and G. Gill (London: Athone, 1993), p. 18.

PART I: THE GREEKS

1 Plato

1. J. Annas, 'Plato's Republic and Feminism', *Philosophy*, vol. 51 (1976), p. 309.
2. See G. Jantzen, *Power, Gender and Christian Mysticism* (Cambridge: Cambridge University Press, 1995), pp. 30–3.

2 Aristotle

1. Cf. A. Baring and J. Cashford, *The Myth of the Goddess* (London: Viking, 1991), ch. 1.
2. For a rejection of this reading of Aristotle, and an alternative feminist account, see Daryl McGowan Tress, 'The Metaphysical Science of Aristotle's Generation of Animals and Its Feminist Critics', in J. K. Ward (ed.), *Feminism and Ancient Philosophy* (London: Routledge, 1996), pp. 31–50.
3. Cf. R. Miles, *Women's History of the World* (London: Paladin, 1992), ch. 1.
4. For example, see Kant's ideas in *Of the Beautiful and Sublime*, where he argues that women cannot/should not be philosophers.

PART II: THE CHURCH FATHERS

3 Tertullian

1. H. von Campenhausen, *The Fathers of the Latin Church*, translated by M. Hoffmann (London: A. & C. Black, 1964), p. 6.
2. Ibid., p. 8.
3. M. Warner, *Alone of All Her Sex* (London: Picador, 1990), p. 58.
4. H. von Campenhausen, *The Fathers of the Latin Church*, p. 7.
5. Quoted on p. 49 of J. Smith, *Misogynies* (London: Faber & Faber, 1989), from 'An Exhortation to Chastity', trans. W. P. Le Saint, in Tertullian, *Treatises on Marriage and Remarriage* (The Newman Press, 1951), p. 58.
6. Quoted on p. 631 of A. Baring and J. Cashford, *The Myth of the Goddess* (London: Viking, 1991).

4 Augustine

1. Cf. K. Power, *Veiled Desire* (London: Darton, Longman & Todd, 1995), ch. 10.
2. Ibid., p. 137.

5 Thomas Aquinas

1. Quoted in A. Kenny, *Aquinas* (Oxford: Oxford University Press, 1980), p. 2.
2. Ibid., p. 2.
3. G. Lloyd, *The Man of Reason* (London: Methuen, 1984), p. 35, quoting from *Summa Theologiae* I, Q. 92, article 1.

6 Heinrich Kramer and James Sprenger

1. See M. Daly, *Gyn/Ecology* (London: Women's Press, 1991), p. 183, for her critical analysis of the way in which the number of deaths is calculated by different scholars.
2. R. Cavendish, *The Powers of Evil* (London: Routledge & Kegan Paul, 1975), p. 211.
3. The Papal Bull of Pope Innocent VIII, issued in December 1484, advocates the work of Kramer and Sprenger, arguing that they are 'applying potent remedies to prevent the disease of heresy . . .' (reproduced in *The Malleus Maleficarum*, translated and introduced by M. Summers (New York: Dover Publications, 1971), p. xliv).
4. Cf. M. Daly, *Gyn/Ecology* (London: Women's Press, 1991); J. Caputi, *The Age of Sex Crime* (London: Women's Press, 1987), ch. 4; M. French, *Beyond Power: On Women, Men and Morals* (London: Cardinal, 1991), ch. 3.
5. Daly, in *Gyn/Ecology*, describes the persecution of the witches as 'gynocide' (p. 196) – the mass murder of women.
6. Ibid., p. 184.
7. Ibid., p. 186.
8. K. Thomas, *Religion and the Decline of Magic* (Harmondsworth: Penguin, 1971).
9. Ibid., p. 669.
10. See Summers, Introduction to *The Malleus Maleficarum*, p. xvii.
11. Ibid., p. xviii.
12. Ibid., p. xxxix.
13. Ibid., pp. ix–x.

PART III: EARLY MODERN PHILOSOPHERS

7 René Descartes

1. E. Harth, *Cartesian Women* (Ithaca: Cornell, 1992), pp. 4–5.
2. For discussion of the correspondence between Descartes and Elisabeth and Christina, and analysis of their respective philosophies, see Andrea Nye, 'Polity and Prudence: The Ethics of Elisabeth, Princess Palatine', in Linda Lopez McAlister (ed.),

Hypatia's Daughters (Indianapolis: Indiana University Press, 1996), pp. 68–91; and Susanna Åkerman, 'Kristina Wasa, Queen of Sweden', in Mary Ellen Waithe (ed.), *A History of Women Philosophers*, vol. 3 (Dordrecht: Kluwer Academic Publishers, 1991), pp. 21–40.

3. For discussion of Margaret Cavendish and her critique of Descartes, see Londa Schiebinger, 'Margaret Cavendish, Duchess of Newcastle', in Mary Ellen Waithe (ed.), *A History of Women Philosophers*, vol. 3 (Dordrecht: Kluwer Academic Publishers, 1991), pp. 1–20.
4. Quoted on p. 60 of J. Grimshaw, *Feminist Philosophers* (Brighton: Harvester Wheatsheaf, 1986).
5. Quoted on p. 69 of Harth, *Cartesian Women*.
6. Quoted on pp. 48–9 of G. Lloyd, *The Man of Reason* (London: Methuen, 1984).
7. Harth, *Cartesian Women*, p. 77.

8 Thomas Hobbes

1. Cf. his 'Objections' to Descartes's 'Meditations' (1641).
2. S. Priest, *The British Empiricists* (Harmondsworth: Penguin, 1990), p. 27.
3. Ibid., p. 42.
4. See Stephen Priest: Hobbes's political theory offers 'a set of prescriptions for the creation of a human society that will escape the state of nature' (ibid., p. 45).
5. Ibid., p. 47.
6. F. C. Hood, *The Divine Politics of Thomas Hobbes* (Oxford: Clarendon Press, 1964), p. 25.
7. Ibid., p. 172.

9 John Locke

1. S. Priest, *The British Empiricists* (Harmondsworth: Penguin, 1990), p. 50.
2. J. Locke, Essay II, XXI, §67.
3. G. Schochet, 'The Family and the Origins of the State in Locke's Political Philosophy', in *John Locke: Problems and Perspectives*, edited by J. Yolton (Cambridge: Cambridge University Press, 1969).
4. K. Green, *The Woman of Reason* (Cambridge: Polity Press, 1995), p. 60.
5. For further details of Mary Astell's critique, and the correspondence between Locke and Trotter and Masham, see Kathleen Squadrito, 'Mary Astell'; Lois Frankel, 'Damaris Cudworth Masham'; and Mary Ellen Waithe, 'Catharine Trotter Cockburn', in Mary Ellen Waithe (ed.), *A History of Women Philosophers*, vol. 3 (Dordrecht: Kluwer Academic Publishers, 1991).

PART IV: THE ENLIGHTENMENT

10 David Hume

1. Cf. D. Z. Phillips, *Religion without Explanation* (Oxford: Blackwell, 1976); Don Cupitt, *Only Human* (London: SCM, 1985).
2. Quoted in E. C. Mossner, *The Life of David Hume* (Oxford: Oxford University Press, 1970), p. 570.

11 Immanuel Kant

1. Carol Gilligan, in her study *In a Different Voice* (Cambridge, Mass.: Harvard University Press, 1982), argues that the different experiences of women and men lead to different approaches to moral decision making. The tendency in western philosophy has been to equate male experience with the norm, leaving women's experience on the margins of moral philosophy.
2. A. MacIntyre, *A Short History of Ethics* (London: Routledge & Kegan Paul, 1967), pp. 192–3.

12 Jean-Jacques Rousseau

1. J. Schwartz, *The Sexual Politics of Jean-Jacques Rousseau* (Chicago: University of Chicago Press, 1984).
2. See S. Okin, *Women in Western Political Thought* (London: Virago, 1980), p. 106; Schwartz, *The Sexual Politics*, ch. 1.
3. Schwartz, *The Sexual Politics*, p. 56.
4. Ibid., p. 58.
5. From Catharine Macaulay-Graham, *Letters on Education*, Letter XXII (1790), quoted in Mary Ellen Waithe (ed.), *A History of Women Philosophers*, vol. 3 (Dordrecht: Kluwer Academic Publishers, 1991), p. 219.
6. M. Wollstonecraft, *A Vindication of the Rights of Woman* (Harmondsworth: Pelican, 1975).
7. J. H. Broome, *Rousseau* (London: Edward Arnold, 1963), p. 99.
8. Ibid., p. 100.

13 G. W. F. Hegel

1. Quoted on p. 11 of P. Singer, *Hegel* (Oxford: Oxford University Press, 1983).
2. Cf. L. Feuerbach, *The Essence of Christianity*, translated by George Eliot (New York: Harper & Row, 1957).
3. Cf. B. Clack, 'God and Language: A Feminist Perspective on the Meaning of 'God', in *The Nature of Religious Language*, ed. S. Porter (Sheffield Academic Press, 1996), pp. 148–58.

PART V: MISOGYNY IN THE MODERN AGE

15 Friedrich Nietzsche

1. See, for example, Don Cupitt, *Only Human* (London: SCM, 1985); Mark C. Taylor, *Erring: A Postmodern A/theology* (Chicago: University of Chicago Press, 1987); R. Rorty, *Contingency, Irony and Solidarity* (Cambridge: Cambridge University Press, 1989).
2. Cf. J. Grimshaw, *Feminist Philosophers* (Brighton: Harvester Wheatsheaf, 1986), pp. 153–61.

16 Sigmund Freud

1. In particular, it is interesting to note that feminists are engaging with his thought. See, for example, N. J. Chodorow, *Feminism and Psychoanalytic Theory* (Cambridge: Polity Press, 1989); T. Brennan (ed.), *Between Feminism and Psychoanalysis* (London: Routledge, 1989).
2. R. Miles, *The Women's History of the World* (London: Paladin, 1989), Chapter 11.
3. Ibid., p. 360.

17 Otto Weininger

1. Cf. S. Griffin, *Made from this Earth* (London: Women's Press, 1982).
2. Cf. B. Clack, 'The Denial of Dualism: Thealogical Reflections on the Sexual and the Spiritual', *Feminist Theology*, 10 September 1995, pp. 102–15.
3. For example, see R. Radford Ruether, *Gaia and God* (London: SCM, 1992), pp. 247–53.

18 Oswald Spengler

1. E. Heller, *The Disinherited Mind* (Harmondsworth: Penguin, 1961).

19 J. R. Lucas

1. Rajlukshmee Debee Bhattacharya, 'Because He is a Man', *Philosophy*, vol. 49 (1974), p. 96.
2. J. R. Lucas, p. 231 (this volume).
3. Cf. Mary Ellen Waithe, 'Finding Bits of Hypatia', in *Hypatia's Daughters*, edited by Linda Lopez McAlister (Indianapolis: Indiana University Press, 1996). Waithe reconstructs the extant writings of Hypatia, whose work survives in fragmentary form.

INDEX